PLACE NAM
CORNWALL
AND SCILLY

Henwyn Plasow yn Kernow ha Syllan

Craig Weatherhill

All rights reserved. No part of this publication may be reproduced, stored in a retrieval system or transmitted, in any form or by any means, electronic, mechanical, photocopying, recording or otherwise, without prior permission of the publishers.

Pub gwyr gwethys. Ny yl ran vyth; an publysyans ma naneyl bos copyes, senjys abarth yn system dascrefyans na truescorrys yn furf vyth oll na dre vayn vyth oll, poken electronek, mechanyk, dre fotocopyans, dre recordyth bo fordh vyth aral, heb cafus cumyas dherag dorn dheworth an dyller.

Published by Wessex Books in association with Westcountry Books, Launceston.

Text and photographs © Craig Weatherhill.

Maps © Craig Weatherhill with thanks to Andrew Climo -Thompson for the lettering.

Cover border by Matthew Harvey.

Designed and produced by Wessex Books.

Design © Wessex Books 2005.

Printed by Eden Print Ltd.

ISBN 1-903035-25-2

CONTENTS
Rol a'n Lyver

FOREWORD
Raglavar

Place Names in Cornwall and Scilly is the ideal source of information for anyone with an interest in Cornwall's unique character and heritage, whether as a visitor or as a resident of the Duchy. Founded upon the most recent research, it gives a valuable insight into the special relationship between the beautiful, varied Cornish landscape and the largely Celtic place names that often describe it.

Cornwall is a very special place, one of Britain's historic nations with its own unique history and language – *Kernuak* (also spelt *Kernewek* and *Kernowek*) – one of the age-old family of Celtic languages still spoken today. Cornish words are found everywhere in the landscape, in family names, in the dialect spoken by many and, of course, in the Cornish language itself which now enjoys protection under the European Charter for Regional and Minority Languages.

Craig Weatherhill brings much of this rich heritage to the reader. A noted scholar and researcher of Cornish place names and the historic environment, he is a well-known specialist in Cornish conservation, archaeology, history, folklore and tradition as well as being a speaker and teacher of the Cornish language. He has produced a number of very fine books on these subjects, notably *Belerion* and *Cornovia*, as well as novels with these studies at their core. His work, especially his detailed surveys of Cornish archaeological sites, is highly acclaimed, both in Cornwall and elsewhere, and he has researched Cornish place names and their individual histories for a quarter of a century.

This book features nearly 3,000 place names within Cornwall and the Isles of Scilly, including those of its ancient 'Hundreds' (more accurately, *Keverangow*), and presents place name lists for each of the modern administrative districts. The author takes full note of acknowledged place name experts such as Dr O. J. Padel, Professor Charles Thomas and the late P. A. S. Pool, as well as drawing upon his own archive of historic place name forms, the largest such compilation in existence. Several of the place names featured are presented here for the very first time, including the Cornish name for the hill of Watch Croft, and the meaning of Newquay's Fistral Bay.

Place Names in Cornwall and Scilly fills a particular need for properly researched, accurate information in order to provide a pleasurable voyage of discovery through the Cornish and Scillonian landscapes as well as providing reliable information for those who may seek to restore Cornish names for display on road signs and maps.

Dalleth agas vyaj omma – omlowena!   *Andrew Climo-Thompson*
                                                        Caderyor / Chairman
                                                        Agan Tavas (Our Language)
                                                        1998–2005

A SENSE OF DIFFERENCE

*Amalveor – Baldhu – Chysauster – Delabole – Egloshayle – Feock –
Goonhilly – Heligan – Kehelland – Liskeard – Marazanvose – Nancledra
– Polyphant – Stencoose – Tredavoe – Warleggan – Zennor*

For many people who cross the Tamar river into the Duchy of Cornwall, the sense
of having moved out of England into another land is immediately apparent as they
catch sight of signposts and nameboards at the roadside. To a very large extent, the
familiar Anglo-Saxon place names like Swindon, Honiton and Plymouth take an
abrupt back seat to thoroughly unfamiliar names like those listed above. Just as
perplexing to many are the roadsigns at the Tamar crossings that declare you are
now in CORNWALL – KERNOW. Cornwall is the English version of the Duchy's
name; Kernow the native name, traceable in that very spelling to c1400 AD and in
other spellings a thousand years before that.

In recent years, bilingual town and village names have begun to spring up all over
Cornwall. St Just is presented as *Lanust*; Penzance as *Pensans*; Helston as *Hellys*;
Hayle as *Heyl* and Mousehole as *Porth Enys*, to mention just a few. This welcome
policy serves to enhance a sense of real difference and one can imagine the further
effect if the names listed above were to be accompanied by their pure linguistic and
historic forms as:

*Amal Vuer – Bal Du – Chysalvester – Delyow Bol – Eglos Heyl – Lan Fyok –
Gun Helghy – Helygen – Kelly Henlan – Lys Kerwys – Marhas an Fos – Nans
Clodry – Pol Lefant – Stumcos – Treworthavo – Worlegan – Eglos Senar*

At least 80 per cent of place names in Cornwall are derived from the Cornish
language (the rest being largely of English and French origin), a tongue that has
survived from prehistory to the present day. Far from being a 'dead' language, a
recent independent survey for the UK Government showed that more than 3,500
people have a working knowledge of Cornish – a number that is steadily growing as
awareness and pride in a very ancient heritage increases.

Closely related to Breton and Welsh, all three tongues evolved from the Celtic
language called Brythonic (British) which was spoken throughout Britain long
before a single word of English was ever uttered on British soil.

In recent years, archaeological and linguistic opinion on the subject of Celtic
languages has radically altered. Until only a few years ago, the established thinking
was that these languages were introduced into Britain and Ireland at the beginning

of the Iron Age, between BC 800 and BC 500. It is now accepted among leading British and European archaeologists and linguists that Celtic languages have been indigenous to Britain since at least the Neolithic era (BC 4,500–BC 2,000) – possibly even earlier – and that all those millennia ago, Celtic first sprang up to become the lingua franca of Atlantic communities along a sea-trading route stretching from the Iberian peninsula to the Hebrides. From then until the Roman invasion of 43 AD, Britain saw no major migrations of peoples to its shores (contrary to the previously fashionable view), only new technologies and beliefs that would largely have arrived by way of those trading routes. The Celtic-speaking peoples of modern Britain and Ireland, along with their native languages (including the Cornish people and their own tongue), are therefore the direct descendants of those first permanent residents of these islands with an unbroken heritage that is at least six thousand years old. As in Wales and other Celtic lands, to see so much of this ancient language in the landscape of Cornwall more than enhances that timeless quality which remains an essential ingredient of Cornwall's unique character.

The place names of Cornwall and the Isles of Scilly not only mystify visitors but also a great many locals who often wonder what they mean. Many of them, when translated, give insights into the landscapes of centuries ago; some give the names or professions of people who lived and worked there all that time ago – or who even committed crimes in places like *Nansladron*, 'thieves' valley'. Some names are purely descriptive of the landscape, others tell of past activities such as mining and hunting, or record animals, both wild and domestic, that once frequented the immediate area. In fact, many Cornish families adopted the name of the place from which they originated as their surname: famous people such as the inventor and engineer Richard Trevithick, or Rick Rescorla who saved so many lives at the expense of his own at the World Trade Centre tragedy in 2001, had surnames derived from Cornish place names.

Place name research is like opening windows upon history and should be viewed in that light. It is neither the sole preserve of the linguist nor of the archaeologist/ historian but lies within the field of both. This book presents the most recent interpretation of the many names it features but it has to be stressed that opinions on some may well alter in the future as previously undiscovered historic spellings are found and shed new light upon a previously established translation. Like the archaeology of which it is a branch, place name research constantly adapts to the increase of knowledge that comes with continuing study and new discoveries.

How do Cornish place names differ from English ones?

By Tre, Ros, Car, Lan, Pol and Pen, shall ye know the Cornishmen

Cornwall has, in fact, both Cornish and English place names, along with a scattering of French ones, a few Old Scandinavian names and even one that is suspected to be from Classical Greek. The Cornish names are generally old: most of those that begin with *Bos-* ('dwelling'), *Car-* (also *Ker-* and *Cayr-*, 'fort, enclosed farmstead') and *Tre(f)-* ('farm, settlement') are known to be a good 1,500 years old and are probably older still. Names with *Ty-* ('house') seem to appear around the ninth century AD and become *Chy-* from about the twelfth century, although the older form was retained by major manorial centres like *Tehidy, Tywarnhayle, Tywardreath, Tybesta* and *Degembris* as though the archaic form was seen as a symbol of prestige.

At the other end of the time scale are names like the West Cornish coastal ones featuring the word *Zawn* (correctly *sawan*), meaning a blind chasm in the cliffs where erosion has eaten away at softer mineral veins to leave these dark, narrow abysses. None of the *Zawn* names appear to predate the Tudor period and may have been coined by the many Breton residents then in Cornwall, perhaps using their own word *saon*, and who were forced to leave by the religious and racial persecutions of the mid sixteenth century.

Some words found in Cornish place names are not easy to translate, the outstanding example being the word *Ros*. Many books translate this as 'heathland' but this is rarely, if ever, applicable to the places where it is found. *Ros* has a number of meanings and the topography of each site has to be checked before the appropriate meaning can be offered. Its earliest meaning was 'promontory', expanding to include 'hillspur' and 'coastal slope'. The scope then widened to bring in 'uncultivated valley' and 'roughland surrounded by farmland'.

Hal is often given as 'moor' and this is generally true if 'moor' is interpreted in its older sense of 'marsh' (although a few rare examples of *hal* do apply to upland areas of wilderness). Many of the places with this element in their name lie close to marshy areas with an extensive growth of willow carr and further research might reveal if there is any relationship between the words *hal* and *helygen* ('willow tree'), and even with *heyl* (see below).

Heyl is often cited to mean 'estuary' but its true meaning is rather more precise than that. It seems to be exclusively applied to tidal estuaries or inlets in which large expanses of sand or mud flats are exposed at low water. It therefore contrasts with *logh* which is applied to inlets and estuaries that retain deep water at all tides (only very rarely applying to inland lakes and pools). Modern dictionaries tend to give *hayl* but a study of the historic forms of the word conclusively shows that the true spelling is *heyl*.

A particular feature of Cornish names is that Old, Middle and Late Cornish spellings are all to be found and generally within definite geographical areas. Old Cornish (roughly pre-1200) featured hard, sometimes guttural, endings like those surviving in Welsh and Breton but, unlike those two languages, a medieval process of softening occurred in Cornish. In eastern parts of the Duchy, where the language became moribund at an early date, the Old Cornish forms remained frozen in time so that one frequently finds *nant*, 'valley' and *cuyt* 'wood'. Further to the west, these forms evolved within the living language to the softer sounds and the same words are found as *nans* and *cos*.

In West Cornwall, the stronghold of the language's survival into modern times, further evolutionary changes took place within Late Cornish (c1550 onwards), the most noticeable of which has been given the grand name of 'pre-occlusion'. This introduced extra sounds into short, stressed syllables; a *b* before *m*, and *d* before *n*. In this way *omma*, 'here', became *obma*, and *lemmyn*, 'now', became *lebmen*. This explains why a name that might appear in East or Mid Cornwall as *Pen Du* might be seen a map in West Cornwall as *Pedn Du* (it does not occur in names like **Penzance** because −*zance* is the part that is stressed). Another feature of Tudor and Late Cornish was the frequent change of −*s*- into −*j*- (and, sometimes, an initial *y*- would become *j*-). This sound was close to the −*s*- of 'pleasure'.

These historical variations are of considerable importance and it is felt by the writer that, when restoring Cornish place names to purer historic forms, the features of Old, Middle and Late Cornish should be retained (unless a recorded spelling shows that the evolutionary change did take place, even if the spelling later reverted to the older form as happened, for example, in the case of **Liskeard** – *Lys Cerruyt* c1010, *Lyskyrrys* 1375, *Lyskeryd* 1380).

The Celtic connection with Wales and Brittany can easily be shown by parallel place names such as **Landewednack** (Cornwall), **Landevennec** (Brittany), and **Pendeen** (Cornwall), **Pendine** (Wales).

How are Cornish place names constructed?

Typically, Cornish place names begin with elements such as *tre*, 'farm, settlement', *pol*, 'pool', and *pen* 'head, end, top'. Normally, these names consist of two elements such as **Trevean** (*tre vyan*, 'little farm'), although simplex (single element) names like **Nance** (*nans*, 'valley'), also occur. Exceptions are found when a conjunction or definite article is inserted between the two elements as in **Perranarworthal**, from *Peran ar wodhel*, 'St Peran facing watery ground', or a compound is used (in this book, compounds are shown as a hyphenated word) as in **Kehelland** (*kelly hen-lan*, 'grove by an old/disused church enclosure'). In names like **Angarrack** (*an garrek*, 'the rock'), the definite article can be the first element but it can never be the final one.

An, 'the' can also never precede an adjective, only a noun, so in names like **Porth Nanven** (*Porthangwin* 1396), the apparent adjective *gwyn*, 'white' must be a noun meaning 'white one' or, more likely in this case, the local surname Angwin which means 'the fair-haired (man)'.

Unlike English names, Cornish ones are usually constructed in 'reverse order'; for example 'little farm' will, in Cornish, be 'farm little', as in **Trevean** above where *vyan* means 'little'. Compounds, though, are usually the other way round, e.g. *hyr-nans*, 'long valley' where *hyr* is 'long', or *hen-dre*, 'old farm, home farm' where *hen* is 'old' and *tre* 'farm'. In a few cases, the compound might be a lost place name: this is certainly the case at **Bosullow** (*bos Chywolow*, 'dwelling at Chywolow') and **Bosigran** (*bos Chygaran*, 'dwelling at Chygaran'). It is interesting to speculate that, in these two cases, the lost place names might have referred to the Late Iron Age courtyard house villages that exist close by.

Also, and unlike English names, some initial letters of the place name's final element may alter. This mutation of initials is a peculiar feature common to all Celtic languages. In the case of **Trevean**, the actual word for 'little' is *byan*. The *b*-softens to *v*- because *tre* is feminine (Cornish nouns are either masculine or feminine) or, with **Angarrack**, *carrek* is feminine singular and will soften after the definite article. Certain other words, like *a*, 'of'; *dew*, 'two' and *war*, 'on, upon', can also cause this softening, which is called lenition and, in compounds like *hen-dre*, the second part of the compound will normally soften, in this case *tre* becoming *dre*.

The letters that become affected in this way are as follows: **B** and **M** soften to **V**; **C** or **K** will become **G**; **CH** will become **J**; **D** softens to **Dh** (spoken like a soft **Th** as in 'this'); **G** becomes **W** or disappears entirely; **P** changes to **B**; **Qu** to **Gw**, and **T** becomes **D**. The sound of **S** will become like that of a **Z**, and the sound of **F** softens to **V**. Some linguists hold that this last example was only spoken, never written, but it is clear from historic place name forms and Late Cornish texts that it was indeed written. In this book, though, **F** will remain unchanged but there is no valid reason why, under the right circumstances, its lenition cannot be shown in writing as **V**. The same argument also applies to the pre-occlusion of Late Cornish which modern linguists say cannot be written, only spoken. Again, place names and Late Cornish texts clearly show it in written form, so there is no reason why their practice cannot be followed.

One or two other mutation types occasionally turn up in place names. One type is 'aspiration', often found after *try*, 'three'. This will turn **C/K** to **H** (so that 'three cats', *try* + *cath* becomes *try hath*). The only other affected letters are **P** to **F**; **Qu** to **Wh**; and **T** to **Th**. Hardening or 'provection' sometimes occurs after a final –s of words like *bos*, *nans* and *ros*, the most commonly found example being the hardening of B to P in, for example, **Nanpean** (*nans* + *byan* > *nans pyan*) and **Rospannel** (*ros* + *banadhel*, 'broom' > *ros panadhel*). To complicate matters, *bos*, 'dwelling' can also soften a following initial but often causes no change at all. *Bos* also retains its Old Cornish form *bod* before the letter R (e.g. **Bodrifty, Bodrugan**).

In revived and written Cornish, the rules of mutation tend to be rigidly observed but, in place names, its use was far from regular and it is not beyond the realms of possibility that there are linguistic or historical reasons for this that are not presently understood. In his suggested reconstructed forms for each Cornish language place name, the writer believes it right to show mutation where it historically occurs (even if it only shows up in one ancient spelling and also where it should not occur in theory), and not to show it where the history of the name never utilised it. It is important to note that *eglos*, 'church' almost never causes lenition in a following name or word but *lan*, 'early church enclosure' nearly always does and yet both words are feminine.

Names of non-Cornish origin

About 20 per cent of Cornwall and Scilly's place names are English, with a few of French origin, a very few from Old Scandinavian and one that may be derived from Classical Greek. None of these have the antiquity of most Cornish names.

Evidence of English settlement in Cornwall is later than generally perceived and may not have occurred until the tenth century. Certainly no English-derived place name in the Duchy can be shown to be any older than the late tenth or early eleventh century: a study of those listed in the Domesday survey of 1086 from within that area north of the Ottery river where English place names predominate, and thought to be the area where the earliest English settlement in Cornwall occurred, shows that none are recorded before the Norman period. Their elements are cited in this book in Old English forms.

The scattering of French language place names undoubtedly find their beginnings under Norman administration but the very few Old Scandinavian ones are something of a mystery. There was a brief Cornu-Viking alliance in AD 838 and Scandinavian visits to the Isles of Scilly in the tenth century (plus a raid on the then Canterbury-controlled priory at Padstow) but no known settlement of these people that could have been permanent enough to have established lasting place names.

Personal names

The names of people frequently crop up in the Duchy's place names and, naturally enough, most of those that occur in Cornish language place names are of Celtic origin. Many of these personal names can be found in documentation from Cornwall, Wales, Brittany and further afield and can be confidently presented in their original forms. Other names are not documented and can only be reconstructed in a conjectural form with the help of historical and linguistic analogy. Names of English and French origin also occur and, in most cases, can be found in documentary sources.

Saints' names are of particular note and the standard has been fully explained by Dr N. J. A. Williams in his paper *Saint in Cornish* (Cornish Studies No 7, 1999). To summarise, the names of Celtic saints and certain other well known ones such as Michael and John are rarely, if ever, preceded by the epithet 'Saint' (*Sent, Sen*) in the language, and place names in particular, although the title was occasionally used for other foreign saints, e.g. the village of St Hilary (Bishop Hilarius of Poitiers) is recorded as *Seynt Eler* c1680, so **Sent Eler**; but the town of St Austell is **Austol** (*Austol* c1150).

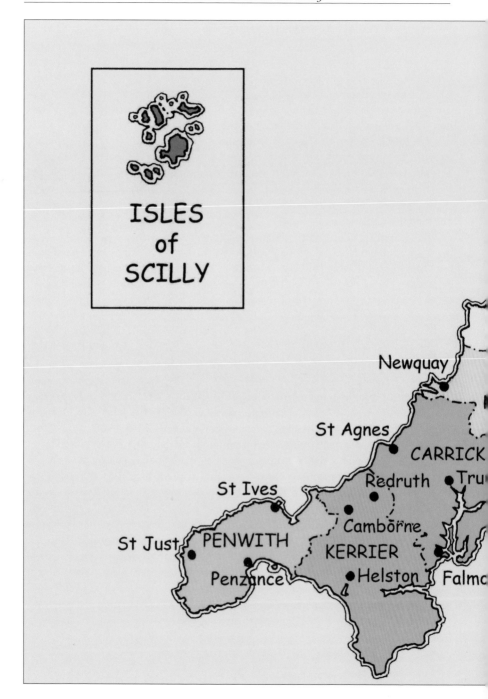

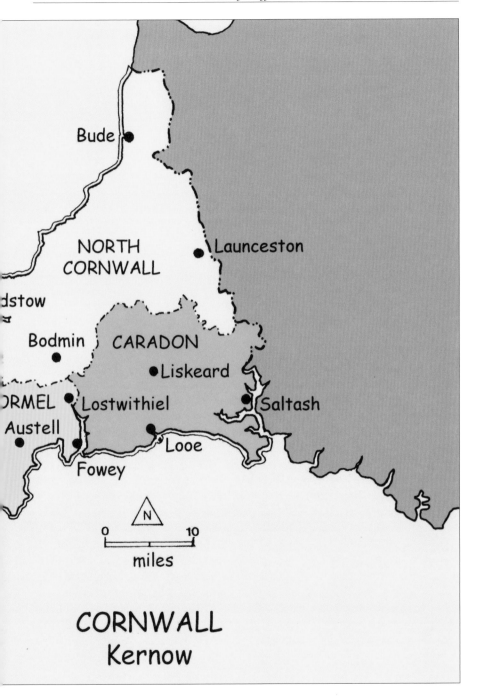

CORNWALL
Kernow

THE CORNISH HUNDREDS
An Keverangow a Gernow

Kerrier: *Keryer* c1250, probably 'place of forts', C. *ker-yer*.

Lesnewth : *Lysnewyth* 1238, 'new court/administrative centre', C. *lys noweth*.

Penwith: *Penwyth* 1236, probably 'end-district', C. *pen-wyth*.

Powder: *Poureder* 1131, 'ploughland region', C. *pow ereder*.

Pydar: *Pydereshyr* 1284, 'fourth (Hundred)', OC *pedera* + OE *scir*.

Stratton: *Straetneat* c881, 'flat-bottomed valley of the river Neet', OC *strad Neth*.

Trigg: *pagus Tricurius* C7, *Tryger* C14, '(land of) three war-hosts', C. *try gor*.

Wivelshire, East: *Estwyveleshyre* 1284, 'eastern part of a twofold shire', OE *est twifeald scir*. Also, *Rilaston* 1084 (from its principal manor), C. *res legh*, 'slab ford' + OE *tun*, 'farm, settlement'.

Wivelshire, West: *Westwyveleshyre* 1284, 'western part of a twofold shire', OE *west twifeald scir*. Also, *Fawiton* 1084 (from its principal manor), C. *faw-y*, 'beech-trees river' + OE *tun*, 'farm, settlement'.

The Cornish Hundreds are of pre-Norman origin and may have been Celtic petty kingdoms under the ancient Kingdom of Dumnonia. This covered much of Britain's south-western peninsula and shrank in the face of Anglo-Saxon advance until, by the tenth century, it was restricted to today's extent of the Duchy and no longer Dumnonia but *Cerniu*. Each termed a *keverang*, a word meaning 'war-host', these were not 'Hundreds' on the Anglo–Norman model but something much more ancient. Originally six in number, the eastern pair of Trigg and Wivelshire later became sub-divided, with Trigg becoming Trigg, Lesnewth and Stratton; and Wivelshire being divided into East and West. Today, they are sadly extinct and only two of the local government districts created in 1974 retain the ancient names (Penwith and Kerrier), even though their boundaries do not coincide with the originals. It is interesting to note that no less than five of the ancient Hundreds were referred to by English sources as 'shires': Powder (1187–1331); Pydar (1130–1539); Trigg (c881–1316); East Wivel (1184–1650) and West Wivel (1201–1428). In addition to this, the Duchy Creation Charters of 1337–38 refer to five counties within Cornwall, these being named as Penwith, Kerrier, Poudar, Trigg and Est Wivelshire. This reinforces Cornwall's claim to a unique constitutional status as no shire county can contain shire counties within itself.

CORNWALL

(Puro)coronavis (for *Durocornovio*) c700 (c400); *Cornubia* c705; *Cornovio* C9; *Cerniu* 878; *Cornwalas* 891; *Cornugallia, Cornualia* 1086; *Cornwal* c1198; *Kernow* c1400. (**Welsh**: *Cernyw*; **French**: *Cornouaille*; **Italian**: *Cornovaglia*; **Spanish**: *Cornualles*; **Breton**: *Kernev Veur*; **Irish**: *Corn na Breataine*). C. *kernow*, 'promontories' + OE *wealas*, 'Britons'.

Duck Street, Mousehole.

Recommended publications

Place name interpretation is a notoriously difficult task. Names invariably change as the years go by, particularly when the mapmaker or documentarian is unfamiliar with the language and writes down what he thinks he hears. This commonly occurred in Cornwall with the result that, all too often, a modern form bears little resemblance to the original; for example, who would ever guess that the name **Bellowal** was once **Boslowen** or that **Scarrabine** was **Roscarrek Byan**?

This is where the search for historical records of the name becomes essential and, for this reason alone, it is not normally advisable to decipher a place name simply by consulting a dictionary. Even with historical research, there have been several cases where a name has been ascribed a meaning with reasonable certainty, only for a newly discovered historical reference to shed a different light upon it. As a result, no place name scholar can ever claim to have everything right. This book fully utilises the very latest research but, even then, some names may have to be reappraised in the future. Such is the nature of place name study.

There have been some unfortunate publications in the field of Cornish place names, some relying more on fantasy than fact and even citing words and place names that do not exist. T. F. G. Dexter's *Cornish Names* (1926 and still available) is among the most misleading of these. The best and most reliable sources are the following:

Gover, J. E. *The Place Names of Cornwall* (1948, unpublished MS volumes at the Royal Institution of Cornwall, Truro) Later research has superceded some of Gover's work which, although generally useful, has to be approached with some caution).

Padel, O. J. *Cornish Place Name Elements* (1985)
A Popular Dictionary of Cornish Place Names (1988)

Pool, P. A. S. *The Place Names of West Penwith* (2nd edition 1985)
The Field Names of West Penwith (1990)
The Field Names of the Manor of Mulfra (Journal of the Royal Institution of Cornwall 1994)

Svensson, Orjan *Saxon Place Names in East Cornwall* (1987)

Thomas, Charles *Exploration of a Drowned Landscape* (1985, giving valuable insight into place names of the Isles of Scilly)
The Coast and Cliff Names of Gwithian (Journal of the Royal Institution of Cornwall 1965, 1967)

Weatherhill, Craig *Cornish Place Names and Language* (1995)
Cornish Place Names Index (unpublished archive files)

Recommended dictionaries are as follows:

Nicholas Williams *English–Cornish Dictionary* (Everson Gunn Teoranta/Agan Tavas 2000, available from Agan Tavas, Gordon Villa, Sunnydale Road, Portreath, Redruth, Cornwall TR16 4NE). This is the most comprehensive dictionary available, revising Nance's Unified spelling system to bring it remarkably close to the appearance of Cornish in the 16th century. Containing 24,000 headwords, it is the first dictionary to allow for regional variations.

R. Morton Nance *A New Cornish–English and English–Cornish Dictionary* (1938/1955, republished 1990, available from AganTavas). The first comprehensive Cornish dictionary, it is valuable in that it gives Old, Middle and Late spellings to augment his Unified spelling which itself closely resembles Middle Cornish.

R. R. M. Gendall *Practical Dictionary of Modern Cornish* (Cornish–English 2nd edition 1997)

A New Practical Dictionary of Modern Cornish (English–Cornish 1998, both available from Teer ha Tavas, Tregrill Vean, Menheniot, Liskeard, Cornwall PL14 3PL). These represent the first ever in-depth research into Late Cornish.

Abbreviations used in the Place Name Lists

Br.	British/Brythonic Celtic		ME	Middle English
C.	Cornish		MF	Middle French
E.	English		Mod.	Modern
F.	French		NF	Norman-French
Gk.	Greek		OC	Old Cornish
LC	Late Cornish		OE	Old English
			OSc.	Old Scandinavian

C12, C13, etc. = 12th century, 13th century, etc.

Abbreviations used in Index of Cornish Place Name Elements

adj.	adjective		LC	Late Cornish
adj. suff.	adjectival suffix		m.	masculine
card. no.	cardinal number		OC	Old Cornish
coll.	collective plural		pl.	plural
comp.	compound		pref.	prefix
def. art.	definite article		prep.	preposition
dim.	diminutive		suff.	suffix
f.	feminine		v.	verb
int.	intensive		v.n.	verb noun

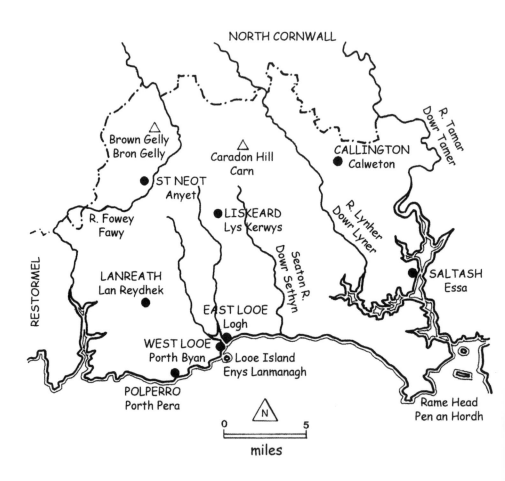

NORTH CORNWALL

R. Tamar
Dowr Tamar

Brown Gelly
Bron Gelly

Caradon Hill
Carn

CALLINGTON
Calweton

ST NEOT
Anyet

R. Lynher
Dowr Lyner

R. Fowey
Fawy

LISKEARD
Lys Kerwys

RESTORMEL

LANREATH
Lan Reydhek

Seaton R.
Dowr Sethyn

SALTASH
Essa

EAST LOOE
Logh

WEST LOOE
Porth Byan

Looe Island
Enys Lanmanagh

POLPERRO
Porth Pera

0   N   5

miles

Rame Head
Pen an Hordh

District of CARADON
Randyr CARN

Place Names of the District of
CARADON

Henwyn Plasow an Randyr
Carn

Addington (SX 2565): 'Eadda's farm', OE *Eaddan tun*.

Albaston (SX 4270): *Alpiston* 1337, 'solitary stone', OE *anlipigan stan*.

Anderton (SX 4152): *Underdon* 1700, 'below a hill,. ME *under don*.

Antony (SX 3954): *Anton* 1195, 'Anta's farm', OE *Anta tun*.

Appledore (SX 3268): *Apelderford* 1315, 'apple-tree ford', OE *apulder ford*.

Ashton (SX 3868): *Aissetone* 1086, 'ash-tree farm', OE *aesc tun*.

Badham (SX 2458): 'Badda's homestead', OE *Badda ham*.

Bake (SX 1854): *Bak* 1356, 'back, ridge', OE *baec*.

Bake (SX 3258): *Bak* 1294, 'back, ridge', OE *baec*.

Barbican (SX 2654): *Barvyan* 1457, 'little summit', C. *bar vyan*.

Barcelona (SX 2253):, so called since C18, presumably after the Catalonian city. It was formerly *Trelawne Cross*, E. 'crossroads at **Trelawne**'.

Bawdoe (SX 1359): *Bodou* 1279, 'dwellings', OC *bodow*.

Bealbury (SX 3766): *Bealdebury* 1361, 'Bealda's fort', OE *Bealda byrig*.

Bearah (SX 3562): *atte Beare* 1337, 'at the grove', ME *atte beare*.

Bearland (SX 3469): *Berland* 1284, 'barley land', OE *bere land*.

Bedwindle (SX 1362): 'dwelling in a fair place', OC *bod wyn-el*.

Beneathwood (SX 3072): *Bynethewode* 1337, 'below the wood', ME *byneth the wode*.

Bephillick (SX 2259): *Bosfilek* 1319, 'Felec's dwelling', OC *bod Felek*.

Berry Down (SX 1968): *Berydon* 1516, 'fort hill', OE *byrig dun*.

Bicton (SX 3169): *Bucaton* 1337, 'Beocca's farm', OE *Beocca tun*.

Bin Down (SX 2757): *Byndon* 1535, 'bees' hill', OE *beona dun*.

Birchenhayes (SX 3966): 'birch tree enclosure/holding', OE *bircan (ge)haeg*.

Bittleford (SX 4064): *Biteliswrthe* 1198, 'Bitela's enclosed settlement', OE *Biteles worthig*.

Blackaton (SX 2960): *the Blakedowne* 1596, 'dark hill', OE *blaecan dun*.

Blackendown (SX 4350), 'dark hill', OE *blaecan dun*. Also recorded in Cornish as *Minadew*, 'dark hillside', C. *menedh du*.

Blacktor Downs (SX 1573): *Blaketorremore* 1401, 'marsh at Black Tor ('black crag', OE *blaec torr*)', OE *blaec torr mor*.

Blunts (SX 3463): *Blunts Shopp* 1687, E. 'Blunt's workshop', after a C16 family.

Bocaddon (SX 1758): *Bodkadwen* 1315, 'Cadwen's dwelling', OC *bod Cadwen*.

Boconnoc (SX 1460): *Boskenech* 1266, 'Cenoc's dwelling', C. *bos Kenek*.

Bodargie (SX 1662): *Bodergi* 1315, 'Wurci's dwelling', OC *bod Worgy*.

Bodbrane (SX 2359): *Bodbran* 1086, 'Bran's dwelling', OC *bod Bran* (personal name from C. *bran*, 'crow, raven').

Bodinnick (SX 1252): *Bosdynek* 1396: 'fortified dwelling', C. *bos dynek*.

Bodway (SX 2962): *Bodewey* 1302, probably 'Dewi's dwelling', OC *bod Dewy*.

Bofarnel (SX 1063): *Bodfernan* 1281, 'Faernan's dwelling', OC *bod Fernan*.

Bofindle (SX 1568): *Bodfelen* c1350, 'Felen's dwelling', OC *bod Felen*.

Bohetherick (SX 4067): *Bohydrek* 1402, 'Hidroc's dwelling', OC *bod Hydrek*

Bokenver (SX 2855): *Bodkenver* 1394, 'Cynvor's dwelling', OC *bod Kenver*

Bonyalva (SX 3059): *Bennavela* 1394, probably 'place of broom', C. *banadhel-va*.

Bosmaugan (SX 1162): *Bosmaelgon* 1284, 'Maelgon's dwelling' , C. *bos Malgon*.

Boturnell (SX 2062): *Botornel* c1320, 'Dornel's dwelling', OC *bod Dornel*.

Botus Fleming (SX 4061): *Bodflumiet* 1318, 'Flumyet's dwelling', OC *bod Flumyet*.

Braddock (SX 1662): *Brodoke* 1422, 'broad oak', OE *brad ac*.

Bray (SX 2757): *Bre* 1306, 'hill', C. *bre*.

Bray Shop (SX 3274): *Bray's Shop* 1728, E. 'Bray's workshop', from a C17 family.

Brendon (SX 2658): *Bremdon* 1296, 'bramble hill', OE *bremel dun*.

Bridals/Bridles (SX 2151): *Brydewille* 1465, 'Bride's spring', OE *Bride wielle*.

Brightor (SX 3561): *Bryghtere* 1326, 'dappled land', C. *brygh-tyr*.

Browda (SX 3071): *Brodewode* 1330, 'broad wood', ME *brode wode*.

Brown Gelly (SX 1972): *Brongelly* 1283, 'grove hill', C. *bron gelly*.

Bucklawren (SX 2755): *Boklowwern* c1200, 'fox's corner', C. *bagh lowarn*.

Bunning's Park (SX 1872) E. 'Bunning's paddock/field', after John Bunnyng, a C15 tenant.

Burraton (SX 4159): *Bureton* 1280, 'peasants' farm', OE *(ge)bura tun*.

Cadson Bury (SX 3467): *Cadokestun* 1175 (referring to the farm of Cadson), *Cadebyre* 1262, 'Cadoc's fort', OC. personal name *Cadoc* + OE *tun*, 'farm' and OE *byrig*, 'fort'.

Caduscot (SX 2063): *Coldruscot* 1418, 'ridge across a wood', OC *kyl dres-cuyt*.

Callington (SX 3569): *Calwetona* 1080, 'farm by a bare hill', OE *calwe tun*, with reference to Kit Hill. Note that Callington is not the *Caellwic* recorded in C10, this most likely being located in the Bodmin–Wadebridge area of North Cornwall.

Calstock (SX 4368): *Kelwistok* 1272: 'Outlying farm near a bare hill', OE *calwe stoc* (see **Callington**).

Canakey (SX 2061): probably 'dog's tor', C. *carn ky*.

Caradon (SX 2770): *Carnedune* c1160. C. *carn*, 'tor', with addition of OE *dun*, 'hill'.

Carburrow (SX 1570): *Carbura* 1256, 'boar's fort', C. *ker/cayr bora*.

Carglonnan (SX 2159): *Kylglynan* 1327, 'ridge by a small deep valley', C. *kyl glynen*.

Cargloth (SX 3354): *Cargluthan* 1432, 'fort by a small ditch', C. *ker/cayr gledhyn.*

Cargreen (SX 4362): *Carrecron* 1018, 'seal rock', C. *carrek ruen.*

Carkeel (SX 4160): *Karkil* 1280, 'ridge fort', C. *ker/cayr kyl.*

Carleon (SX 2858): *Carleghion* 1339, 'fort of slabs', C. *ker/cayr leghyon*

Carracawn (SX 3257): *Caricon* 1291, 'lamb's rock', C. *carrek on*; or 'rock by ash-trees', C. *carrek on.*

Cartole (SX 1954): *Cruktoll* 1284, 'hollow barrow/tumulus', C. *crug toll.*

Cartuther (SX 2663): *Cructuther* 1328, 'Teudar's barrow/tumulus',C. *crug Teudar.*

Castle Dewey (SX 1670): *Castelduy* 1327, 'castle on the river **Dewey**', C. *castel Duy.*

Castlewich (SX 3668): *Castlewyk* 1284, 'castle at a forest settlement', C. *castel wyk.*

Catchfrench (SX 3059): *Cachefrenshe* 1458, 'free chase/hunting ground', F. *chasse franche.*

Cawsand (SX 4350): *Couyssond* 1405, E. 'cow's sand'.

Cheesewring, The (SX 2672): *Cheswring Rock* 1584, E. 'rock like a cheese-press'.

Chilsworthy (SX 4172): *Chilesworthi* 1337, 'Ceol's holding', OE *Ceoles worthig.*

Cholwell (SX 3368): *Choldewylle* 1428, 'cold well/stream', OE *ceald wielle.*

Clampit (SX 3075): 'muddy hollow, claypit', OE *clam pytt.*

St Cleer (SX 2468): *St Clarus* 1202, after St Clair, a male European saint.

Cleese (SX 2656): *Cleys* 1420, 'ditch', C. *cleys.*

Clennick (SX 3160): *Clunyok* 1284, 'place of meadows', C. *clunyek.*

Clicker Tor (SX 2861): C. *clegar*, 'crag' + addition of OE *torr*, 'crag' (itself borrowed from W. *twr*, 'tower').

Cliff (SX 1255): 'steep slope, cliff, river bank', OE *clyf.*

Clowne (SX 1560): 'meadow', C. *clun.*

Coldrenick (SX 2961): *Kyldreynak* 1302, 'thorny nook', C. *kyl dreynek.*

Coldrinnick (SX 2057): *Kyldreynak* 1302, 'thorny nook', C. *kyl dreynek.*

Colliford (SX 1871): *Colaford* C13, 'Cola's ford', OE *Cola ford.*

Colloggett (SX 4162): 'ridge of mice', OC *kyl logot.*

Colquite (SX 3567): *Kilcoit* 1175, 'wood ridge', OC *kyl cuyt.*

Corneal (SX 3869): *Cornhele* 1305, 'crane's corner', OE *corna healh.*

Cotehele (SX 4268): *Cutheyle* 1484, 'wood on an estuary with tidal flats', OC *cuyt heyl.*

Couch's Mill (SX 1458): E. 'Couch's mill' from C14 family whose name derives from C. *cough*, 'red, scarlet'.

Crafthole (SX 3654): *Crofthol* 1348, 'hollow in enclosed arable land', OE *croft holh.*

Cremyll (SX 4553): *Crimel* 1249, 'fragment of land', OE *crymel.*

Criffle (SX 3260): *Cryffyl* 1451, 'wrinkled place', C. *crygh-el.*

Crockett (SX 3672): *Knoket* 1348, 'knoll at a wood',OC *knogh cuyt.*

Crow's Nest (SX 2669): C17 E. 'crow's nest' for an elevated site with extensive views.

Crumplehorn (SX 2051): *Tremylhorne* 1565, 'Maelhoern's farm', C. *tre Malhorn* (C. personal name from Br. *maglo-isarnos*, 'iron prince').

Cuddenbeak (SX 3657): *Cotynbeke* 1330, 'little point-wood', OC *cuydyn byk.*

Cutbrawn (SX 1258): *Cutbrayn* 1476, 'crow's wood', OC *cuyt bran.*

Cutcare (SX 2767): *Cutkayrowe* 1600, 'wood with forts', OC *cuyt kerrow/ cayrow.*

Cutkieve (SX 2867): 'stump wood', OC *cuyt kyf.*

Cutmere (SX 3260): 'great wood', OC *cuyt muer.*

Cutparrett (SX 2859): *Cut Pervet* 1324, 'middle wood', OC *cuyt pervet.*

Cuttivet (SX 3662): *Cuttyvet* 1334, 'cultivated wood, plantation', OC *cuyt tyvet.*

Dannett (SX 3265): *Dounant* 1303, 'deep valley', OC *down-nant.*

Darite (SX 2569): *Daryet* 1506, 'deer gate', OE *deor geat.*

Darley (SX 2773): *Durklegh* 1296, 'dark clearing',OE *deorc leah.*

Deviock (SX 3155): *Deviek* 1311, perhaps 'the cultivated one', C. *an devyek*, most likely a stream name.

Dobwalls (SX 2165): *Dobbewalles* 1619. E. 'Dobbe's walls' after a C14 Liskeard family.

Doddycross (SX 3062): *Doddacrosse* 1516. E. 'Dodda's cross', from a C14 family.

St Dominick (SX 4067): *St Dominica* 1263, after a female saint.

Doublebois (SX 1964): *Dobelboys* 1293, 'double wood', F. *double bois*. Note nearby place name **Twelvewood** (*Twyfeldewode* 1375), 'two-fold wood', OE *twifeald wudu*).

Downderry (SX 3157): C17 E. name of uncertain meaning, possibly 'dairy on a hill', E. *down dairy.*

Downgate (SX 3672): C19 E. name, 'gate to downland'.

Dozmary Pool (SX 1974): *Thosmery* c1170, 'pleasant drinking bowl', ME *tos mery.*

Drakewalls (SX 4171) C19 E. 'Drake's walls' after a local family.

Draynes (SX 2169): *Draynez* C13, 'overgrown with thorns', C. *dreynys.*

Duloe (SX 2358): *Deulo* 1327, 'two **Looe** rivers' or 'two deep water inlets', C. *dew logh*. An alternative name was recorded as *Lankyp* 1286, 'St Kybi's church enclosure', C. *lan Kyby.*

Dupath (SX 3769): *Thieuespath* 1195, 'thieves' path', OE *theofa path.*

Eddystone (SX 3834): *Ediston* 1405, 'stone in eddying water', ME *edy stone.*

Eglarooze (SW 3454): *Eglosros* 1360, 'church of the Rame peninsula', C. *eglos Ros*. See **Rame Peninsula**.

Ellbridge (SX 4063): *Thelebrigge* 1324, 'plank bridge', OE *thel brycg.*

St Erney (SX 3759): *S. Ternin* 1434, after St Ternin, a male saint.

Erth (SW 3856): 'ploughland', OE *ierth.*

Fairy Cross (SX 1262): *Faircros* 1359, 'fair cross', OE *faegar cros.*

Fawton (SX 1668): *Fawiton* 1205, C. river name *Fawy*, C. *faw-y*, 'beech-trees river' + addition of OE *tun*, 'farm, settlement'.

Forder (SX 4158):, 'at the ford', ME *atte forde.*

Fowey (river): *Fawe* c1210-1306, *Fawi* 1241, *Fawy* 1241-1339, 'beech-trees river', C. *faw-y* (some modern sources give **Fawydh* but this is not borne out by historical references except the late [C17] *Foath*). A late name for the estuary, *Uzell* c1680, may be an LC or dialect word meaning 'windpipe'.

Freathy (SX 4052): *Vridie* 1286, after the Fridia family.
Frogwell (SX 3468): *Frognewilla* 1175, 'frog stream/spring', OE *frocgena wielle*.
Fursdon (SX 2659): 'furze hill', OE *fyrs dun*.
Fursnewth (SX 2267): *Fosneweth* 1196, 'new wall/bank',C. *fos noweth*.
Furzenapp (SX 3367): *Vorsknapp* 1365, 'furze hill', OE *fyrs cnaepp*.
St Germans (SX 3557): after St Germanus of Auxerre. The alternative C. name was *Lannaled, Lanalet* C10, 'Aled's church enclosure', OC *lan Aled*.
Glasdon (SX 3358): *Glazon* 1748, 'greensward, verdure', C. *glasen*.
Golberdon (SX 3271): *Golberdon* 1659, *Goldburne* 1691, 'hill by a marigold stream', OE *golde burna dun*.
Golitha Falls (SX 2268): *Galetha* C19, perhaps 'cataract', C. **golytha*, possibly a cognate of W. *gorlifo*.
Gonamena (SX 2670): *Gunnemaine* 1473, 'downland with stones', C. *gun meyn/menow*.
Goonzion (SX 1767): *Gonsyan* 1516, probably 'waterless downs', C. *gun sehen*.
Gooseford (SX 3867): *Goseford* 1305, 'goose ford', OE *gos ford*.
Gormellick (SX 2462): *Gonmaylek* 1327, 'Maeloc's downs', C. *gun Maylek*.
Gunnislake (SX 4371): *Gunnalake* 1608, 'Gunna's stream', OE *Gunna lacu*.
Halbathick (SX 2560): *Halbothek* 1338, 'humped marsh', C. *hal bothek*.
Hall (SX 1768): *Halle* 1401, 'at the nook', OE *aet thaem hale*.
Halwinnick (SX 3074): 'marsh of the white one', C. *hal Wynnek* (a stream name).
Hammett (SX 3265): *Hamet* 1086, 'summer grazing, shieling', OC *havod* (the historic form retains some of the original Br. *sami-bot*).
Hannafore (SX 2552): *Henofer* 1642, *Hanaver* 1654, 'cock fair/market', OE *hana feire*.
Harewood (SX 4469): *Hergarth* 1351, 'long ridge', C. *hyr-yarth*.
Harrowbarrow (SX 3970): *Harebeare* 1313, either 'hare's wood', OE *hara bearu*, or 'grey wood', OE *har bearu*.
Hatt (SX 3962): *La Hatte* 1305, 'hat (-shaped hill)', OE *haett*.
Haye (SX 3569): *Heye* 1327, 'smallholding, enclosure', OE *(ge)haeg*.
Hendersick (SX 2352): *Hendresuk* 1314, *Hendrasick* 1866, 'waterless home farm', C. *hendre segh*.
Hendrabridge (SX 2665): *Hendrabrigge* 1418, E. 'bridge at Hendra'. **Hendra** is from C. *hendre*, 'home farm, old farm'.
Hendrifton (SX 2369): *Hendreneythyn* 1362, 'Hendra ('home farm', C. *hen-dre*) at the furze', C. *hendre'n eythyn*.
Henwood (SX 2673): *Hennewode* 1338, 'hens' wood', OE *henn wudu*. 'Hen' here refers to wild birds rather than the domestic hen.
Herodsfoot (SX 2160): E. *foot*, 'foot of', added to C. place name **Hiriard*, OC *hyr-yard*, 'long-ridge' (see **Herodshead**).
Herodshead (SX 2060): *Bronhiriard* 1284, 'long-ridge hill', OC *bron hyr-yard*.
Heskyn (SX 3359): *Hiskyn* 1314, 'sedge', C. *heskyn*.

Hessenford (SX 3057): *Heceneford* 1280, 'hags' ford',OE *haegtsena ford*.

Holwood (SX 3463): *Holewode* 1263, 'hollow wood',OE *holh wudu*.

Honicombe (SX 4170): 'honey valley', OE *hunig cumb*.

Hornifast (SX 4165): *Herdenefast* 1200, 'herdsmen's stronghold', OE *hierdena faesten*.

Horningtops (SX 2760): 'top of a horn-shaped hill',OE *horning top*.

Hurlers, The (SX 2571): *The Hurlers* 1584, E. 'the hurlers' from the likeness of the stone circles to men engaged in hurling.

Ince Castle (SX 4056): E. 'castle at Ince'. **Ince** (*Enys* 1427) is C. *enys*, 'island'.

Insworke (SX 4352): *Eniswork* 1361, C. *enys*, 'island' + addition of OE *geweorc*, 'fortification'.

St Ive (SX 3167): *S. Yvone* 1201, *S. Ivon* 1251, after a male saint Ivo or Ivon.

St John (SX 4053): *Seynt Johan* 1375, after St John the Apostle.

Keason (SX 3167): *Kestyngtun* 1175, 'farm of Caest's people', OE *Caestinga tun*.

Kellow (SX 2052): *Kelyou* 1325, 'groves', C. *kellyow*.

Kelly Bray (SX 3571): *Kellibregh* c1286, 'dappled grove', C. *kelly bregh*.

Kernock (SX 3763): *Kernek* 1302, 'little corner', C. *kernyk*.

Kersbrook (SX 3075): *Carsbroc* 1229, 'cress stream', OE *caerse broc*.

Kerslake (SX 3754): 'cress stream', OE *caerse lacu*.

Keveral (SX 2955): *Keverel* 1299, 'place of joint-tillage', C. *kevar-el*.

St Keyne (SX 2460): *Cayne* 1342, *Seynt Kayn* 1525, after female saint Kayn.

Killigarth (SX 2151): *Kylgath* 1214, 'cat's ridge',C. *kyl gath*.

Kilminant (SX 1561): *Kylmenaunt* 1476, 'awl-shaped ridge', OC *kyl menawed*.

Kilquite (SX 3361): *Kylguit* 1327, 'wood ridge', OC *kyl guyt*.

Kingbath (SX 1456): *Kynburgh* 1427, 'royal barrow/tumulus', OE *cyne beorg*.

Kingsand (SX 4350): E. 'King's sand', from C16 family.

Knatterbury (SX 4250): *Nattlebury* c1840, 'fort of nettles', OE *netele byrig*.

Lamellion (SX 2463): *Nansmelin* 1298, 'mill valley', C. *nans melyn*.

Lamellyon (SX 1352): *Lammelyn* 1278, 'mill valley', C. *nans melyn*.

Lammana (SX 2551): *Lamana* 1300, 'monk's church enclosure', C. *lan managh*. This name was transferred to the mainland site from the nearby **Looe Island**.

Lampen (SX 1867): *Lanpen* 1250, perhaps 'end valley', C. *nans pen*.

Landlooe (SX 2559): 'valley of the river **Looe**', OC *nant Logh*.

Landrake (SX 3760): *Lanrach* 1291, 'clearing', C. *lanergh*.

Landulph (SX 4361): *Landelech* 1086, 'Dilic's church enclosure', C. *lan Dylyk*.

Langunnett (SX 1557): *Langenewit* 1086, 'Cyneuit's church enclosure', OC *lan Genewyt*.

Lanlawren (SX 1653): *Nanslowarn* 1356, 'fox's valley', C. *nans lowarn*.

Lanreath (SX 1856): *Lanredoch* 1086, *Lanreythou* 1266, 'Reidoc's church enclosure', C. *lan Reydhek*.

Lansallos (SX 1751): *Lanselewys* 1302, 'Selewys's church enclosure', C. *lan Selewys*.

Lantallack (SX 3560): *Lantollek* 1329, probably 'hollowed valley', OC *nant tollek*.

Lanteglos (SX 1451): *Nanteglos* 1284, 'church valley', OC *nant eglos*.

Lantewey (SX 1668): *Nandywy* 1284, 'valley of the river **Dewey**', OC *nant Duy*.

Lantivet Bay (SX 1650): *Namtiuat* 1086, E. 'bay at Lantivet'. **Lantivet** is 'cultivated valley', OC *nant tyvet*.

Latchley (SX 4073): *Lacheleie* 1341, 'clearing by boggy ground', OE *laecc leah*.

Lawhippet (SX 1453): *Lawhybbet* 1592, 'valley of gnats',OC *nant wybed*.

Lerryn (SX 1457): after the **Lerryn** river (see below).

Lerryn (river): *Leryon* 1289, apparently, 'floods', OC *leryon*.

Lesquite (SX 1754): 'tail of a wood', OC *lost cuyt*.

Lewarne (SX 1765): *Lanwern* 1184, 'alder-trees valley', OC *nant gwern*.

Ley (SX 1766): *Lay Crosse* 1515, E. 'cross at Ley'. **Ley** is 'clearing', OE *leah*.

Linkindale (SX 1768): *Lenkeyndeyrn* 1507, 'Cyndaern's pool', C. *lyn Kyndern*.

Linkinhorne (SX 3173): *Lankynhorn* 1269, 'Cynhoern's church enclosure', C. *lan Kynhorn*.

Liskeard (SX 2564): *Lys Cerruyt* c1010, *Lyskerrys* 1375, 'Kerwyd's court/administrative centre', C. *lys Kerwys*.

Lithiack (SX 3558): *Leydek* 1394, 'muddy', OC *leydek*.

Looe (river): *Loo* 1298–1635, *Lo* 1411, 'deep water inlet, ria', C. *logh*.

Looe, East (SX 2553): *Lo* 1257–1335, 'deep water inlet, ria', C. *logh*.

Looe, West (SX 2553): *Porthbighan* 1280, 'little cove/landing place', C. *porth byan*.

Looe Island (SX 2551): *Insula S.Michaelis de Lammana* c1250, 'island of a monk's church enclosure', C. *enys lan-managh*. The island has been named after Saints Michael (C13–C16) and George after 1584.

Lord's Waste (SX 1774): E. 'lord's waste ground', after Lords of Cardinham.

Lydcott (SX 2957): *Lotcoyd* 1302, 'grey wood', OC *lot cuyt*.

Lynher (river): *Linar* 1018, *Lyner* c1120-1669, probably 'lake-like', C. *lyn-er*, with reference to the appearance of its estuary. The estuary itself was *Hallamore* (undated), perhaps 'marsh of the sea', C. *hal an mor*.

Maders (SX 3471): *Metheros* 1325, 'middle hillspur', C. *medhros*.

Maker (SX 4451): *Macuir* c1000, 'ruin', C. *magor*.

Manaton (SX 3473): 'common farm', OE *(ge)maenen tun*.

Markwell (SX 3658): *Aelmarches wylle* 1018, 'Aelmarch's spring/stream', OE *Aelmarches wielle*.

St Martin-by-Looe (SX 2555): *Martistowe* c1220, *Kayne the More* 1547. The C13 reference is 'St Martin's holy place', OE *Martin stow*, with a C16 dedication to St Kayn (see **St Keyne**).

St Mellion (SX 3865): *S. Melan* 1199, after Melaine, bishop of Rennes (see **Mullion** [Kerrier]).

Mendennick (SX 4153): *Myndenack* 1546, 'fortified tip', C. *myn dynek*.

Menheniot (SX 2962): *Mahynyet* 1311, 'Hyniet's land', OC. *ma-Hynyet*.

Merrymeet (SX 2766): C17 E. 'pleasant meeting place'.

Metherell (SX 4069): *Middylhille* 1327, 'middle hill', ME *myddel hille.*

Middlehill (SX 2869): E. 'middle hill'.

Millbrook (SX 4152): *Milbrok* 1342, 'mill brook', OE *myln broc.*

Millcombe (SX 2255): *Plenentmylle* 1390, E. 'mill at Pelynt' (see **Pelynt**), now E. 'mill valley'.

Millendreath (SX 2654): *Melendrayth* 1329, 'beach mill', C. *melyn dreth.*

Minions (SX 2671): *Miniens* 1613, difficult to interpret for lack of early forms. It may be an archaic plural of C. *men*, 'stone' (as *menyon*) or even 'cold stone', C. *men yeyn*, if it were not for the apparently consistent final *-s*. Alternatively, C. *myn*, 'muzzle, tip' might be involved.

Mixtow (SX 1252): *Michaelstowe* 1502, 'St Michael's holy place', OE *Micheles stow.*

Moditonham (SX 4161): *Modetone* 1306-1428, 'muddy farm', OE *muddig tun*, with –ham (from OE *ham*, 'homestead') being added in the C17.

Molenick (SX 3361): *Melionach* 1309, 'clover patch', C. *mellyonek.*

Moorswater (SX 2364): mod. E. 'stream between marshes'.

Mornick (SX 3172): *Mirinook* 1175, 'ant-infested', C. *muryonek.*

Morval (SX 2656): *Morwell* 1474, 'marsh stream/spring', OE *mor wielle.*

Mount (SX 1468): a contraction of the C17 E. name Mount Pleasant, 'pleasant hill'.

Mount Edgcumbe (SX 4552): E. 'Edgcumbe family's hill', built and named by Sir Richard Edgecomb c1550.

Muchlarnick (SX 2156): *Lanner* 1086, *Muchellanrek* 1382, 'clearing', C. *lanergh*, with the addition of ME *micel*, 'great'.

Narkurs (SX 3255): *Knockers Hole* 1659, E. 'slaughterman's hollow'.

St Neot (SX 1867): *S. Aniet* 1084, after a male saint Aniet, rather than the usually assumed St Neot.

St Neot River: E. 'river of St Neot' since C18. Formerly *Loneny* 1238, *Lonyn/Loneyn* 1241, meaning unknown unless a diminutive of C. *lon*, 'bush, grove', with a river name suffix in *-y*; perhaps 'river of small groves', C. *lonyn-y.*

Netherton (SX 2269): *Nitheraton* 1332, 'lower farm', OE *nitherra tun.*

Newbridge (SX 3467): *Newebrygge* 1496, 'new bridge', ME *new brigge.*

Newton Ferrers (SX 3465): Originally *Neweton* 1086, 'new farm', OE *niwan tun*, the surname *Ferrers* being added when the family held the estate in the C17.

Notter Tor (SX 2773): 'bare crag', OE *hnotte torr.*

Okeltor (SX 4468): *Tokelyng Torre* 1351, 'at the crag with an oak tree', OE *aet thaem acen torr.*

Padderbury (SX 3161): *Padirdabury* 1364, 'fort at Padreda', OC *pedreda*, 'four-fords/watercourses' + OE *byrig*, 'fort'.

Padreda (SX 3355): 'four fords/watercourses', OC *pedreda.*

Pantersbridge (SX 1567): *Pontyesu* 1241, 'Jesus's bridge', OC *pont Yesu*

Patrieda (SX 3073): 'four fords/watercourses', OC *pedreda.*

Pelynt (SX 2055): *Plunent* 1086, 'St Nenyd's parish', C. *plu Nenyd.*

Penadlake (SX 1758): *Penhylek* 1394, 'top/end of willows', C. *pen helyk*.

Pencarrow Head (SX 1550): *Pencarowe* c1480, 'stag's head(land)', C. *pen carow*.

Pencrebar (SX 3568): *Crewabere* 1284, 'crows' grove', OE *craewena bearu*. The addition of C. *pen*, 'head, end, top' is recent.

Pendrym (SX 2655): *Pendrum* 1237, 'ridge top', C. *pen drum*.

Pengover Green (SX 2865): *Pengover* 1334, 'head of a stream', C. *pen gover*, with a modern addition of E. 'green'.

Penhale (SX 4153): 'head of a marsh', C. *pen-hal*.

Penkestle (SX 1463): *Penkastel* c1535, 'castle top', C. *pen castel*.

Penlee Point (SX 4448): *Penlegh* 1359, 'slab/ledge head(land)', C. *pen legh*.

Penpoll (SX 1454): 'head of a creek', C. *pen-pol*.

Penquite (SX 3661): *Pencoet* 1286, 'end/top of a wood', OC *pen cuyt*.

Pensilva (SX 2969): Coined in C19, apparently after the nearby Silver Down. *Pensivillowe* 1592 belongs to a site in Newlyn East parish and not to Pensilva.

Pentillie Castle (SX 4064): C18 name coined by Sir James Tillie, C. *pen*, 'head, end, top' + family name.

Perdredda (SX 3355): *Pydrede* 1306, 'four fords/watercourses',OC *pedreda*.

Pillaton (SX 3664): 'farm defended by stakes', OE *pila tun*.

St Pinnock (SX 2063): *Pynnoke* 1442, after a male saint Pinnoc.

Plashford (SX 2557): 'marshy ford', OE *plaesc ford*.

Plushabridge (SX 3072): *Plysshabrygge* 1428, 'bridge over a marshy spot', OE *plysc brycg*.

Polbathic (SX 3456): *Polbarthek* 1365, *Polvethick* 1699. C. *pol*, 'pool' + uncertain second element, possibly a stream name. The C17 form suggests a personal name *Budoc*, but this is not supported by the earlier form.

Polborder (SX 3864): *Polbother* 1200, 'pool of dirty water', C. *pol bodhowr*.

Poldrissick (SX 3859): *Poldrysoc* 1275, 'brambly pool', C. *pol dreysek*.

Polmenna (SX 1866): *Penmene* 1275, 'hill top',C. *pen menedh*.

Polperro (SX 2050): *Porthpera* 1355, 'Pera's cove/landing place', C. *porth Pera*.

Polruan (SX 1250): *Porthruan* 1284, *Polruen* 1371, 'seal cove/landing place', C. *porth ruen*, rather than the second element representing St Rumon, as often suggested. There is no tradition of St Rumon in this area.

Polveithan (SX 1553): *Penvuthyn* 1330, 'end/top of a meadow', C. *pen vuthyn*.

Polventon (SX 1568): *Penfenten* 1435, 'spring-head',C. *pen-fenten*.

Pont (SX 1452): 'bridge', OC *pont*.

Port Eliot (SX 3657): C16 E. name, 'port of the Eliots' coined by the (then) Ellyot family after acquiring the estate.

Porthallow (SX 2251): *Portatland* 1086, 'cove/landing place at **Talland**', C. *porth Tallan*.

Portlooe (SX 2452): *Porthlo* 1302, 'gateway/entrance to **Looe**', C. *porth Logh*.

Portnadler Bay (SX 2451): C. *porth*, 'cove, landing place' + unknown qualifier that might include C. *an*, 'the, of the, at the'.

Portwrinkle (SX 3553): *Port Wrickel* 1605, 'cove/landing place at a small forest settlement', C. *porth wykkel* (see **Trewrickle**).

Quarle (SX 3666): *atte Quarrere* 1337, 'at the quarry', ME *atte*, 'at the' + MF *quarrere*, 'quarry'.

Queener Point (SX 4148): *Queana Point* 1748, C. *kewn-a*, 'place of moss' + E. 'point, headland'.

Quethiock (SX 3164): *Quedoc* 1241, 'wooded', OC *cuydek*.

Rame (SX 4249): *Rama* 1086, either 'wild garlic', OE *hramma*, or 'border, barrier', OE *rama*.

Rame Head (SX 4148): E. 'headland at Rame'. An alternative C. name, almost certainly a back-formation, was *Pendenhar* c1680, 'the ram's headland', C. *pen an hordh*.

Rame Peninsula (centred at SX 3953): *Ros* c1000, 'promontory', C. *ros*.

Raphael (SX 1950): *Resfrawel* 1284, C. *res*, 'ford' + stream name **Frawel*, of unknown meaning.

Redgate (SX 2268): C18 E. 'red gate'.

Respryn (SX 0963): *Ridpryne* 1270, 'timber ford', C. *res pren*.

Rilla Mill (SX 2973): E. 'mill at **Rillaton**'.

Rillaton (SX 2973): *Ridlehtune* c1150, *Rislestone* 1086, 'slab ford', C. *res legh* + addition of OE *tun*, 'farm, settlement'.

Rosecraddock (SX 2667): *Rescaradec* 1249, 'Caradoc's ford', C. *res* + OC personal name *Caradoc*.

Roselyon (SX 1661): *Elyn* 1444, 'elbow, bend' + late addition of C. *ros*, 'uncultivated valley'.

Rytha (SX 3256): *atte Rytha* 1349, 'at the streamlet', OE *aet thaem ritha*.

Saltash (SX 4358): *Aysh* 1284, 'ash-tree', OE *aesc*, with C14 addition of ME *salt*, 'salt', from the local saltpans.

Sandplace (SX 2556): E. 'place where sand is stored'.

Sclerder Abbey (SX 2253): modern name from Bret. *sklaerder*, 'clarity'.

Sconner (SX 3656): *Rosconeuer* 1311, 'Cynvor's promontory', C. *ros Kenvor*.

Scraesdon (SX 3954): *Creulisdon* 1349, 'weir by a ruin', C. *crew lys*, with addition of OE *dun*, 'hill'.

Seaton (SX 3054): *Seythyn* 1302, after the river name, possibly 'little arrow', C. *sethyn*.

Seaton River: *Seythyn* 1302, *Seythen* 1441, perhaps 'little arrow', C. *sethyn*.

Sharp Tor (SX 2673): 'sharp/pointed crag', OE *scearp torr*.

Sheviock (SX 3755): *Sevioc* 1226, 'strawberry land', C. *sevyek*.

Shortacross (SX 2857): *Short Cross* 1732. E. 'short cross'.

Siblyback (SX 2372): *Sibliback* 1590, 'Sybyly's ridge', from C15 family name + OE *baec*, 'back, ridge'.

Sillaton (SX 3963): *Seleton* 1349, 'farm with a hall', OE *sele tun*.

South Hill (SX 3272): *Suthhynle* 1306, 'south *Henlea', from OE *suth*, 'south, southern' + *hean leah*, 'high clearing' (see **North Hill**, North Cornwall).

St Stephens (SX 4158): *S. Stephanus* 1265, after St Stephen.

Stockadon (SX 4063): *Stocaton* 1321, 'farm built from logs', OE *stocca tun*.

Stoketon (SX 3860): 'outlying farmstead', OE *stoc tun*.

Talland (SX 2251): *Tallan* 1205-1523, 'hill-brow with a church enclosure', C. *tallan*. See also **Porthallow** and **Talland Bay**.

Talland Bay (SX 2251): *Por Tallant* 1699, 'cove/landing place at Talland', C. *porth Tallan*.

Tamar (river): *Tamar, Tamaros* C2, *Tamer* 997-1870, an early Celtic name with common element *tam-*, possibly 'flowing' (as also in Thames, Thame, Tame, etc.) + *-ar, -er* suffix also found in the river **Lynher**.

Taphouse, East (SX 1863): C16/17 E. 'eastern tap-house (alehouse)'.

Taphouse, Middle (SX 1763): C16 E. 'central tap-house (alehouse)'.

Taphouse, West (SX 1563): C16 E. 'western tap-house (alehouse)'.

Tencreek (SX 1458): *Trencruke* 1309, 'farm at the barrow/tumulus', C. *tre'n crug*.

Tencreek (SX 2352): *Kyencruke* 1447, 'ridge with a barrow/tumulus', C. *keyn crug*.

Tencreek (SX 2663): *Trencruk* 1328, 'farm at the barrow/tumulus', C. *tre'n crug*.

Thanckes (SX 4355): from C14, named after the Thonkes family. Previously, it was named *Pengelly* C13, 'end of a grove', C. *pen gelly*.

Tiddy (river): *Tudi* 1018, *Tudy* 1395, apparently 'people's river', OC *tud-y*.

Tideford (SX 3459): E. 'ford on the river **Tiddy**'. The correct pronunciation (often argued about) is 'tid'i-ford' as shown by *Tediford* 1345 and *Tidiford* 1813.

Tilland (SX 1598): *Tyllon* 1598, 'useful land', OE *til land*.

Torpoint (SX 4455): a corruption of *Stertpoynt* 1608, originally OE *steort*, 'tail of land, promontory', with later addition of a tautologous E. *point*, 'headland'.

Trago (SX 1864): *Treiagu* 1277, 'Jago's (Jacob's/James's) farm', C. *tre Yago*.

Trebrownbridge (SX 2959): E. 'bridge at Trebrown'. Trebrown was *Trefron* 1327, *Trebron* 1413, 'hill farm', C. *tre vron*.

Tredarrup (SX 1666): *Tretharap* 1401, 'very pleasant farm', C. *tre wortharap*.

Tredinnick (SX 1666): *Trethynek* 1345, 'farm by a fort', C. *tre dhynek*.

Tredinnick (SX 2357): *Trethynek* 1302, 'farm by a fort', C. *tre dhynek*.

Tredinnick (SX 2957): *Treveythynek* 1300, 'farm at a furze-brake', C. *tref eythynek*.

Tredrossel (SX 3555): *Tredrysell* c1450, 'bramble-grown farm', C. *tre dreys-el*.

Tregantle (SX 3952): *Argantell* 1521, 'silver stream', OC *arhant-el*.

Tregarland (SX 2557): *Crugalan* 1201, 'barrow/tumulus by the Alan stream', C. *crug Alan*.

Tregarrick (SX 2370): *Tregadock* 1552, 'Cadoc's farm', OC *tre Gadek*.

Tregonhawke (SX 4051): *Trekynheauk* 1357, 'Cynhafoc's farm', C. *tre Gynhavek.*

Tregrill (SX 2863): *Tregrilla* 1284, 'Crylla's farm', C. *tre Grylla.*

Trehan (SX 4058): *Trehanno* 1306, 'Hanno's farm', C. *tre Hanno.*

Trehunist (SX 3163): *Trenanast* 1327, *Trenanyst* c1510, C. *tre,* 'farm, settlement' + unknown element, perhaps a personal name.

Trelaske (SX 2253): 'farm on burnt/swaled land', C. *tre losk.*

Trelawne (SX 2253): *Trevelowen* 1284, 'elm-tree farm', C. *tref elowen.*

Trelay (SX 2154): *la Leye* 1305, 'at the clearing', ME *ate lege.*

Trelowia (SX 2956): *Trelewyan* 1303, 'Leuien's farm', C. *tre Lewyen.*

Tremar (SX 2568): *Tremargh* 1284, 'March's farm', C. *tre Margh* (the personal name is the more likely option than C. *margh,* 'horse').

Tremarcoombe (SX 2568): mod. E. 'valley at **Tremar**'.

Trematon (SX 3959): *Trementon* 1187–1346, C. *tre men,* 'stone farm', with addition of OE *tun,* 'farm, settlement'.

Trembraze (SX 2565): *Trembras* 1338, 'farm of the big man', C. *tre'n bras* (*bras* must here be a descriptive noun as the definite article *an,* represented here by *'n,* never precedes an adjective).

Trenant (SX 2168): 'valley farm', OC *tre nant.*

Trenewan (SX 1753): *Trenewyen* 1421, 'Newyen's farm', C. *tre Newyen.*

Trenode (SX 2858): *Trenoda* c1260, perhaps 'Noda's farm', C. *tre Noda.*

Trequite (SX 3261): *Trequit* 1327, 'wood farm', OC *tre cuyt.*

Trerulefoot (SX 3258): E. 'foot of hill at Trerule'. Trerule (*Trerewal* 1310) is 'Riwal's farm', C. *tre Rywal* (personal name from Br. *rigo-ualos,* 'worthy king').

Trethevy (SX 2668): *Trethewy* 1284, 'Dewi's farm', C. *tre Dhewy.*

Trethevy Quoit (SX 2668): *Trethevy-stones* 1584, E. 'stones at Trethevy'.

Trevelmond (SX 2063): *Trevelemount* 1338, 'at the fair hill', ME *atte,* 'at the' + MF *bel mont,* 'fair hill'.

Treverbyn (SX 2067): 'Erbin's farm', C. *tref Erbyn.*

Trevigro (SX 3369): *Trevigora* 1175, 'openings farm', C. *tref egorow.*

Trewartha (SX 2167): 'higher farm', C. *tre wartha.*

Trewashford (SX 3664): *Washford* 1360, 'ford at a washing place', OE *waesce ford* but, since C18, preceded by ME *atte,* 'at the', now represented as *tre.*

Trewidland (SX 2559): *Trewythelon* 1298, 'Gwytelan's farm', C. *tre Wythelan.*

Trewint (SX 2963): 'wind(y) farm', OC *tre wynt.*

Trewoodloe (SX 3271): 'at the wood', ME *atte wode* + C. river name **Looe**, from C. *logh,* 'deep water inlet, ria'.

Treworgey (SX 2456): *Trewurgy* 1438, 'Wurci's farm', C. *tre Wurci.*

Upton (SX 2772): 'higher farm', OE *uppe tun.*

St Veep (SX 1454): *S. Vep* 1262, after St Vepe.

Warleggan (SX 1569): *Worlegan* c1260, possibly C. *wor-legan,* 'watch-place'.

Warleggan River: now E. 'river at Warleggan' but formerly *Mindaldur* 1230, *Bedalder* 1600, perhaps 'quiet water', C. *medhel-dowr*.

Whitsand Bay (centred at SX 3952): *Whitesand Bay* 1813, mod. E. 'bay with white sand'.

Widegates (SX 2857): C17 E. 'wide gates'.

Widlake (SX 2858): *Wythelake* 1340, 'willow stream', OE *withig lacu*.

Wilcove (SX 4256): 'well/stream cove', ME *wille cove*.

St Winnolls (SX 3455): *S. Wynwole* 1386, after St Winwalo.

St Winnow (SX 1157): *San Winnuc* 1086, from St Winnoc (most likely a pet form of the saint's name *Winwalo*).

Withey Brook (stream): *Withebrook Water* 1613, 'willow brook', OE *withig broc*.

Woolston (SX 2968): *Ullavestone* 1086, 'Wulflafe's farm', OE *Wulflafes tun*.

Wringworthy (SX 2658): *Wryngeworthy* 1294, 'cheese-press farmstead', OE *wryng worthig*.

Yolland (SX 2871): *Oldelande* 1377, 'old land/holding', OE *ealde land*.

Caradon: "Welcome to LISKEARD" sign.

District of CARRICK
Randyr CARREK

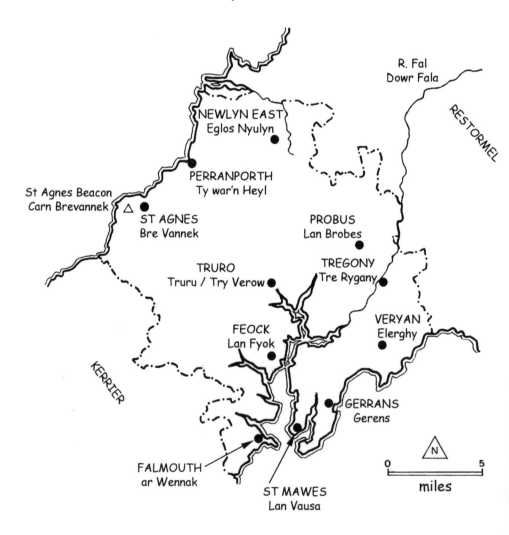

R. Fal
Dowr Fala

RESTORMEL

NEWLYN EAST
Eglos Nyulyn

PERRANPORTH
Ty war'n Heyl

St Agnes Beacon
Carn Brevannek

ST AGNES
Bre Vannek

PROBUS
Lan Brobes

TRURO
Truru / Try Verow

TREGONY
Tre Rygany

VERYAN
Elerghy

FEOCK
Lan Fyok

KERRIER

GERRANS
Gerens

FALMOUTH
ar Wennak

ST MAWES
Lan Vausa

N

0   5

miles

Place Names of the District of CARRICK

Henwyn Plasow an Randyr
Carrek

St Agnes (SW 7250): after St Agnes. The settlement's C. name was *Brevannek* 1261–1415, 'pointed/prominent hill', C. *bre vannek*.

St Agnes Beacon (SW 7050): now E. 'beacon (hill) at St Agnes'. The C. name of the hill was *Carne Bryanick* c1720, 'cairn on a pointed/prominent hill', C. *carn brevannek*.

Allen (river): *St Allen River* 1748, perhaps the ancient, widespread Celtic river name **Alan*, from Br. *alaunos*, probably meaning 'shining, brilliant', rather than being named after the parish. Its source was *Ventoneage* (undated), which may be 'little spring', C. *fentenyk*.

St Allen (SW 8250): after a male saint Alun. The C. name was *Eglosalon* 1302, 'St Alun's church', C. *eglos Alun*.

Allet (SW 7948): *Aled, Alet* 1284, from stream name meaning 'nourisher', OC. *alet*.

Angarrick (SW 7937): 'the rock',C. *an garrek*.

St Anthony-in-Roseland (SW 8532): *S. Antoninus* 1170, after St Entenin, a male Cornish saint (see also **Roseland**).

Ardevora (SW 8740): *Ardevro* 1430, 'facing waters/rivers', C. *ar devrow*.

Arwenack (SW 8132): *Arwennek* 1285, 'facing the stream called **Gwennek*', C. *ar wennek*. The stream name means 'fair/white one' and derives from C *gwen*, the feminine form of *gwyn*, 'white/fair'.

Baldhu (SW 7743): *Baldue* 1755, 'black/dark diggings', C. *bal du*.

Barkla Shop (SW 7350): E. 'Barkla's workshop', from C17 family.

Barteliver (SW 9247): *Baghtylever* 1338, C. *bagh*, 'nook, corner' + a lost place name **Tylever*, OC *ty Lyver*, 'Lyfr's house'.

Bawden Rocks (SW 7053): E. 'rocks off Bawden', the farm name being *Boden* 1748, 'little dwelling', C. *bodyn*. The rocks are also called **Man and his Man** (*the Manrocke* 1587), probably E., but may involve C. *men*, 'stone'.

Benny Mill (SW 8458): E. 'Bennye's mill' after Robert Bennye, recorded in 1572.

Besore (SW 7844): *Boswoer* 1303, 'sister's dwelling', C. *bos whor*.

Bessy Beneath (SW 9242): lack of early forms make this difficult, but possibly a corruption of C. *bos venedh*, 'hill dwelling'.

Bissoe (SW 7741): *Besowe* 1327, 'birch trees', C. *besow*.

Black Rock (SW 8331): now E. 'black rock' but formerly *an garrak ruen* c1400, *Caregroyn* 1540, 'seal rock', C. *carrek ruen*.

Blackwater (SW 7346): E. 'dark stream'.

Blouth Point (SW 9238): C. *blogh*, 'bare, bald' + E. *point*, 'headland'.

Blowinghouse (SW 7451): C18/19 E., 'smelting works'.

Bohortha (SW 8632): *Behorthou* 1302, 'cow-yards', C. *buorthow*. Locally pron. 'b-huh'ra'.

Bolingey (SW 7653): *Mellingy* 1516, 'mill-house', C. *melynjy*.

Bolster (SW 7149): *Bothlester* 1398, 'boat (-shaped) hump', after detached portion of the **Bolster Bank** linear earthwork, C. *both lester*.

Bolster Bank (SW 7149): now E. 'bank at Bolster'. The earthwork has C. names: *Gorres* c1720, 'the weir/dam', C. *an gores*; and *Kleth* 1740, 'ditch', C. *cledh*.

Bosloggas (SW 8434): *Boslogos* 1327, 'dwelling of mice', C. *bos logos*.

Boslowick (SW 7931): *Bodelewyth* 1301, 'Leuit's dwelling', C. *bos Lewyth*.

Bosvigo (SW 8145): *Bosveygou* 1284, C. *bos*, 'dwelling' + unknown word or name.

Buckshead (SW 8346): E. 'buck's hill-brow'.

Calenick (SW 8243): *Clunyek* 1334–1370, 'meadow place', C. *clunyek*.

Callestick (SW 7150): *Kellestoc* 1286, apparently a hybrid name with C. *kelly*, 'grove' + addition of OE *stoc*, 'holding'.

Camels (SW 9234): *Cammals* 1359, 'crooked cliff', C. *cam-als*.

Camerance (SW 8437): *Camweres* 1303-1325, 'crooked slope', C. *cam-weres*.

Caragloose Point (SW 9439): 'grey rock', C. *carrek los*.

Carclew (SW 7838): *Crucleu* 1311, 'colour(ed) barrow/tumulus', C. *crug lyw*.

Cargoll (SW 8156): *Cargaul* 1302, 'fort by a road-fork', C. *ker/cayr gawl*.

Carines (SW 7959): *Crowarthenys* 1398, 'hut by detached land', C. *crow orth enys*. Note the nearby **Colgrease** (*Crowgres* 1498), 'middle *Crow*', C. *Crow gres*; and **Carevick** (*Crowarthevycke* 1567), C. *crow orth*, 'hut by' + unknown word or name.

Carland (SW 8453): *Cowland* 1813, E. 'cow land'.

Carlyon (SW 8242): *Carleghion* 1287, 'fort of slabs', C. *ker/cayr leghyon*.

Carn Clew (SW 7555): probably 'bell (-shaped) crag', C. *carn clogh*.

Carne (SW 9138): 'cairn', C. *carn*, here referring to the huge barrow of Carne Beacon.

Carn Gowla (SW 6951): perhaps 'lookout crag', C. *carn golva*, or a corruption of C. *carn golowva*, 'beacon crag'.

Carn Haut (SW 7555): 'hat (-shaped) crag', C. *carn hot*.

Carnon Downs (SW 7940): *Goon Carnon* 1782, 'downland at Carnon', C. *gun Carnen*. **Carnon** is 'little cairn',C. *carnen*, after one of the Bronze Age barrows here.

Carn Pednathan (SW 9440): *Cabaneithan* 1866, 'the furze cape', C. *capa'n eythyn*. Now 'the furze headland', C. *pen* (LC *pedn*) *an eythyn*.

Carrick Calys (SW 8236): 'hard rock', C. *carrek cales*.

Carricknath Point (SW 8432): *Caregnah Point* 1584, 'hewn rock',C. *carrek nath*.

Carrick Roads (centred at SW 8335): *Careck Rode* 1584, C. *carrek*, 'rock' (here referring to **Black Rock**) + ME *rode*, 'anchorage, haven'.

Carrine (SW 7943): *Caryeyn* 1280, 'cold/bleak fort', C. *ker/cayr yeyn.*
Carsawsen (SW 8038): 'Saxon's fort', C. *ker/cayr Sawsen.*
Carvedras (SW 7231): *Carvodret* c1250, 'Modret's fort', C. *ker/cayr Vodres.*
Carvinack (SW 8147): *Carveynek* 1327: 'stony fort', C. *ker/cayr veynek.*
Carvinack (SW 7935): *Kerwynnec* 1288, 'fort by a stream called Wynnek' (stream name meaning 'white/fair one'), C. *ker/cayr wynnek.*
Carvossa (SW 9148): *Carawoda* 1302, *Carwosa* 1480, perhaps 'fort of bloodletting', C. *ker/cayr wosa.*
Carwarthen (SW 8437): *Carwenran* 1314): 'Uuenran's fort', C. *ker/cayr Wenran.*
Castlezens (SW 9242): *Kestelsens* 1360, 'holy men's fort', C. *castel sens.*
Chacewater (SW 7544): E. 'chase (hunting ground) stream'.
Chapel Porth (SW 6949): *Porth Chapell* 1699, 'chapel cove/landing place', C. *porth chapel*, now in E. word order.
Chirwyn (SW 8041): 'house on a slope', C. *chy ryn.*
Chiverton (SW 7447): 'house on pastureland', C. *chy war ton.*
Chybucca (SW 7848): *Guenbuck* 1714, 'buck's downland', C. *gun bogh*, now altered to appear like: 'ghost's/scarecrow's house', C. *chy bukka.*
Chycoose (SW 8038): *Chiencoys* 1378, 'house at the wood', C. *chy an cos.*
Chycowling (SW 7941): *Chycowlyng* 1554, 'Cowlyng's house' after a C16 family.
Chynhale (SW 7849): *Chyenhale* 1356, 'house at the marsh', C. *chy an hal.*
Chyvelah (SW 7945): *Chywela* 1836, 'beetle-infested house', *chy whyl-a.*
Chyverton (SW 7951): *Chywarton* 1324, 'house on pastureland', C. *chy war ton.*
Chyvogue (SW 7739): *Chifoage* 1634, 'furnace house', C. *chy fog.*
St Clement (SW 8543): *Clemens* 1464, after St Clement.
Cligga Head (SW 7353): *Clegar* 1588, 'crag', C. *clegar.*
Cocks (SW 7652): E. 'Cooke's holding' after the C17 Cooke family.
Coldharbour (SW 7548): E. 'wayside shelter'. So called since 1715, replacing *Gyllyveor* c1600, 'great grove', C. *kelly vuer.*
Comprigney (SW 8145): *Gwele Cloke-prynnyer* 1597, 'gallows field', C. *gwel cloghprenyer.*
Coosebean (SW 8145): *Cusbyan* c1400, 'little wood', C. *cos byan.*
Coosewartha (SW 7246): *Coozwarra* 1748, 'higher wood', C. *cos wartha.*
Cornelly (SX 9145): after St Cornelius.
Costislost (SW 8051): C19 E., for unprofitable land.
Cowlands (SW 8340): *Cownance* 1631, 'enclosed valley', C. *kew-nans.*
Creegbrawse (SW 7443): 'great barrow/tumulus', C. *crug bras.*
Cregoe (SW 9142): *Crugou* 1284, 'barrows/tumuli', C. *crugow.*
Crofthandy (SW 7342): *Croft Hendy* 1794, 'enclosed rough grazing with an old/ruined house', C. *croft henjy.*
Crowsmeneggus (SW 7538): *Rosemenewas* 1660, 'awl-shaped hillspur', C. *ros menawes*, now so changed as to appear as C. *crows venegys*, 'blessed cross'.
Crugsillick (SW 9439): *Crugsulec* 1302, 'Suloc's barrow/tumulus', C. *crug Sulek.*

Cubert (SW 7857): after St Cuthbert. The churchtown had two C. names: *Egloscubert* 1622, 'St Cuthbert's church', C. *eglos Cubert*; and *Lanowyn* 1622, 'Owein's church enclosure', C. *lan Oweyn* (this now appears as a farm name Lanlovey).

Cuby (SW 9245): *S. Kybi* 1282, after St Kybi.

Curgurrel (SW 8837): *Crugeler* 1314, 'coffin barrow/tumulus', C. *crug geler*. This altered to *Crukgorall* 1585, with the appearance of 'ship barrow', C. *crug gorhel*, as if to echo the local legend of King Gerent's burial in a golden ship.

Cusgarne (SW 7640): *Coysgaran* 1277–1542, 'crane's/heron's wood', C. *cos garan*.

Degembris (SW 8556): *Tikenbret* 1201, 'Cynbret's manorial centre', C. *ty Kenbres*.

Devichoys (SW 7737): *Kilcoys* 1652, *Deviscoys* 1652, earlier 'ridge-wood', C. *kylcos*; then 'cultivated-wood, plantation', C. *tevys-cos*.

Devoran (SW 7939): *Dephryon* 1275, 'waters, rivers', C. *devryon*.

Dingerein Castle (SW 8837): C18 name coined by Revd. Whitaker to connect with the local traditions of King Gerent, 'Gerent's fortress', C. *dyn Gerens*.

Elerkey (SW 9139): *Elerghy* 1349, 'swans' place/stream', C. *elergh-y*. See also **Veryan**.

Ellenglaze (SW 7757): *Eylin* 1213, *Elynglas* 1302, 'green Elyn', C. *Elyn glas*. *Elyn*, 'elbow, bend' is likely to have been the stream name.

Engelley (SW 8052): *Gilly* 1404, 'the grove', C. *an gelly*.

St Erme (SW 8449): *Egloserm* 1345, 'St Hermes's church', C. *eglos Erm*.

Fal (river): an ancient name that was *Faele* 969, *Fala* 977–c1540. This is an early Celtic name, the meaning of which has become lost. Its source, now Pentevale (in Restormel Borough), was *Penfenten fala* 1320, 'spring-head of the Fal', C. *penfenten Fala*. The Fal might have been the *Cenionis fluvii* of Ptolemy (C2 AD), placed by him in the approximate position of the Fal. The mouth of the Fal proper, between Tregothnan and Tolverne at SW 8540 and as far upstream as Tregony (SW 9244), was *Hafaraell* 1049, seemingly 'water at the summer fallow land', C. *havar-el*.

Falmouth (SW 8032): *Falesmuth* 1234, E. 'mouth of the Fal river'. The name was only adopted for the infant town in C17 (it formerly belonged to the harbour mouth and bay), all that formerly existed being the house and estate of **Arwenack**, and a village named Smithick (OE *smith wic*, 'smith's village'). Apart from Arwenack, the place does not seem to have had a C. name. Some modern revivalists, though, have coined **Aberfal*, even though (unlike Wales and Brittany), the element **aber* (as 'river-mouth') features in not one C. place name. Perhaps **Loghfala* might have been a better option, as *logh* is the word used in C. place names to denote a deep-water estuary or ria; or maybe **ar Wennek* to retain an historical connection.

Fentongollan (SW 8643): *Fentengollen* 1201, 'hazel-tree spring', C. *fenten gollen*.

Feock (SW 8238): *Lanfioc* c1165, 'St Fioc's church enclosure', C. *lan Fyok*.

Fernsplatt (SW 7641): mod. E. 'ferns plot'.

Flushing (SW 8033): named after the Dutch port of Vlissingen. It was formerly *Nankersis* 1590, 'reedy valley', C. *nans kersys*.

Four Burrows (SW 7648): C16 E. 'four barrows'. A C. name is known: *Bethcywrc* 960, 'grave mound', C. *bedh crug*.

Frogpool (SW 7640): C19 E. 'frog pool'.

Gerrans (SW 8735): after St Gerent, traditionally one of the C6 and C8 Dumnonian kings so named.

Gerrans Bay (centred at SW 9037): now E. 'bay of Gerrans', replacing earlier *Gwyndraith Bay* 1588, 'bay at **Gwendra**'.

Glasney (SW 7834): *Glasneyth* 1291, 'verdure', C. *glasneth*.

Gloweth (SW 7944): *Glowyth* 1485, 'trees used for charcoal', C. *glow-wedh*.

St Gluvias (SW 7834): after St Glyviac, but known as *Behethlan* 1230–1342, perhaps 'dwelling in a pleasant valley', C. *bos hueth-nans* (this name survives as Bohelland).

Golden (SW 9246): *Wolvadon* 1327, 'wolf's hill', OE *wulfa dun*. It was formerly called *Trewygran* C12, C. *tre*, 'farm' + a word or name of uncertain meaning, possibly C. *kygbran*, 'carrion-crow' in either its literal sense or as a personal name.

Goonbell (SW 7249): 'far downs', C. *gun bell*.

Goon Gumpas (SW 7442): 'level downs', C. *gun gompes*.

Goonhavern (SW 7853): *Goenhavar* 1290, 'downs of summer fallow', C. *gun havar*.

Gooninis (SW 7250): *Goenenys* 1404, 'isolated/remote downs', C. *gun enys*.

Goonlaze (SW 7250): *Goonlas* c1720, 'green downs', C. *gun las*.

Goonown (SW 7249): 'downs of fear', C. *gun own*.

Goonpiper (SW 8139): 'Piper's downs', after a local family, C. *gun Pyper/Pyber*.

Goonvean (SW 7944): 'little downs', C. *gun vyan*.

Goonvrea (SW 7049): 'hill downs', C. *gun vre*.

Gorrangorras (SW 7934): *Goneangoras* C16, 'downs at the weir/dam', C. *gun an gores*.

Grampound Road (SW 9150): C19 E. 'road to Grampound' coined when railway station was built. See **Grampound**, Restormel.

Greeb Point (SW 8733): *The Greeb* 1732, 'the reef', C. *an gryb*.

Greensplat (SW 7740): *The Green Plot* 1754, C18 E. 'green plot', now with dialect word *splat*, 'plot of land'.

Grogarth (SW 9145): *Crugoyt* 1278, 'barrow/tumulus in a wood', OC *crug cuyt*.

Gull Rock (SW 9236): now E. 'gull rock', replacing *The Gray* 1720, perhaps 'the flock/herd', C. *an gre*.

Gummow's Shop (SW 8657): C17 E. 'Gummow's workshop', after a local family.

Gwarnick (SW 8148): *Gwernek* c1400, 'alder-grove', C. *gwernek*.

Gwendra (SW 9038): *Gwyndreth* 1343, 'white sand', C. *gwyn-dreth*.

Gwennap (SW 7340): after St Gwenap; earlier *Lanwenap* 1328, 'St Gwenap's church enclosure', C. *lan Wenap*.

Gyllyngdune (SW 8131): *Gillindowne* 1597, 'the deep inlet', C. *an gylen down*.

Gyllyngvase (SW 8131): *Gillenvaes* 1540, 'the shallow inlet', C. *an gylen vas*.

Halbullock (SW 7944): *Halbothek* 1338, 'humped marsh', C. *hal bothek*.

Harcourt (SW 8137): *Harcrake* 1549, 'facing a crag', C. *ar crak*.

Hendra (SW 7855): 'old farm/home farm', C. *hendre*. Cornwall's most common place name with more than 34 instances.

Hendra Croft (SW 7955): *Hendrekiogh* 1338, 'snipe's home farm', C. *hendre kyogh* (although *kyogh* might here be a personal name).

Hendravossan (SW 7755): *Hendrefosen* 1479, 'home farm at a little wall/ bank', C. *hendre fosyn*.

Hick's Mill (SW 7641): E. 'Hick's mill' from local family.

Holywell Bay (SW 7659): now E. 'bay with a holy well', earlier *Porraylen* 1688, 'cove/landing place with small tidal flats', C. *porth heylyn*.

Hugus (SW 7743): 'high wood', C. *uh-gos*.

Idless (SW 8247): *Ethles* C13, *Etheles* 1301, 'place of aspens', C. *edhel-ys*.

Jacka Point (SW 9339): *Jacka* 1866, 'jackdaw, chough', C. *choca*.

Jolly's Bottom (SW 7544): E. 'Jolly's valley bottom', after a local family.

St Just-in-Roseland (SW 8432): after St Just (Yestin); earlier *Lansyek* 1342, 'Sioc's church enclosure', C. *lan Syek*. See also **Roseland**.

Kea (SW 8142): C19 name, after St Kei. See also **Old Kea, Porthkea**.

Kelsey Head (SW 7660): E. 'headland in the manor of Kelsey'. Kelsey was *Kelse* 1349, apparently C. *kelgh-jy*, 'circle-house'.

Kennall (river): *Kennel* 1201, *Kenel* 1278, *Kynal* 1302, possibly 'reedy one', C. *kuen-el*.

Kenwyn (SW 8145): *Keynwyn* 1316, 'white/fair ridge', C. *keyn wyn* ('St Kenwyn' is fictitious).

Kenwyn (river): now apparently named after the village of Kenwyn (although the similarity of name to Ptolemy's *Cenionis fluvii* C2 AD is hard to discount). Alternative names were: *Dower Ithy* (undated), 'ivy river',C. *ydh-y* + addition of C. *dowr*, 'water, river'; and *Dourtrurubighan* 1339, 'river of little Truro', C. *dowr Truru (Tryveru) vyan*. The source of the river, at SW 7547, was *Venton Wicorriar* 1613, evidently 'traders'/merchants' spring', C. *fenten wycoryon*.

Kerley Downs (SW 7644): E. 'downland at Kerling'. The farm name, variously Kerling and Kerley, was *Crugbleth* 1306, 'wolf's barrow/tumulus', C. *crug bleydh*.

Kiberick Cove (SW 9238): 'timber strewn', C. *keberek*.

Killifreth (SW 7343): *Kellyvregh* 1345, 'dappled grove',C. *kelly vregh*.

Killiganoon (SW 8040): *Kellygnohan* 1291, 'nut grove', C. *kelly gnowen*.

Killigerran Head (SW 8732): 'St Gerent's ridge', C. *kyl Gerens* (a *St Girrian's rock* was marked here in 1597).

Killigrew (SW 8452): *Kelligreu* 1175–1378, 'grove by a weir', C. *kelly grew*.

Killiow (SW 8042): 'groves', C. *kellyow*.

Killiserth (SW 8551): 'steep grove', C. *kelly serth*.

Killivose (SW 8049): *Kylivos* 1314, 'grove by a wall/bank', C. *kelly fos.*
Ladock (SW 8951): from the female saint Ladoc. *Egloslagek* 1354, 'St Ladoc's church', C. *eglos Lajek*, shows an early softening of <d> to <j>.
Ladock Water (stream): a small tributary of the Tresillian River just north of Ladock. It was *Besek* 1547, apparently C. *besek*, 'finger-like', perhaps from the shape of its valley.
Lambessow (SW 8444): *Lanbedou* 1308, *Lambesoe* 1662, apparently 'church enclosure by birch-trees', C. *lan besow.*
Lambourne (SW 7651): *Lanbron* 1231, 'church enclosure on a hill', C. *lan bron.*
Lamorran (SW 8741): *Lanmoren* 1187-1359, 'Moren's church enclosure', C. *lan Moren.*
Lamouth Creek (SW 8340): now E. 'creek at Lamouth'. Lamouth is 'pigs' valley', C. *nans mogh.*
Langarth (SW 7845): *Lenengath* 1365, 'the cat's strip field', C. *leyn an gath.*
Lanteague (SW 8053): *Lanleke* 1452, perhaps 'valley with a slab/ledge', C. *nans legh.*
Ligger Point (SW 7558): uncertain due to lack of forms prior to 1818. Arguments that it may derive from C. *clegar*, 'crag', although apt, are weak on the evidence currently available.
Loe Beach (SW 8238): *Loo* 1327, 'deep water inlet, ria', C. *logh.*
Malpas (SW 8442): 'bad passage', F. *mal pas.*
Manare Point (SW 9338): probably 'stone on a height', C. *men ardh.*
Marazanvose (SW 8050): *Marrasanvose* 1541, 'market at the wall/bank', C. *marhas an fos.*
St Mawes (SW 8433): after St Maudet, a male saint widely celebrated in Brittany. The C. name was *Lanvausa* 1445, 'St Maudet's church enclosure', C. *lan Vausa.*
Mawla (SW 7045): *Mola* 960, 'pigs' place', C. *mogh-la.*
Melinsey (SW 9030): 'mill-house', C. *melynjy.*
Menagissey (SW 7146): *Milgysy* 1330, 'house where hunting dogs are bred', C. *mylgy-jy.* An earlier name was *Meny-utheck* 1256, 'terrible hillside', C. *menedh uthek.*
Merther (SW 8644): *Eglosmerther* 1201, 'church with a saint's grave/relics', C. *eglos merther.*
Messack Point (SW 8435): E. 'headland at Messack'. Messack (*Meysek* 1296) is 'place of an open field', C. *mesek.*
St Michael Penkevil (SW 8542): *Penkevel* c1210, 'St Michael' added to original name Penkevil, 'horse's head', C. *pen kevyl.*
Mingoose (SW 7148): *Meyngoys* 1327, 'stones in a wood', C. *meyn gos.*
Mitchell (SW 8654): *Meideshol* 1239, 'maid's hollow', OE *maegd holh.*
Mithian (SW 7450): *Mydyan* 1284, *Midhyan* 1302, unknown meaning, unless a derivative of C. *myth*, 'whey'.
Moresk (SW 8543): *Moreis* c1150, 'marsh'. F. *morais.*

Mount Hawke (SW 7147): E. 'Hawke's hill', from C18 local family.
Mylor (SW 8235): after St Melor. The C. name was *Lanwythek* 1277, 'church enclosure in a place of trees', C. *lan wedhek*.
Mylor Bridge (SW 8036): E. 'bridge at Mylor', replacing *Ponsnowythe* 1562, 'new bridge', *pons noweth*.
Mylor Creek (SW 8135): E. 'creek at Mylor', replacing *Polscatho* 1866, 'pool for boats', C. *pol scathow*.
Nampara (SW 7553): 'bread (-producing) valley', C. *nans bara*.
Nancarrow (SW 8050): *Nanskarow* 1476, 'stag's valley', C. *nans carow*.
Nancassick (SW 8239): *Nanscasek* 1416, 'mare's valley', C. *nans casek*.
Nancemabyn (SW 8945): *Namabon* c1470, 'Mabon's valley', C. *nans Mabon*.
Nansalsa (SW 8748): *Nansalwester* 1284, 'Sylvester's valley', C. *nans Salvester*. It is interesting to note that the C. form of the personal name Sylvester is shown by historic forms of this name and **Chysauster** (Penwith) to be *Salvester*.
Nansavallen (SW 8143): 'apple tree valley', C. *nans avallen*.
Nansough (SW 8750): *Nanshogh* c1350: 'pig's valley', C. *nans hogh*.
Nare Head (SW 9136): *Penare Point* c1540, 'prominent headland', C. *penardh*.
Newbridge (SW 7944): C19 E. 'new bridge'.
Newham (SW 8244): *Neweham* 1266, 'new homestead', OE *niwe ham*.
Newlyn East (SW 8256): after the female saint Neulin, with E. 'east' to distinguish it from **Newlyn**, Penwith (the derivation of which is entirely different). The C. name was *Eglosnyulyn* 1415, 'St Neulin's church', C. *eglos Nyulyn*.
Newmill (SW 8045): C18 E. translation of *Melynneweth* 1366, 'new mill', C. *melyn noweth*.
Newmills (SW 8952): C16 E. 'new mills' replacing *Melyneweth* 1364, 'new mill', C. *melyn noweth*.
Old Kea (SW 8441): *Landegei* c1184, 'church enclosure of thy St Kei', C. *lan de Gey*.
Parkengear (SW 9047): 'field of the fort', C. *park an ger/gayr*.
Parkengew (SW 7734): 'field of the enclosure',C. *park an gew*.
Pednvadan (SW 8835): *Pentalvan* c1540, 'brow-height headland', C. *pen* (LC *pedn*) *tal-van*.
Pen-a-Gader (SW 7352): 'headland of the chair', C. *pen an gadar*.
Penair (SW 8445): *Penarth* 1650, 'prominent hilltop', C. *penardh*.
Penarrow Point (SW 8134): *Pencarreu point* 1597, 'stag's head(land)', C. *pen carow*.
Pencabe (SW 8735): *The Cabe* 1732, 'cape', C. *capa*, with later addition of C. *pen*, 'head(land)'.
Pencalenick (SW 8545): *Penkelynnec* 1296, 'end of a holly-grove', C. *pen kelynek*.
Pencoose (SW 8146): 'top of a wood', C. *pen-cos*.
Pencoose (SW 9444): 'top of a wood', C. *pen-cos*.
Pendennis (SW 8231): 'fort head(land)', C. *pen dynas*.
Pendower (SW 9038): *Bondowar* 1558, 'foot of a stream', C. *ben dowr*.

Penelewey (SW 8140): *Penhalewey* 1308, C. *pen-hal*, 'top of a marsh' + stream name **Ewy*, C. *ew-y*, 'yews stream'.

Pengreep (SW 7438): 'end of a hillcrest', C. *pen cryb*.

Penhale (SW 7658): 'end of a marsh', C. *pen-hal*.

Penhale (SW 8851): 'top of a marsh', C. *pen-hal*.

Penhallow (SW 7651): 'top of marshes', C. *pen hallow*.

Penhellick (SW 8346): 'hilltop with willows', C. *pen helyk*.

Penhesken (SW 9142): 'end of sedge', C. *pen hesken*.

Penmount (SW 8247): a late C19 contrived name with E. 'mount' preceded by C. *pen*, 'head, end, top'. Previously *Penhellek vyan* 1429, 'little Penhellick' (see **Penhellick**).

Pennance Point (SW 8031): *Carne penans* 1590, 'crag at Pennance', C. *carn Pennans*. Pennance (SW 7930) is 'head of a valley', C. *pen-nans*.

Penpol (SW 8139): 'head of a creek', C. *pen-pol*.

Penryn (SW 7834): 'hill-spur, promontory', C. *pen-ryn*.

Penstraze (SW 7545): *Penstras* 1340, 'head of a flat-bottomed valley', C. *pen stras*.

Penvose (SW 9541): 'end of a wall/bank', C. *pen fos*.

Penwartha (SW 7552): 'higher end', C. *pen wartha*.

Penwerris (SW 8033): *Penweres* 1285, 'head of a slope', C. *pen weres*.

Perbargus Point (SW 9540): E. 'headland at Perbargus'. Perbargus is 'buzzard's cove/landing place', C. *porth bargos*.

Percuil (also spelt Porthcuil) (SW 8534): *Porthcule* 1613, 'narrow cove/landing place', C. *porth cul*.

Perranarworthal (SW 7738): *Peran Arwothall* 1584, 'St Peran facing watery ground', C. *Peran ar wodhel*. The name of St Piran is, historically, usually referred to as Peran.

Perrancoombe (SW 7552): *Piran Coombe* c1810, E. 'St Peran's valley'.

Perranporth (SW 7554): C18 name in E. word order, *St Peran* + C. *porth*, 'cove, landing place'. The town centre was the location of the manorial centre of **Tywarnhayle**, 'manor on the tidal flats', C. *ty war'n heyl*.

Perranwell (SW 7752): *Fenton Berran* 1680, 'St Peran's spring', C. *fenten Beran*.

Perranwell Station (SW 7839): C17 E. 'St Peran's well', with '(railway) station' added in C19. The holy well is at Perran-ar-Worthal near the Norway Inn.

Perranzabuloe (SW 7752): 'St Peran in the sands', Lat. *Peran in sabulo*. The C. version was recorded c1608 as *Piran treth*, 'St Piran's sand', C. *Peran treth*; although the church site (actually the second church at SW 7756) was *Lanberan* 1281, C. *lan Beran*, 'St Peran's church enclosure'.

Peterville (SW 7250): 'Peter's town (F. *ville*)', from C18 Peter family.

Philleigh (SW 8739): after St Fili. The C. name was *Eglosros* 1311, 'church of Roseland', C. *eglos Ros*.

Pibyah Rock (SW 8937): 'piper', C. *pyber*.

Pill (SW 8338): 'creek', ME *pyll*.

Place Manor (SW 8532): 'mansion', C. *plas.*

Playing Place (SW 8141): *Kea Playing Place* 1813, E. 'arena at Kea', referring to an amphitheatre otherwise known in Cornwall and Cornish place names as a *plen an gwary.*

Polhendra (SW 8536): *Polhendre* 1302, 'pool at a home farm', C. *pol hendre.*

Polstain (SW 7844): *Polstene* 1522, 'tin-pit', C. *pol sten.*

Polsue (SW 8546): 'dark/black pool', C. *pol du.*

Polsue (SW 8839): *Bosu* 1349, *Bossue* 1538, 'dark dwelling', C. *bos du.*

Polwhele (SW 8347): *Polwhyl* 1350, 'pool of beetles', C. *pol whyl.*

Ponsharden (SW 7934): *Ponshardy* 1677, C. pons, 'bridge' + surname Hardy.

Ponsmere (SW 7654): *Pons* 1338, originally simple 'bridge', C. *pons*; now 'great bridge', C. *pons muer.*

Porthbean (SW 8836): 'little cove/landing place', C. *porth byan.* Locally pron. 'per-bain'.

Porthbeor (SW 8631): 'cove/landing place at Bohortha', C. *porth Buorthow.* Locally pron. 'pol-beer'.

Porth Curnick (SW 8735): 'cove/landing place in a corner', C. *porth kernyk.*

Porthgwidden (SW 8237): *Porthgwyn* 1584, 'white/fair cove or landing place', C. *porth gwyn* (LC *gwidn*).

Porth Kea (SW 8242): *Porthkey* 1614, 'gateway to Kea', C. *porth Key.*

Porth Joke (SW 7760): *Porthlejooacke* 1636, 'plant-rich cove/landing place', C. *porth losowek.*

Porthmellin Head (SW 8632): E. 'headland at Porthmellin'. Porthmellin is 'mill cove', C. *porth melyn.*

Porthtowan (SW 6948): 'cove/landing place for the manor of **Towan**', C. *porth Tewyn.*

Portloe (SW 9339): *Portlo* 1254, 'cove/landing place in a deep water inlet', C. *porth logh.*

Portscatho (SW 8755): *Porthskathow* 1592, 'cove/landing place for boats', C. *porth scathow.*

Presingoll (SW 7249): *Presencoll* 1461, 'copse of the hazel trees', C. *prys an coll.*

Probus (SW 8947): *Lanbrobes* 1302, 'St Probus's church enclosure', C. *lan Brobes.*

Pulla Cross (SW 7549): C. *pollow*, 'pools', with addition of E. 'cross' (for 'crossroads').

Redinnick (SW 8243): 'fern-brake', C. *redenek.*

Reen (SW 7754): *Run* 1338, 'slope', C. *run, ryn.*

Rejerrah (SW 8056): *Resworow* 1538, 'Goreu's ford', C. *res Worow.*

Restronguet (SW 8136): *Rostronges* 1346, 'promontory of a hill-spur wood', C. *ros tron-gos.*

Rose (SW 7754): 'roughland', C. *ros.*

Rosecliston (SW 8159): *Reskylistyn* 1334, apparently 'pebble ford', C. *res kellestron.*

Roseland (centred at SW 8738): *Ros* 1261, 'promontory', C. *ros*, now with E. 'land' added.

Rosemundy (SW 7250): *Rosmundy* 1751, 'roughland with an ore-house', C. *ros mon-dy*.

Rosen Cliff (SW 9237): 'little promontory', C. *rosyn*.

Rosevallen (SW 9343): *Rosavallen* 1359, 'hillspur with an apple tree', C. *ros avallen*.

Rosevine (SW 8736): *Rosvreyn* 1302, 'putrid hillspur', C. *ros vreyn*.

Roseworthy (SW 7947): *Rosworgi* 1327, 'Wurci's hillspur', C. *ros Worgy*.

Rosteague (SW 8733): *Rostek* 1400, 'beautiful promontory', C. *ros teg*.

Round Wood (SW 8340): E. 'wood with a round', with reference to the Iron Age earthwork here.

Ruan Lanihorne (SW 8942): *Lanryhorn* 1270, the name of St Rumon, added to 'Rihoern's church enclosure', C. *lan Ryhorn*.

Saveock (SW 7544): *Sevyek* 1365, 'strawberry land', C. *sevyek*.

Saveock Water (stream): now E. 'stream at Saveock', but formerly *Dowr Meor* C17, 'great water/river', C. *dowr muer*.

Shortlanesend (SW 8047): now E. 'Short's lane end', after a C16 family. Formerly *Penfounder* 1541, 'lane end', C. *pen vownder*.

Silverwell (SW 7448): C18 E. 'silver well'.

Skinner's Bottom (SW 7246): E. 'Skinner's valley bottom' after a C18 family.

Sparnock (SW 7942): *Spernek* 1280, 'thorn-brake', C. *spernek*.

Stampas (SW 7855): 'tin-stamping mill', C. *stampys*.

Suffree (SW 9045): *Resvreghy* c1500, C. *res*, 'ford' + C. river name *Breghy*, 'dappled stream'.

Swanpool (SW 8031): *Levine* (for *Lenine*) *Prisklo* c1540, C. *lyn yeyn*, 'cold pool' + place name Prislow, which was *Priskelou* 1317, 'copse of elms', C. *prysk elow*. Its present name is E. 'swans' pool' although it was briefly (1748), *Goose Pool*.

Three Burrows (SW 7446): C18 E. 'three barrows/tumuli'.

Threemilestone (SW 7844): C19 E. 'milestone at the third mile (from Truro)'.

Tippett's Shop (SW 9342): E. 'Teppet's workshop' from C17 family.

Tolgullow (SW 7343): *Talgolou* 1284, 'hill-brow of light', C. *tal golow*.

Tolverne (SW 8539): *Talvron* 1275, 'brow of a hill', C. *tal vron*.

Towan (SW 6948): *Tewyn* 1284–1439, probably not C. *tewyn*, 'sand-dunes' at this inland site, but a cognate of W. stream name *Tywyn*, 'radiance'.

Towanwroath (SW 6950): 'the giant's hole', C. *toll an wragh* (in LC, *gwragh*, normally 'hag, crone', came to also mean 'giant'). The site is linked with the legend of the giant Bolster, the hole in which he bled himself to death being nearby.

Treamble (SW 7856): *Taranbol* 1316, 'thunder pool/pit', C. *taran-bol*.

Trebisken (SW 7857): *Trebryskyn* 1403, 'farm by a small copse', C. *tre bryskyn*.

Trebowland (SW 7338): *Trebowlan* 1391, 'farm with a cow-pen', C. *tre bowlan*.

Tredeague (SW 7238): *Trethaeg* 1311, 'beautiful farm', C. *tre theg*.

Tredinnick (SW 8656): *Treredenek* 1288, 'farm at a fern-brake', C. *tre redenek*.

Tredinnick (SW 9242): *Trethynicke* c1470, probably 'farm by a fort', C. *tre dhynek.*
Tredrea (SW 7738): *Tredrue* 1301, 'yonder farm', C. *tre dru.*
Treffry (SW 8645): *Trefry* 1320, 'Fri's farm', C. *tre Fry.*
Trefronick (SW 8251): *Trevronek* 1334, 'hilly farm', C. *tre vronek.*
Trefusis (SW 8034): *Trefusys* 1356, uncertain derivation, perhaps 'well-used farm',
    C. *tref usys.*
Tregair (SW 8258): *Tregayr* 1249, 'farm by a fort', C. *tre ger/gayr.*
Tregassa (SW 8735): 'Cada's farm', C. *tre Gasa.*
Tregassick (SW 8634): *Tregerasek* 1454, 'Caradoc's farm', C. *tre Garasek.*
Tregavethan (SW 7847): *Treganmedan* 1086, 'Cynfedan's farm', C. *tre Genvedhan.*
Tregeagle (SW 8646): *Tregagel* 1241, 'dung farm', C. *tre gagel.*
Tregear (SW 8650): *Tregaer* 1304, 'farm by a fort', C. *tre ger/gayr.*
Tregellas (SW 9149): *Tregellest* 1280, 'Celest's farm', C. *tre Gelest.*
Tregenver (SW 7932): *Tregenvor* 1590, 'Cynvor's farm', C. *tre Genvor.*
Tregew (SW 8034): *Tregeu* 1208, 'farm by an enclosure', C. *tre gew.*
Tregolls (SW 8345): *Tregollas* 1302, 'farm by a hazel-grove', C. *tre golles.*
Tregongon (SW 9141): *Tregongan* 1360, 'Congan's farm', C. *tre Gongan.*
Tregoniggie (SW 7932): *Tregenegy* 1316, 'farm by a reed-bed', C. *tre genegy.*
Tregony (SW 9244): *Trerigani* 1086, 'Rigani's farm', C. *tre Rygany.*
Tregothnan (SW 8541): *Treguythenan* 1280, 'Guithenan's farm', C. *tre Gwythenan.*
Tregye (SW 8040): *Tregy* 1327, 'dog (-breeding?) farm', C. *tre gy.*
Trehane (SW 8648): *Treyahan* 1302, 'Iahan's farm', C. *tre Yahan.*
Treheveras (SW 8146): *Trethyverys* 1379, 'well-watered farm', C. *tre dheverys.*
Trelagossick (SW 9241): *Trelogosek* 1284, 'mouse-infested farm', C. *tre logosek.*
Trelassick (SW 8752): *Treloysek* 1345, 'Loidoc's farm', C. *tre Loysek.*
Trelew (SW 8135): *Treleu* 1470, 'Leu's farm', C. *tre Lew.*
Treliske (SW 8045): *Trelosk* 1311, 'farm on burnt/swaled land', C. *tre losk.*
Trelissick (SW 8339): *Trelesyk* 1275, 'Leidic's farm', C. *tre Lesyk.*
Trelonk (SW 8941): 'farm by a gully', C. *tre lonk.*
Trelowthas (SW 8846): *Treloudat* 1280, 'Leudat's farm', C. *tre Lowdhas.*
Treluggan (SW 8838): *Trelogan* 1334, probably 'Ylocan's farm', C. *tre Ylogan.*
Trendeal (SW 8952): *Tyndel* 1284, 'rounded hill with leaves', C. *tyn del.*
Trengrouse (SW 9241): *Trengrous* 1373, 'farm at the cross', C. *tre'n grows.*
Trenithan (SW 9048): *Treneydhyn* 1284, 'farm at the furze', C. *tre'n eythyn.*
Trenithan Bennett (SW 9049): as **Trenithan** above but with addition of a family
    name. It was originally *Hendrenydyn* 1284, 'home farm at the furze', C. *hendre'n*
    eythyn.
Trennick (SW 8344): *Trewythenek* 1305, 'Guithenoc's farm', C. *tre Wydhenek.*
Trerice (SW 8251): *Trereys* 1317, 'farm at a watercourse', C. *tre reys.*
Trerice (SW 8458): *Treres* 1326, 'farm at a ford', C. *tre res.*
Tresawle (SW 8946): *Tresawel* 1297, 'Sawel's farm', C. *tre Sawel.*
Tresawsen (SW 7849): 'Saxon's farm', C. *tre Sawsen.*

Trescobeas (SW 7933): *Treskubays* 1356, difficult in spite of a wealth of early forms: C. *tre*, 'farm, settlement' + uncertain second element, perhaps C. *scubys*, 'swept'. C. *epscop*, 'bishop' is unlikely to be involved.

Tresean (SW 7858): *Tresevion* c1200, 'strawberry farm', C. *tre sevyen*.

Tresemple (SW 8445): *Tresympel* 1338, 'farm of the Sympel family' (family recorded in C13/14), C. *tre Sympel*.

Tresillian (SW 8646): *Tresulyan* 1315, 'Sulgen's farm', C. *tre Sulyen*.

Tresillian River: now E. 'river at Tresillian', but *Seugar* 1297, *Sowgar* 1530. This is of unknown meaning but might be linked with the C. verb *sewya*, 'to follow'.

Trestrayle (SW 9046): *Trestrael* 1278, 'farm where mats are made', C. *tre strayl*.

Trethem (SW 8536): *Trethrym* 1309, 'ridge farm', C. *tre dhrum*.

Trethurffe (SW 8950): *Trederveu* c1200, 'oak wood farm', *tre dherva*.

Trevalso (SW 8152): *Trevalda* c1310, 'Maelda's farm', C. *tre Valsa*.

Trevaskis (SW 7647): 'Maelscuit's farm', C. *tre Valscos*.

Trevaunance (SW 7251): *Trefuunans* 1302, 'beech-valley farm', C. *tre faw-nans*.

Treveal (SW 7858): *Trevael* 1291, 'Mael's farm', C. *tre Vayl*.

Trevellas (SW 7452): *Trevelles* 1302, 'Meled's farm', C. *tre Veles*.

Trevethan (SW 8032): *Trefuthen* 1327, 'meadow farm', C. *tre vuthyn*.

Treviglas (SW 8947): 'church farm, churchtown', C. *tref eglos*.

Treviles (SW 9041): *Trevaelus* 1293, 'Maelod's farm', C. *tre Vaylos*.

Treviskey (SW 7339): *Trevrysky* 1404, 'Britci's farm', C. *tre Vrysky*.

Trevoll (SW 8358): *Treroval* 1345, 'Riwal's farm', C. *tre Rywal*.

Trevolland (SW 9248): *Trevolghan* 1338, 'farm at a small gap', C. *tre volghen*.

Trewarthenick (SW 9044): *Trewethenec* 1326, 'Guethenoc's farm', C. *tre Wedhenek*.

Trewirgie (SW 8845): *Trewythgi* 1298, 'Guidci's farm', C. *tre Wydhgy*.

Trewithen (SW 9147): *Trewythyan* 1327, 'Guidien's farm', C. *tre Wydhyen*.

Trewithian (SW 8737): *Trewythyan* c1270, 'Guidien's farm', C. *tre Wydhyen*.

Treworga (SW 8940): *Treworge* 1314, 'Wurci's farm', C. *tre Worgy*.

Treworgan (SW 8349): *Trewothgan* 1338, 'Goethgen's farm', C. *tre Wodhgen*.

Treworgans (SW 7858): 'Wurcant's farm', C. *tre Worgans*.

Treworlas (SW 8938): 'Gorlas's farm', C. *tre Worlas*.

Treworthal (SW 8838): *Trewoethel* 1292, 'farm on watery ground', C. *tre wodhel*.

Treworthen (SW 7856): *Treworyn* 1284, 'Uuorin's farm', C. *tre Woryn*.

Trispen (SW 8450): *Tredespan* 1325, *Trethespan* 1382, 'Despan's farm', C. *tre Dhespan*.

Truro (SW 8244): *Triveru* 1201, C. *try*, 'three' + uncertain second element, perhaps C. *berow*, 'boiling' i.e. 'three turbulent streams'. Modern revivalists tend to use *Truru*, a form found in 1278 but *Tryverow* might be closer to the historical original.

Turnaware Point (SW 8338): *Coresturnan* 1323, 'weir at a little turning', C. *cores tornen*.

Twelveheads (SW 7542): C17 E. 'twelve-headed tin-stamping mill'.

Two Burrows (SW 7346): C18 E, 'two barrows/tumuli'.

Tywarnhayle (SW 7554): 'manorial centre at the tidal flats',C. *ty war'n heyl* (see also **Perranporth**).

Ventonarren (SW 8355): *Fentonworen* 1548, 'St Goron's (Guron's) spring', C. *fenten Woron*.

Venton Gassic (SW 8535): *Fontenkadok* 1223, 'St Cadoc's spring', C. *fenten Gasek*.

Ventongimps (SW 7851): *Fentongempes* 1296, 'spring in a flat place', C. *fenten gompes*.

Ventonglidder (SW 9049): *Fentengleder* 1327, 'St Clether's spring', C.*fenten Gleder*.

Venton Vaise (SW 7650): *Funtenvaes* 1311, 'shallow spring', C. *fenten vas*.

Ventonveth (SW 9541): *Vyntonvergh* 1370, 'horses' spring', C. *fenten vergh*.

Ventontrissick (SW 8150): *Ventondrissick* 1766, 'brambly spring', C. *fenten dreysek*.

Veryan (SW 9139): *S. Symphorian* 1278, *Severian* 1525, after St Symforian. The manor centred in Veryan was *Elerchi* 1086, *Elerghy* 1349, 'swans' place/stream', C. *elergh-y*.

Voskelly (SW 8434): 'wall/bank by a grove', C. *fos kelly*.

Wheal Jane (SW 7742): C. *whel*, 'mine, works' + either C. *yeyn*, 'cold, bleak' or personal name *Jane*.

Wheal Kitty (SW 7251): C. *whel*, 'mine, works' + personal name *Kitty*.

Wheal Rose (SW 7244): C. *whel*, 'mine, works' + either C. *ros*, 'uncultivated valley' or personal name *Rose*.

Wheal Vlow (SW 7655): 'blue mine', C. *whel vlou*.

Zelah (SW 8151): *Sele* 1311, 'hall', OE *sele*.

Zone Point (SW 8530): a contraction of its former name, *Savenheer* 1597, 'long cliff-chasm', C. *sawan hyr*.

Carrick: site of Glasney College, Penryn (now the new university town)

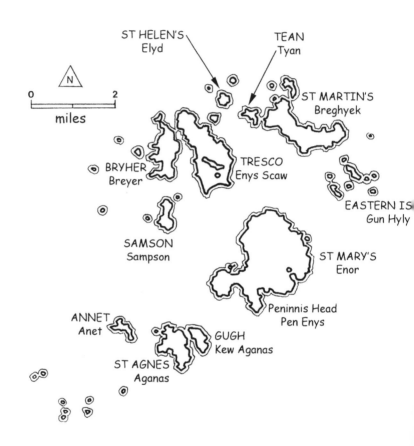

ST HELEN'S
Elyd

TEAN
Tyan

ST MARTIN'S
Breghyek

BRYHER
Breyer

TRESCO
Enys Scaw

EASTERN IS
Gun Hyly

SAMSON
Sampson

ST MARY'S
Enor

ANNET
Anet

Peninnis Head
Pen Enys

GUGH
Kew Aganas

ST AGNES
Aganas

Bishop Rock
Men an Epscop

Isles of SCILLY
SYLLAN

Place Names of the Isles of SCILLY

Henwyn Plasow an Enesow
Syllan

To explain the meaning of various place names in the Isles of Scilly (they should never be called 'The Scilly Isles') requires some background knowledge of their history. In brief, these beautiful islands are gradually sinking. At the end of the Neolithic era, 4000 years ago, the main islands of St Mary's, Samson, Bryher, Tresco, St Martin's, the Eastern Isles and the various islets in between formed one single landmass. Gugh and St Agnes formed a peninsula to the main island while, to the south west, Annet and the Western Rocks formed smaller islands. Archaeology suggests that a large part of the main Neolithic island was wooded and supported a herd of red deer.

By the end of the Roman period, c400 AD, the main island had become a little smaller, with St Agnes and Gugh being sundered from it to become another island. The low-lying centre of the large island was only protected from the sea by natural lines of sand dunes that still exist as submerged sand bars but, in time, the sea forced its way in. Beneath the shallow central waters lie prehistoric settlements, cairns and field boundaries and the submergence of so much of Scilly may explain the origin of the legend of the lost land of Lyonesse.

Place names show that Cornish was extensively spoken in the islands but its use probably ceased before 1700.

St Agnes (SV 8808): *Aganas* 1193, 'off-island', Br. **ek-enes*. The 'Saint' prefix was added in C16.

Annet (SV 8608): *Anet* 1302, 'kittiwake', C. *anet*.

Arthur (SV 9413): *Artur* 1500, *Arthures Isle* 1570, 'Arthur's island', Br. personal name from Lat. *Artorius*.

Bant's Carn (SV 9012): C. *carn*, 'tor, cairn' + family name *Bant*, OC *pant*, hollow', according to Dr W. Borlase 1752.

Bar Point (SV 9113): *Pendrathen* 1652, 'end of a sand-bar', C. *pen drethen*.

Biggal (SV 8512): 'shepherd', C. *bugel*.

Biggal (SV 9413): 'shepherd', C. *bugel*.

Bishop Rock (SV 8016): *Maen Escop* 1284, *Maenenescop* 1302, 'the bishop's stone', C. *men an epscop*.

Borough (SV 8914): *Cheyncruk* 1314, 'house at the barrow/tumulus', C. *chy an crug*.

Broad Sound (centred at SV 8409): *Haylue Gawen* c1588, *The brode sownde* c1540, now E. 'broad sound', replacing a C. name consisting of C. *heyl*, 'inlet with tidal flats' and an apparent C. personal name *Gawen*.

Bryher (SV 8715): *Brayer* 1336, *Brear* 1500, 'place of hills', C. *bre-yer*.

Camber Rocks (SV 9017): 'meeting of currents',C. *kemper*.

Camper Porth (SV 9217): 'cove/landing place at a meeting of currents', C. *porth kemper*, now in E. word order.

Carn Ithen (SV 8405): 'furze crag', C. *carn eythyn*.

Carn Kimbra (SV 8908): 'Welshman's crag', C. *carn Kembro*.

Carn Leh (SV 9105): 'slab/ledge crag', C. *carn legh*.

Carn Mahael (SV 9009): 'Michael's crag', C. *carn Myhal*.

Carn Morval (SV 9012): 'whale's crag', C. *carn morvyl*.

Carrickstarne (SV 9109): 'framework rock', C. *carrek starn*.

Castella (SV 8707): 'castles', C. *castylly*, probably from shape of natural outcrops.

Clodgie Point (SV 9116): C. *clojy*, 'lazar-house, hospital' + E. 'point'.

Cragyellis (SV 9114): *Trigga Hilles* 1689, 'old ruin of a dwelling', C. *tregva henlys*, from nearby submerged prehistoric settlements.

Crebawethan (SV 8307): 'reef of a tree', C. *cryb an wedhen*, evidently from an era when a greater area stood above water and was able to support the growth of a tree.

Crebinicks (SV 8106): *Crebinack* 1744, 'place of small reefs', C. *crybynek*.

Creeb (SV 9012): 'reef', C. *cryb*.

Crim Rocks (SV 8009): probably 'little reef', C. *crybyn*.

Crow Sound (centred at SV 9313): named after the Crow Rock, 'hut', C. *crow*, from submerged prehistoric buildings. This was evidently the original *Heyl Vuer* ('great inlet with tidal flats'), after which the St Mary's settlement of **Helvear** is named.

Dolphin Town (SV 8915): E. 'Godolphin's settlement', from the influential Godolphin family in ownership during the C17.

Eastern Isles (SV 9414): E. 'eastern islands' since C19. Prior to submergence, the whole area of the Eastern Isles was known as *Goenhili* (see **Ganilly**).

Ennor (SV 9110): *Enoer* 1306, the probable original name of the former main island of which St Mary's (itself called *Enor* 1194) was the southernmost part. Now a minor place name on St Mary's, 'the land, mainland', OC. *en noer*.

Ganilly (SV 9414): *Guenelly* 1500, *Gwenhele* 1570, 'saltwater downs', C. *gun hyly*.

Ganinick (SV 9313): *Kenenick* 1650, 'place of wild garlic',C. *kenynek*.

Garrison, The (SV 8910): C17 E, 'the garrison'. Formerly *The Hew* c1535 (see **Hugh Town**]

Giant's Castle (SV 9210): *Hengastel* 1305, 'old castle', C. *hen-gastel*.

Grimsby, New & Old (SV 88/8915): *Grymsey* c1540, 'Grimr's (i.e. Odin's) island', OSc. *Grimrs ey*.

Gugh (SV 8908): *Agnes Gue* 1652, 'enclosure of St Agnes island', C. *gew Aganas* (rendered in E. word order in 1652).

Gweal (SV 8615): *Gwithiall* 1652, 'place of trees', C. *gwedh-yel*. Another name that must refer to a pre-submergence era as this is now a wave-embattled islet.

Halangy (SV 9012): *Hallingy* 1910, 'pool-house marsh', C.*hal lyn-jy*.

Hanjague (SV 9515): *Ingeak* 1655, 'the windy one', C. *an wynjak*.

St Helen's (SV 9017): *Seynt Elyd* c1500, after St Elid, perhaps the Welsh bishop Ilid. A chapel of the early Celtic church still survives on this island.

Hellweathers (SV 8607): *Hellveraz* 1655, perhaps 'tidal flats to watch for', C. *heyl veras*.

Helvear (SV 9212): *Hayle Veor* c1500, 'great tidal flats', *heyl vuer*.

High Cross (SV 9111): E. 'high cross'.

Higher Town (SV 8808): E. 'higher settlement'. ·

Higher Town (SV 9215): E. 'higher settlement'.

Holy Vale (SV 9111): *La Val* 1301, 'at the foot, low-lying', NF *la val*.

Hugh Town (SV 9010): named after the peninsula now called **The Garrison**, formerly *The Hew* 1585, 'heel of land, promontory', OE *hoh*.

Illiswilgig (SV 8513): *Inniswelsick* 1584, 'grassy island', C. *enys weljak*.

Innisidgan (SV 9212): *Inezegon* 1744, perhaps 'ox island', C. *enys ojyon*.

Innisvouls (SV 9514): 'wether sheep's island', C. *enys vols*.

Isinvrank (SV 8607): 'Frenchman's island', C. *enys Frynk*.

Izzacumpucca (SV 9109): 'the Bucca's chasm', Bucca having been the traditional Cornish sea-god venerated by fishermen, C. *yslonk an Bukka*.

Kittern Rock (SV 8908): 'kite's nest', OE *cyta aern*.

Lethegus Rocks (SV 8707): 'milky ones', C. *letheges*, from their foamy surroundings.

Longstone (SV 9112): E. 'long stone, standing stone' from the Bronze Age menhir that remains at the site.

Lower Moors (SV 9110): Mod. E. 'lower marshes', replacing *Gwernewgavell* 1652, 'snipe's/woodcock's alder-marshes', C. *gwernow gavarhal* (*gavarhal*, 'snipe/woodcock', literally means 'marsh-goat').

Maiden Bower (SV 8514): probably 'water stone', C. *men dowr*.

St Martin's (centred at SV 9315): E. 'St Martin's (island)' since C16. The C. name was *Brechiek* 1390, probably 'dappled', C. *breghyek*.

St Mary's (centred at SV 9111): E. 'St Mary's (island)' since C15. The C. name was *Enor* 1194, this being thought to have originally been the name of the former large island of which St Mary's was the southern part, 'the land, mainland', OC. *en-noer*.

Melledgan (SV 8606): 'ledge stone', C. *men lehen* (earlier *leghen*).

Men-a-Vaur (SV 8917): *Menavorth* 1689, 'stone facing a hump (i.e. Round Island)', C. *men ar voth*.

Menawethan (SV 9513): *Mynangwython* c1588, 'stone of the tree', C. *men an wedhen*.

Menbean (SV 8608): 'little stone', C. *men byan*.

Middle Town (SV 8708): E. 'central settlement'.

Middle Town (SV 9216): E. 'central settlement'

Minalto (SV 8711): 'stone of cliffs', OC *men altow* (a rare survival of Old Cornish so far west).

Mincarlo (SV 8512): 'rayfish stone', C. *men carlyth*.

Mouls (SV 9514): 'wether sheep', C. *mols*.

Newford (SV 9112): *Newfort* 1650, E. 'new fort'.

Nornour (SV 9414): *Nonore* 1655, probably 'facing the mainland', C. *ar nor*.

Northwethel (SV 8916): *Arwothel* 1570, 'facing watery ground', C. *ar wodhel*.

Old Town (SV 9110): *Church Towne* 1650, originally E. 'church town', then E. 'old town' when the 'new' town (**Hugh Town**) was built.

Old Town Bay (SV 9110): *Porthenor* C12, *Pereglis* 1708, originally 'cove/landing place for Enor (St Mary's)', C. *porth Enor*; later 'church cove', C. *porth eglos*.

Outer Head (SV 9109): *Carnmur* 1655, 'great crag', C. *carn muer*.

Parting Carn (SV 9110): *The Perkin Carne* 1652, 'the crag field', C. *park an carn*.

Pednbean (SV 9116): 'little head(land)', C. *pen* (LC *pedn*) *byan*.

Pednbrose (SV 9116): 'great head(land)', C. *pen* (LC *pedn*) *bras*.

Pelistry Bay (SV 9211): *Porthlistrye* 1650, 'cove/landing place for ships', C. *porth lystry*.

Peninnis Head (SV 9109): *Penenis* 1652, 'end of an island', C. *pen enys*.

Pernagie (SV 9117): 'cove/landing place at the gap', C. *porth an ajy*.

Periglis (SV 8708): *Porteglos* 1652, 'church cove', C. *porth eglos*.

Polreath (SV 9515): 'red pool', C. *pol rudh*.

Pool (SV 8714): *Sturtom* 1652, now E. 'pool', formerly 'homestead at a tail of land/promontory', OE *steort ham*.

Popplestone Bay (SV 8715): 'pebblestones bay', OE *popelstanas*.

Porth Cressa (SV 9010): *Porthcresse* 1652, probably 'most peaceful (sheltered) cove/landing place', C. *porth cressa*.

Porth Hellick (SV 9210): 'willow-trees cove', C. *porth helyk*.

Porth Loggos (SV 9210): 'cove of mice', C. *porth logos*.

Porthloo (SV 9011): *Porthloe* 1712, 'landing place in a deep water inlet', C. *porth logh*.

Porth Mellon (SV 9217): *Porthmelyn* 1305, 'mill cove', C. *porth melyn*.

Porth Minick (SV 9310): *Porthmeynek* 1314, 'stony cove', C. *porth meynek*.

Porth Morran (SV 9217): *Porthmoren* 1708, 'berry cove' or 'maiden's cove', both C. *porth moren*.

Porth Warna (SV 8707): 'St Awana's cove', C. *porth Awana*.

Puffin Island (SV 8813): C17 E. 'puffin island', although, on Scilly, 'puffin' refers to the Manx Shearwater.

Rosevean (SV 8305): 'little promontory', C. *ros vyan*.

Rosevear (SV 8306): 'great promontory', C. *ros vuer*.

Round Island (SV 9017): now E. 'round island' but the name of nearby **Men-a-Vaur** implies that the island was formerly C. *an voth*, 'the hump'.

Samson (SV 8712): *S. Sampson* c1160, *Sampsons iland* 1650, E. 'St Sampson's island', after St Sampson of Dol.

Scilly: the name of the archipelago is not easy to unravel, its present form being clearly corrupt. Its ancient forms: *Silimnus* C1, *Sillina* C3, *Sulling* C12 and *Syllingar* (with OSc. plural), support the correctness of the C18 LC name *Sillan* and the current Cornish rendering of the name as *Syllan*. Professor Charles Thomas suggests that the islands are named after the British Celtic goddess Sulis (pron. 'sil'is'), also found at Aquae Sulis (Bath). The goddess's Celtic name appears to mean 'she who watches'. The C. word for a Scillonian (inhabitant of Scilly) is found as *Sullouk* 1523 (for *Syllowek, Sylluak*).

Seven Stones: so called on charts since C16, this dangerous reef between Land's End and Scilly had a C.name recorded in C17 as *Lethas* and *Lethowsow*, 'milky', C. *lethes*; and 'milky ones', C. *lethesow*, from the foam that constantly churns about the reef. *Lethowsow* was also the C. name for the semi-mythical lost land of Lyonesse.

Shipman Head (SV 8716): *Shepene* (undated), 'barn', OE *scypen*, with modern E. 'head(land)'.

Smith Sound (SV 8708): E. 'Smith sound' from rocks called Great and Little Smith. The name is of C16 origin and can have no link with the first Lord Proprietor of the islands, Augustus Smith, who did not assume his post until 1834. The Sound was also called *Awana Sound* 1652, after St Awana (St Warna on the neighbouring island of St Agnes), patroness of shipwrecks.

Tarbarrel Rock (SV 8712): E. 'tar barrel rock', coined in 1869 after the wreck of the Swedish brigantine *Otto*, laden with barrels of Stockholm tar.

Tean (SV 9116): *S. Theona* 1193, *Tyan* c1540, after St Theona, about whom little is known. The ruins of an early Celtic chapel remain on the island whose name is pron. 'tee'an'.

Tolmen Carn (SV 9110): 'hole-stone crag', C. *carn toll-men* (now in E. word order).

Town, The (SV 8715): E. 'the settlement', although this may be the site of *Bantham* 1652, 'homestead by rushes', OE *bent ham*.

Tremelethen (SV 9210): *Tremolefyn* 1310, apparently 'Molefyn's farm', C. *tre Molefyn*.

Trenoweth (SV 9112): 'new farm', C. *tre noweth*.

Tresco (centred at SV 8915): in C12, this was *St Nicholas's island* (after the priory whose ruins remain in Tresco Abbey gardens). This superceded the obsolete C. name *Rentemen* (possibly 'promontory of sand-dunes', C. *ryn tewyn*) which had covered the then conjoined Tresco and Bryher. *Trescau* 1305, 'elder-trees farm', C. *tre scaw*, was a holding on the island which in 1540 became *Iniscaw*, 'elder-trees island', C. *enys scaw*.

Trewince (SV 9111): *Trewins* 1650, 'wind(y) farm', C. *tre wyns*.

White Island (SV 9217): *Whites Iland* 1652, E. 'White's island', probably with a personal name. An alternative C.name was *Nornower* 1652, probably identical with the name of **Nornour**, 'facing the mainland', C. *ar nor*.

Isles of Scilly: Hugh Town (aerial shot)

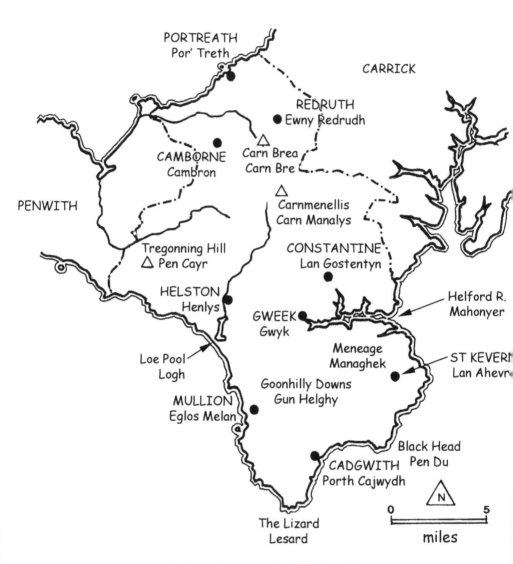

District of KERRIER
Conteth KERYER

Place Names of the District of
KERRIER

Henwyn Plasow an Conteth
Keryer

Angrouse (SW 6719): *Crous* 1317, 'cross', C. *crows*.

Anhay (SW 6522): *Enhee* 1584, 'the enclosure', C. *an hay* (borrowed from OE *(ge)haeg*).

St Anthony-in-Meneage (SW 7822): *Lanyntenyn* 1344, 'St Entenin's church enclosure', C. *lan Entenyn*.

Antron (SW 6327): 'the nose (i.e. 'hillspur')', C. *an tron*.

Antron (SW 7633): *Anter, Antrenon* C13/14, 'retreat at the downs', C. *anter'n wun*.

Anvoase (SW 7114): *Voage* 1866, probably C. *an vos*, 'the dwelling'.

Argal (SW 7632): 'retreat', C. *argel*. Argal (manor) was *Argel Woen* 1262, 'A. of the downs'; Higher Argal was *Argeldu* 1401, 'black A.'; and Lower Argal was *Argelwyn* 1284, 'white A.'.

Arrowan (SW 7517): *Arawon* c1510, perhaps 'acre place', C. *erow-an*.

Ashton (SW 6023): C19 E. 'ash-tree settlement'.

Balrose (SW 6042): *Balrosa* 1571, 'diggings with (water)wheels', C. *bal rosow*.

Balwest (SW 5929): 'western diggings', C. *bal west*

Bareppa (SW 7829): 'fair retreat', F. *beau repair*.

Barncoose (SW 6841): 'wood hill', C. *bron cos*.

Barrimaylor (SW 7323): *Merther Melor* 1587, 'St Melor's grave/relics', C. *merther Melor*.

Barripper (SW 6338): *Beaurepere* 1397, 'fair retreat', F. *beau repair*.

Beacon (SW 6539): E. 'place where beacons are lit'.

Berepper (SW 6522): *Beureper* 1327, 'fair retreat', F. *beau repair*.

Binnerton (SW 5933): *Bynner* 1293, apparently C. of unknown derivation, with addition of OE *tun*, 'farm, settlement'.

Black Head (SW 7716): Mod. E. directly translating the original C. name *Peden-due* 1699, 'black head(land)', C. *pen* (LC *pedn*) *du*.

Blowinghouse (SW 6841): E. mining term for a tin-smelting house.

Bochym (SW 6921): C. *bos*, 'dwelling' + unknown word or name. Early forms show *–chim/-chym* consistently except for *Bossim* c1400.

Boden (SW 7623): 'little dwelling', C. *bodyn*.

Boderlogan (SW 6831): *Bodulugan* 1313, 'Ylocan's dwelling', OC *bod Ylogan*.

Boderwennack (SW 6830): C. *bos*, 'dwelling' + place name Trevennack, 'stony farm', C. *tre veynek*.

Bodilly (SW 6731): *Bodyly, Bodely* 1338, 'Yli's dwelling', OC *bod Yly*.

Bodrivial (SW 6536): 'farm-place dwelling', C. *bos drev-yel*.

Bolenowe (SW 6737): *Bolleynou* 1356, 'dwelling by strip fields', C. *bos leynow*.

Bolitho (SW 6634): *Bolleythou* 1278, 'Leithou's dwelling', C. *bos Leythow*.

Bonallack (SW 7126): *Benathelek* 1321, 'broom-brake', C. *banadhlek*.

Bonython (SW 6921): *Bosneythan* 1296, C. bos, 'dwelling' + personal name *Nechtan*, rather than C. *a'n eythyn*, 'at the furze'.

Boquio (SW 6633): 'snipe's dwelling', C. *bos kyogh*. Here, *kyogh* may be a personal name rather than the bird, so 'Kyogh's dwelling'.

Borgwitha (SW 7516): *Bargwythar* c1510, 'workman's summit', C. *bar gweythor*.

Borthog (SW 6335): *Bosworthogo* 1330, 'dwelling at a cave', C. *bos orth ogo*.

Bosahan (SW 7625): 'waterless dwelling (i.e. one with no independent water supply)', C. *bos sehen*.

Boscadjack (SW 6730): *Boscadek* 1350, 'Cadoc's dwelling', C. *bos Cajek*.

Bosleake (SW 6740): 'Laoc's dwelling', C. *bos Laek*.

Bospebo (SW 6041): *Boospeeby* 1700, 'piper's dwelling', C. *bos pybyth* (with common unvoicing of final *-th*).

Bosvathick (SW 7530): *Boswodek* 1330, 'stream-place dwelling', C. *bos wodhek*.

Boswidjack (SW 7129): 'sow-farm dwelling', C. *bos wysak* (western C. *wyjak*).

Boswyn (SW 6636): 'white/fair dwelling', C. *bos wyn*.

Brea (SW 6640): 'hill', C. *bre*.

Breage (SW 6128): *Eglosbrek* 1181, *Eglospenbro* 1207, C. *eglos*, 'church' + saint's name *Breaca*; also + place name **Penbro**, 'end of a region', C. *pen bro*. Pronounced 'braig'.

Bridge (SW 6744): *Tresulyan* 1699, probably C. *res Julyan*, 'ford of St Julian', also *St Julyan's bridge* 1584.

Brill (SW 7229): *Brehelgh* 1304, 'hunt hill', C. *bre helgh*.

Budock (SW 7832): *Eglos Budock* (undated), 'church of St Budoc', C. *eglos Budhek*.

Budock Vean (SW 7627): *Eglosbuthekbyan* 1469, 'little Budock' (see **Budock**), C. *Eglosbudhek byan*.

Budock Water (SW 7832): C19 E. 'stream at Budock', formerly *Roseglos* C18, 'roughland near a church', C. *ros eglos*.

Burncoose (SW 6923): *Broncoys* 1277, 'wood hill', C. *bron cos*.

Burras (SW 6734): *Berres* 1337, 'short ford', C. *ber-res*.

Buscaverran (SW 6434): *Boskeveren* 1302, 'Hundred ('keverang') dwelling', C. *bos keverang* (this farm lay on the border of Penwith and Kerrier Hundreds).

Busveal (SW 7141): *Bosvael* 1356, 'Mael's dwelling', C. *bos Vayl*.

Cadgwith (SW 7214): *Porthcaswyth* 1540, *Por Cadgewith* 1699, 'cove/landing place at a thicket', C. *porth cajwydh* (earlier *caswydh*).

Caerthillian Cove (SW 6912): *Gothillan* 1760, 'stream bend', C. *godh elyn* (*elyn* is literally 'elbow').

Caervallack (SW 7224): *Carmailoc* C11/12, 'Maeloc's fort', C. *ker/cayr Vaylek*.

Calamansack (SW 7426): *Kilmonsek* 1338, 'mounded ridge', C. *kyl monsek*.
Calvadnack (SW 6936): 'pointed hill', C. *cal vannek* (LC *vadnek*) (literally 'penis-peaked').
Camborne (SW 6440): *Cambron* c1100–c1700, 'curve-hill, crook-hill', C. *cam-bron* (although *cam-vron* would normally be expected).
Cambrose/Cambridge (SW 6845): *Cambres* 1286, 'crooked copse', C. *cam-brys*.
Cardrew (SW 7043): *Caerdro* 1311, *Caerdreu* 1356, 'yonder fort', C. *ker/cayr dru*.
Cargenwen (SW 6636): *Cargenwyn* 1375, 'Cynwen's fort', C. *ker/cayr Genwyn*.
Carharrack (SW 7841): *Cararthek* 1250, probably 'Arthoc's fort', C. *ker/cayr Ardhek*, rather than an adjective of *ardh*, 'a height'.
Carleen (SW 6130): *Carleghyon* 1262, 'fort of slabs', C. *ker/cayr leghyon*.
Carleen (SW 7124): *Carleyn* 1548, 'fort by a strip-field', C. *ker/cayr leyn*.
Carlidnack (SW 7729): *Carlunyek* 1333, probably 'meadow-place fort', C. *ker/cayr glunyek*.
Carminow (SW 6623): *Kaermenou* 1300, 'fort of stones', C. *ker/cayr menow*.
Carn Arthen (SW 6639): *Carnarthur* 1454, 'Arthur's tor', C. *carn Arthur*.
Carn Brea (SW 6840): 'tor at Brea', C. *carn Bre*.
Carnebone (SW 7031): *Carnebwen* 1298, 'Ebwyn's tor', C. *carn Ebwyn* (personal name, Br. *epo-uindo-s*, 'white horse').
Carnkie (SW 6839): 'dog's tor', C. *carn ky*.
Carnkie (SW 7134): 'dog's tor', C. *carn ky*.
Carn Marth (SW 7140): *Carnmargh* 1584, 'horse's tor', C. *carn margh*.
Carn Meal (SW 6229): *Carnmele* 1501, 'honey tor', C. *carn mel*.
Carnmenellis (SW 6936): 'stacked/heaped tor', *carn manalys*.
Carnpessack (SW 7417): 'decayed crag', C. *carn pesak*.
Carnsew (SW 7634): *Carnduwyou* 1309, 'gods' tor', C. *carn dewyow*.
Carrag-a-Pilez (SW 6620): 'crag of the naked oats (*avena nuda*)', C. *carrek an pylas*.
Carrag Luz (SW 6618): 'grey rock', C. *carrek los*.
Carrag Luz (SW 7516): 'grey rock', C. *carrek los*.
Carthew (SW 6836): 'black/dark fort', C. *ker/cayr dhu*.
Carvannel (SW 6444): *Kaervanathel* 1302: 'broom (plants) fort', C. *ker/cayr vanadhel*.
Carveth (SW 7534): *Carvergh* 1538, 'horses' fort', C. *ker/cayr vergh*.
Carvolth (SW 6535): *Carvolgh* c1400, 'gap fort', C. *ker/cayr volgh*.
Carwinion (SW 7828): *Caerwenkein* 1297, 'white-ridge fort', C. *ker/cayr wen-geyn*.
Carwynnen (SW 6537): 'fort of bees', C. *ker/cayr wenen*.
Carwythenack (SW 7128): *Kayrwethenec* 1303, 'Guethenoc's fort', C. *ker/cayr Wedhenek*.
Castle Pencaire (SW 6030): now 'castle of Pencaire (the former name of **Tregonning Hill**), formerly *Cair Gonyn, Cair Conin* c1540, 'Conan's fort', C. *ker/cayr Gonan*.

Chegwidden (SW 7230): *Chygwen* 1304, 'white house', C. *chy gwyn* (LC *gwidn*).
Chenhalls (SW 7818): 'house at the cliff', C. *chy'n als.*
Church Cove (SW 6620): now E. 'church cove', formerly *Porth Lingie* c1580, 'pool-house cove', C. *porth lyn-jy.*
Church Cove (SW 7112): now E. 'church cove', formerly *Perran Vose* 1851, 'cove of the wall/bank', C. *porth an fos.* The Ordnance Survey has transferred this name to a cove 300 metres to the north.
Chyanvounder (SW 6522): 'house at the lane', C. *chy an vownder.*
Chynhalls (SW 7817): 'house at the cliff', C. *chy'n als.*
Chynoweth (SW 7633): 'new house', C. *chy noweth.*
Chypons (SW 6820): 'bridge house', C. *chy pons.*
Chyreen (SW 8022): *Chywarrin* 1419, 'house on a slope', C. *chy war ryn.*
Chyvarloe (SW 6523): *Chywarlo* 1300, 'house on **Loe Pool**', C. *chy war Logh.*
Chywoone (SW 7820): *Chyenwoen* 1300, 'house at the downs', C. *chy an wun.*
Clijah (SW 7040): 'ditches', C. *cleyjow.*
Clowance (SW 6335): *Clewyns* 1362, apparently 'hear-wind', C. *clow-wyns.*
Cober (river): this name has appeared as *Clohar* 1259, *Coffar* 1283, *Cofar* 1323 and *Cohor* 1354 before becoming *Cober* 1584. On this evidence, it would appear to be C. *cough-ar*, 'red one'.
Cogegoes (SW 6339): *Cozejegowe* C17, 'ducklings' wood', C. *cos heyjygow.*
Comfort (SW 7329): seemingly E. '(place of) comfort', unless evidence emerges to support C. *com-fordh*, 'vale-road'.
Condurrow (SW 6639): *Kendorou* 1327, 'meeting of waters/streams', C. *kendowrow.*
Constantine (SW 7329): *Langostentin* 1574, 'St Constantine's church enclosure', C. *lan Gostentyn.*
Coombe (SW 6242): E. 'valley', OE *cumb*, itself borrowed from C. *com*, W. *cwm*, 'valley'.
Corgerrick (SW 7216): *Kugurryk* 1342, 'little **Kuggar**', C. *cogeryk.*
Cosawes (SW 7637): *Cosawyth* 1284, 'stream wood', C. *cos aweth.*
Coverack (SW 7818): *Porthkoverec* 1284, apparently 'stream-abundant cove/landing place', C. *porth goverek*, although the provected initial would be odd. A stream name *Coverek* might be involved instead.
Coverack Bridges (SW 6630): E. 'bridge' (later made plural), added to C. *Cougharyk*, 'little **Cober** river'.
Cow-y-jack (SW 7719): *Kewedyk* 1312, *Cowesyk* c1430, 'hollowed', C. *kewesek* (LC *kewejak*).
Crane (SW 6339): *Caervran* c1260, 'crow's or Bran's fort', C. *ker/cayr vran.*
Crenver (SW 6333): *Caergenver* 1201, 'Cynvor's fort', C. *ker/cayr Genvor* (personal name from Br. *cuno-moro-s*, 'sea hound').
Croft Michell/Michael (SW 6637): 'Michael's enclosed rough grazing', C. *croft Myhal.*

Croft Pascoe (SW 7220): 'Pascoe's enclosed rough grazing', C. *croft Pasco* (from Richard Paskoe 1698).

Crousa (SW 7618): *Crouswrach* 977, 'hag's cross', C. *crows wragh*.

Crowan (SW 6434): *Egloscraweyn* 1580, 'St Crewenna's church', C. *eglos Crewen*.

Crowgey (SW 7116): 'hut', C. *crowjy*.

Crowntown (SW 6330): Mod. E., 'settlement at the Crown Inn'.

Culdrose (SW 6726): 'thin/narrow roughland', C. *cul-ros*.

Cury (SW 6721): *Egloscury* C16, 'St Corentyn's church (Cury being a pet form of Corentyn), C. *eglos Cury*.

St Day (SW 7342): *Seynt Dey* 1358–1511, after St Dei.

Degibna (SW 6525): *S. Degamannus* 1427, after a former chapel to St Decuman.

Dennis Head (SW 7825): *Dinas* 1610, 'fort', C. *dynas*.

Devil's Frying Pan (SW 7214): Mod. E. name replacing *Huggadridge* 1726, 'low-water cave', C. *ogo dryg*.

Dolcoath (SW 6540): 'old ground', C. *dor coth*.

Dollar Ogo (SW 7213): 'sea-stack cave', C. *ogo dalar*, now in E. word order.

Dolor Point (SW 7818): C. *talar*, 'sea-stack (literally, 'auger') + E. 'point.

Dowha (SW 6736): *Dyuuer* 1317, apparently 'water, stream', C. *dowr*.

Downas Cove (SW 7616): *Downance Cove* 1866, C. *down-nans*, 'deep-vale' + E. 'cove'.

Drym (SW 6233): *Trem* 1327, 'ridge', C. *trum*.

Durgan (SW 7727): *Dourgen* 1813, apparently '(place of) otters', C. *dowrguen*.

Durra (stream): apparently a well-shortened form of *Cendefrion* 967, 'meeting of waters/streams', C. *kendevryon*.

Eathorne (SW 7431): A baffling name in spite of a number of early forms such as *Eytron* 1392 and *Ethron* 1417. The second syllable might be C. *tron*, 'nose, hillspur'.

Edgcumbe (SW 7253): named after the Edgcome family (so spelt in parish registers).

St Elvan (SW 6827): named after St Helven, perhaps a Breton saint.

Enys (SW 7936): 'isolated, remote', C. *enys*.

Erisey (SW 7117): *Erysy* 1284, 'ploughland place/stream', C. *erys-y*.

Flushing (SW 7825): an Anglicisation of the transferred name of the Dutch port of Vlissingen (see **Flushing**, Carrick).

Forge (SW 7045): *Forge Wash* 1301, *Forges* 1641, E. 'forge, forges'.

Four Lanes (SW 6240): E. 'where four lanes meet'.

Gadles (SW 7636): 'the bailey/courtyard', C. *an gadlys*.

Gaider, The (SW 7616): 'the chair', C. *an gadar*.

Garlidna (SW 6932): *Gerlynnow* 1461, 'herd/flock-ponds', C. *grelynnow* (LC *grelidnow*).

Garras (SW 7023): *Garros* c1320, a contraction of C. *garow-ros*, 'rugged roughland'.

Gear (SW 6438): *Kaervran* 1283, 'crow's, or Bran's, fort', C. *ker/cayr vran*.

Gear (SW 7224): *Caer* 1086, 'fort', C. *ker/cayr*.

Germoe (SW 5829): *Germogh* 1289–1347, pron. with a hard G and named after St Germoch.

Gernick (SW 6336): *Kernic* 1229, 'little corner', C. *kernyk*.

Gew (SW 6336): *Kew* 1456, 'paddock, enclosure, hollow', C. *kew*.

Gew Graze (SW 6714): 'central hollow', C. *kew gres*.

Gilbert's Coombe (SW 6943): E. 'valley of the Gilbert family'.

Gillan (SW 7825): *Gillyn* 1327, *Kellian* 1507, 'creek, inlet', C. *kylen*.

Gilly Gabben (SW 6827): *Kyllygam* 1506, 'crooked grove', C. *kelly gam* (LC *gabm*).

Gillywartha (SW 7824): 'higher grove', C. *kelly wartha*.

Glendurgan (SW 7727): a modern name consisting of C. *glyn*, 'deep valley' + place name **Durgan**.

Godolphin (SW 6031): a supposed C. word * *godolghan*, 'tump', does not exist and can be ruled out. Early forms: *Godholkan* c1210 and *Gotholgan* 1284–1346 strongly suggest C. *godh*, 'stream' + C. *olcan*, 'metal, tin', i.e. 'tin-stream'.

Godolphin Hill (SW 5931): *Carne Godolcan* c1538, 'tor at Godolphin', C. *carn Godholcan*.

Goodagrane (SW 7432): *Gothowgran* 1451, 'bracken/scrub streams', C. *godhow gran*.

Goongillings (SW 7328): *Goon Gillin* 1649, 'downs at a tidal creek/inlet', C. *gun gylen*.

Goonhilly Downs (centred at SW 7219): *Gonhely* 1284, *Gonelgy* 1315, 'hunting downs', C. *gun helghy*.

Goonhingey (SW 7535): *Goynhensy* 1342, 'downs with an old/ruinous house', C. *gun henjy*.

Goonhusband (SW 6625): C. *gun*, 'downs' + C14 family name Hosebond.

Goonlaze (SW 7237): 'green downs', C. *gun las*.

Goonreeve (SW 7737): *Gonruth* 1613, 'red downs', C. *gun rudh*.

Goonvean (SW 7435): 'little downs', C. *gun vyan*.

Goonwin (SW 6826): 'white downs', C. *gun wyn*.

Grade (SW 7114): named after St Grada.

Grambla (SW 6828): *Cromlegh* 1327, 'dolmen', C. *cromlegh*.

Grambler (SW 7041): *Gromleth* c1610, 'the dolmen', C. *an gromlegh*.

Gregwartha (SW 6938): 'higher barrow/tumulus', C. *crug wartha*.

Grugwith (SW 7520): *Crukwaeth* 967, 'barrow/tumulus by trees', C. *crug wedh*.

Gullyn Rock (SW 6747): 'gull', C. *gwylan*.

Gunwalloe (SW 6522): *Wynwala* 1499, after St Winwalo.

Gunwalloe Church Cove (SW 6620): *Porth Lingie* c1580, 'pool-house cove', C. *porth lyn-jy*.

Gunwalloe Fishing Cove (SW 6522): *Gunwalloe Cove* 1794, E. 'cove/landing place at Gunwalloe'.

Gunwalloe Stream: now E. 'stream at Gunwalloe' but *Lofhal, Lovel* 1380. Although evidently a Celtic name, the meaning of this is uncertain.

Gwarder (SW 7836): *Gwerthour* 1312, 'green-water', C. *gwer-dhowr*.

Gwarth-an-Drea (SW 7025): 'top of the settlement', C. *gwarth a'n dre*.

Gwavas (SW 6529): 'winter dwelling', C. *gwavos*.

Gwavas (SW 7113): 'winter dwelling', C. *gwavos*.

Gwealavellan (SW 5941): probably 'the mill field', C. *gwel an velyn*, rather than 'apple-tree field', C. *gwel avallen*.

Gwealdues (SW 6628): *Gweale due* 1691, 'black/dark field', C. *gwel du*.

Gwealeath (SW 6922): *Guaenelegh* 1288, 'slab downs', C. *gun legh*.

Gwealmellin (SW 7428): 'mill field', C. *gwel melyn*.

Gweek (SW 7026): *Gwyk* 1358, 'forest settlement', C. *gwyk*.

Gwendreath (SW 7316): *Gwyndreth* 1343, 'white-beach', C. *gwyn-dreth*.

Gwenter (SW 7147): *Gwynter* 1519, 'white-land', C. *gwyn-tyr* (although *gwyn-dyr* would have been expected).

Halabezack (SW 7034): *Halwebesek* 1338, 'gnat-infested marsh', C. *hal webesek*.

Halliggye (SW 7323): *Helygy Whethlowe* 1457, C. *helyg-y*, 'place/stream of willows' + C. *whethlow*, 'tales, stories' or personal name *Gwetheleu*.

Halvosso (SW 7433): *Hafossowe* 1532, 'summer farms, shielings', C. *havosow*.

Halzephron (SW 6521): *Alseyeffarn* 1488, 'Hell cliff', C. *als Yfern*.

Hantertavis (SW 7433): *Hantertavas* 1522, farm named after a rock formation, 'half-a-tongue', C. *hanter tavas*.

Hayle Kimbro (SW 6916): *Halkimbra* 1841, 'Welshman's marsh', C. *hal Kembro*.

Hayle River: *Heyl* 1265, 'estuary with tidal flats', C. *heyl*.

Helford (SW 7526): C. *heyl*, 'inlet with tidal flats' + E. 'ford'. A 1732 reference to *Helford alias Penkestle* gives a tenuous alternative name, 'castle headland', C. *pen castel*. The *heyl* of the name is probably the small creek on which the village is sited rather than the Helford River itself.

Helford Passage (SW 7626): *Haylford Treath* (undated), C. *treth*, 'ferry' + place name **Helford**.

Helford Point (SW 7526): now E. 'point (headland) at Helford' but probably the *Penkestle* referred to under **Helford** above.

Helford River: the present name is an extension of that of the inlet and village on the southern side of the estuary, the former name of which is given as *Monhonyer/Mahonyer* C13 and *Mawonieck/Mawoniek* C14. The correct form and meaning of this name is not known.

Helland (SW 7531): 'ancient/disused church enclosure', C. *hen-lan*.

Hell's Mouth (SW 6042): probably E. 'hell's mouth' although there is an unsubstantiated chance of it being C. *als mogh*, 'pigs' cliff'.

Helston (SW 6527): *Henliston* 1086, *Hellys* 1396, C. *hen-lys*, 'old administrative centre' (often contracted to *hellys*) + addition of OE *tun*, 'settlement'.

Hendra (SW 5927): 'old/home farm', C. *hen-dre*.

Hendra (SW 6931): 'old/home farm', C. *hen-dre*.
Hendra (SW 7017): 'old/home farm', C. *hen-dre*.
Hendra (SW 7237): 'old/home farm', C. *hen-dre*.
Henscath (SW 6618): 'slipway', C. *hens-scath*.
Herland (SW 6031): *Hyrleyn* 1283, 'long strip-field', C. *hyr-leyn*.
Herniss (SW 7334): *Hyrnans* 1290-1428, 'long valley', C. *hyr-nans*.
Hoe Point (SW 5727): a contraction of *Pengersick How* C19, E 'promontory/heel of land at **Pengersick**', OE *hoh* + C. place name. It was *Peden Due* 1794, 'black/dark head(land)', C. *pen* (LC *pedn*) *du*.
Holestrow (SW 6912): 'broken cliff', C. *als trogh*.
Holseer (SW 6912): 'tall/long cliff', C. *als hyr*.
Hugo Mesul (SW 6618): 'mussels cave', C. *ogo mesel*.
Huthnance (SW 6131): 'pleasant-valley', C. *hueth-nans*.
Hyrlas Rock (SW 7716): 'tall green/grey one', C. *hyr-las*.
Illogan (SW 6743): after St Ylocan. The churchtown was formerly *Egloshallow* 1700, 'marshes church', C. *eglos hallow*.
Inow (SW 7427): *Iwenau* 1269, 'yew-trees', C. *ewenow*.
Jangye-Ryn (SW 6520): 'promontory with an ice house', C. *ryn yeyn-jy* (now in E. word order)'.
Kaledna (SW 6923): *Kelenneu* 1315, a curious double plural, 'hollies', C. *kelynnow* (LC *kelidnow*).
Kehelland (SW 6241): *Kellyhellan* 1284, 'grove at an old/disused church enclosure', C. *kelly hen-lan*.
Kennack Sands (SW 7316): *Porth Kunyk* 1538, 'reed-bed cove'. C. *porth kenak*.
Kennall (river): *Kennel* 1201, *Kenel* 1278, *Kynal* 1302, possibly 'reedy one', C. *kuen-el*.
Kenneggy (SW 5528): 'reed beds', C. *kenegy*.
Kergilliack (SW 7733): *Kegulyek* 1327, 'cockerel's hedge', C. *ke gulyek*.
Kernewas (SW 7420): *Kynyavos* 1513, 'autumn dwelling', C. *kynyavos*.
Kerthen (SW 5833): *Kerthyn* 1284-C15, 'rowan tree', C. *kerdhyn*.
St Keverne (SW 7921): *Lanachebran* 1086, *Lanhevran* 1504, 'St Achebran's church enclosure', C. *lan Ahevran*.
Killivose (SW 6438): *Kyllyvos* 1480, 'grove by a wall', C. *kelly fos*.
Kuggar (SW 7216): *Coger* 1324, 'winding (stream)', C. *coger*.
Kynance (SW 6714): *Keynance* 1620, 'ravine',C. *keynans*.
Kynance Cove (SW 6813): *Penkynans* 1619, 'foot of a ravine', C. *ben keynans*.
Laddenvean (SW 7821): *Lanvyghan* 1369, 'small church enclosure', C. *lan vyan*, referring to a C13 monastic grange 150m away at Tregonning.
Laden Ceyn (SW 6617): *Lappen Kean, Ladn Keyn* 1876, 'leap-back', C. *lam* (LC *labm*) *keyn*.
Laity (SW 6744): 'dairy', C. *lety*.
Lanarth (SW 7621): *Lannergh* 1357, 'clearing', C. *lanergh*.

Lancarrow (SW 6938): *Nanscarou* 1338, 'stag's valley', C. *nans carow*.

Landewednack (SW 7112): 'thy St Winnoc's church enclosure', C. *lan de Wynnek*. *Winnoc* is a recognised pet form of the saint's name Winwalo, who also founded the Breton monastery of Landevennac.

Landrivick (SW 7524): *Hendrevyk* 1324, 'little home farm', C. *hendrevyk*.

Lannarth (SW 7624): *Lannargh* 1413, 'clearing', C. *lanergh*.

Lanner (SW 6426): *Lanergh* 1305, 'clearing', C. *lanergh*.

Leedstown (SW 6034): C19 E. 'settlement founded by the Duke of Leeds'.

Lesneage (SW 7722): *Lismanahec* 1150, 'administrative centre of the Meneage district' (see **Meneage**), C. *lys Manahek*.

Lestowder (SW 7924): *Lesteudar* c1400, 'Teudar's court/ruin/administrative centre', C. *lys Teudar*. *Teudar* is the name of a semi-legendary Cornish king.

Lezerea (SW 6834): *Lesgre* 1284, 'herd/flock court', perhaps an ironic name, C. *lys gre*.

Lizard, The (SW 6913): *Lesard* c1250–1348, doubtfully OC *lys ard*, 'high court/administrative centre' as there is no noticeably high spot in this flat-topped landscape, nor an explanation for the failure of OC *ard* to soften to MC *ardh* as it should have done this far west. The name may be an E. or F. mariner's name, 'lizard' from the resemblance of its outline seen from the sea to a lizard's tail. Early forms seem far closer to F. *lesard*, 'lizard' than to any supposed C. origin. An early Celtic name for the Lizard may survive in **Predannack**.

Loe Pool (SW 6424): 'deep water inlet', C. *logh* (which rarely applies to an inland pool as often mistakenly thought. Loe Pool was once an arm of the sea).

Mabe (SW 7532): *Lanvabe* (undated), 'St Mab's church enclosure', C. *lan Vab*.

Mabe Burnthouse (SW 7634): *Burnt House* 1813, C19 E. 'burnt house', now 'burnt house at Mabe'.

Maenporth (SW 7929): *Mayne porte* 1584, probably 'cove of stones', C. *porth meyn*, now in E. word order.

Magor (SW 6342): 'ruin', C. *magor*, probably from the Romano-Cornish villa rediscovered here in 1931.

Manaccan (SW 7625): *Managhan* 1395, 'monkish place', C. *managh-an*. An alternative name was *Mynstre* 1283, 'endowed church', C. *mynster*.

Manacles, The (SW 8120): the traditional pronunciation, 'mean-a'klz', given in 1808 and the form *Mannahackles* 1619 tip the balance in favour of this being 'church stones', C. *meyn eglos*.

Manhay (SW 6930): *Menihy* 1327, 'church land', C. *menehy*.

Mankea (SW 7636): *Maenke* 1288, 'hedge stones', C. *meyn ke*.

St Martin-in-Meneage (SW 7323): *Dydemin* 1385, 'St Dedymin' the original church saint, replaced after 1385 by St Martin.

Mawgan-in-Meneage (SW 7025): *S. Maugan* C14, *Pluvogan* 1523, 'St Maugan's parish', C. *plu Vaugan*.

Mawnan (SW 7827): *Seynt Maunan* 1398, after St Maunan.

Mawnan Smith (SW 7728): C17 E. 'smith's Mawnan'.

Mean Toll (SW 7331): 'tax/tithe boundary stone', C. *men toll* (rather than 'holed stone', C. *men toll*, as this and similarly named bound stones in Penwith are unperforated).

Medlyn (SW 7033): 'middle pool', C.*medh-lyn*.

Mehal Mill (SW 7722): *Melyn Myhall* 1474, 'St Michael's mill', C. *melyn Myhal* (formerly owned by the priory of St Michael's Mount).

Mellangoose (SW 6428): *Melyn Goys* 1535, 'wood mill', C. *melyn gos.*

Mellangoose (SW 6826): *Melingoys* 1339, 'wood mill', C. *melyn gos.*

Menadarva (SW 6141): *Mertherderwa* 1285, 'St Derwa's grave/relics', C. *merther Derwa.*

Men Amber (SW 6532): 'balance stone', C. *men omborth* (a sensitive loggan stone until dislodged during the Civil War).

Meneage (district centred at SW 7524 and pron. 'm'n-aig'): *Manahec* 1269, 'monkish (place)', C. *manahek.*

Menehay (SW 7832): *Menehy* 1327, 'church land', C. *menehy.*

Menerdue (SW 7235): *Menethdu* 1356, 'dark/black hillside', C. *menedh du.*

Menherion (SW 7036): 'standing stones', C. *menhyryon.*

Men-te-heul (SW 6516): *Mean Tale* 1794, 'brow stone', C. *men tal.*

Menwinnion (SW 6442): *Menwynyon* 1303, *Meinwinion* 1318, 'white stones', C. *meyn wynyon*, with unusual adjectival plural.

Meres (SW 6719): *Methros* 1386, 'mid-roughland', C. *medh-ros.*

Merrose (SW 6643): *Methros* c1200, 'mid-roughland', C. *medh-ros.*

Merthen (SW 7226): *Merthyn* 1213, 'sea-fort', C. *merdhyn.*

Mertheruny (SW 7029): *Merther Ewny* 1291, 'St Euny's grave/reliquary', C. *merther Ewny.*

Methleigh (SW 6226): 'mid-place', C. *medh-le.*

Millewarne (SW 6722): *Maenlewern* 1289, 'foxes' stone', C.*men lewern.*

Morah, The (SW 8121): 'dolphin, porpoise', C. *morhogh.*

Mount Ambrose (SW 7143): C16 E. 'James Ambrose's hill', after the tenant of Trefula 1501.

Mount Hermon (SW 7015): E. 'hill at Hervan' (from C. *hyr-ven*, 'standing stone').

Mudgeon (SW 7324): *Mudion* c1250, *Mogyon* 1385, 'ox place', C. *ma ojyon* (OC *odion*).

Mullion (SW 6719): *S. Melan* 1262, *Eglosmeylyon* 1274, 'St Melan's church', C. *eglos Melan.*

Mullion Cove (SW 6617): *Porthmellyn* C18, 'mill cove', C. *porth melyn*. It is tempting to see this as 'St Melan's cove/landing place' but early spellings indicate C. *melyn*, 'mill'.

Mullion Island (SW 6617): *Inispriven* c1540, 'worm island', C. *enys pryven.*

Nance (SW 6644): 'valley', C. *nans.*

Nancegollan (SW 6332): *Nannsygollen* 1356, early spellings and pron. 'nansy-goll'en' favour C. *nans ygolen*, 'whetstone valley' over C. *nans an gollen*, 'valley of the hazel tree'.

Nancekuke (SW 6846): *Nancoig* c1170, 'empty/worthless valley', C. *nans cog*.

Nancemerrin (SW 6825): *Nansmerion* 1338, 'Merien's valley', C. *nans Meryen*.

Nancenoy (SW 7328): 'Noy's valley' (personal name that is the C. form of *Noah*), C. *nans Noy*.

Nanplough (SW 6821): *Nansblogh* 1334, 'bare valley', C. *nans blogh*.

Nansidwell (SW 7828): *Nansudwall* 1540, 'Iudhael's valley', C. *nans Yudhal*.

Nansloe (SW 6526): 'valley of Loe Pool', C. *nans Logh*.

Nantithet (SW 6822): *Nanstedeth* 1535, 'Tudet's valley', C. *nans Tudheth* (C. personal name containing Br. *toto-s*, OC *tud*, mod. C. *tus*, 'people').

Nare Head (SW 7924): *Penare Point* c1540, 'prominent headland', C. *penardh*.

Newham (SW 6528): *Newenham* 1327, 'new homestead', OE *niwan ham*.

Newtown (SW 5729): C19 E. 'new settlement'.

Newtown (SW 7423): *Neweton* 1620, 'new farm', ME *newe ton*.

Nine Maidens (SW 6836): *Naw-vos, Naw-whoors* c1880, C. *naw mowes*, 'nine maids' and C. *naw whor*, 'nine sisters'.

North Country (SW 6943): mod. E., presumably 'country to the north of Redruth'.

Ogo-Dour (SW 6615): *Ugethowr* 1794, 'water cave', C. *ogo dhowr*.

Ogo Pons (SW 6714): 'bridge cave', C. *ogo pons*.

Padgagarrick Cove (SW 7825): C. *pajer carrek*, 'four rocks' + E. 'cove'.

Parc-an-Ithon (SW 6328): 'the furze field', C. *park an eythyn*.

Parc-an-Tidno (SW 7922): *Parkfyntynowe* 1419, 'springs field', C. *park fentynyow*.

Paynters Lane End (SW 6743): E. 'end of a lane' + surname Paynter.

Pednandrea (SW 7042): 'top/end of the settlement', C. *pen* (LC *pedn*) *an dre*.

Pedn Boar (SW 7716): *Pedenbore* 1699, 'swollen head(land)', C. *pen* (LC *pedn*) *bor*.

Pedn Crifton (SW 6516): 'headland with wrinkled turf', C. *pen* (LC *pedn*) *crygh-ton*.

Pedngwinian (SW 6520): 'head(land) at the manor of **Winnianton**', C. *pen* (LC *pedn*) *Gwynan*.

Pedn Myin (SW 7919): 'end of the stones', C. *pen* (LC *pedn*) *meyn*.

Pedn Tiere (SW 8023): 'promontory', C. *pentyr*.

Pencoose (SW 7337): *Broncoys* 1278, 'wood hill', C. *bron cos*.

Pencoys (SW 6838): 'end/top of a wood', C. *pen-cos*.

Pendarves (SW 6437): *Penderves* c1320, 'end/top of an oak wood', C. *pen derves*.

Pengegon (SW 6539): 'end/top of a ridge', C. *pen gygen*.

Pengelly (SW 6432): 'end/top of a grove', C. *pen gelly*.

Pengersick (SW 5828): 'end of a reed marsh', C. *pen gersek*.

Pengwedna (SW 6231): 'head of the Gwedna stream', C. *pen Gwena* (LC *Gwedna*); the stream name is 'white stream', C. *gwen-a* (LC *gwedn-a*), containing the fem. form of *gwyn/gwidn*, 'white').

Penhale (SW 6918): 'end/top of a marsh', C. *pen-hal.*

Penhale-an-Drea (SW 6231): '**Penhale** by the farm', C. *Penhal an dre.*

Penhale Jakes (SW 6028): 'Jakes's **Penhale**', from a C15 tenant.

Penhallick (SW 6740): *Penhelek* 1314, 'end/top of willows', C. *pen helyk.*

Penhalurick (SW 7038): 'Penhale with a rampart', C. *Penhal luryk* (*Penhal* is 'end/top of a marsh'; *luryk* is literally 'breastplate').

Penhalvean (SW 7037): 'little Penhale', C. *Penhal* ('end/top of a marsh') *vyan.*

Penhalveor (SW 7037): 'great Penhale', C. *Penhal vuer.*

Penjerrick (SW 7730): *Pennanseyryk* 1333, C. *pen-nans*, 'head of a valley' + unknown word, probably a stream name.

Penmarth (SW 7035): *Pengarth* 1337, 'end of a ridge', C. *pen garth.*

Penmenor (SW 7237): *Penmeneth* 1512, 'top/end of a hillside', C. *pen menedh.*

Pennance (SW 7140): 'head of a valley',C. *pen-nans.*

Pen Olver (SW 7111): 'lookout head(land)', C. *pen golva.*

Penpoll (SW 7728): 'head of a creek', C. *pen-pol.*

Penponds (SW 6339): 'bridge end', C. *pen-pons.*

Penrose (SW 6129): 'end/top of a hillspur', C. *pen-ros.*

Pentreath (SW 5728): 'head of a beach', C. *pen treth.*

Penventon (SW 6426): 'spring-head', C. *pen-fenten.*

Penwarne (SW 7730): 'end/top of alder trees', C. *pen wern.*

Perprean Cove (SW 7817): 'putrid cove', C. *porth breyn.*

Piece (SW 6739): E. 'piece (i.e. plot of land, smallholding)'.

Piskey Hall (SW 7230): now represented as E. 'hall of Piskey (a Cornish sprite)' or even wholly Anglicised as *Pixie's Hall* but in fact coined from the name of the field containing this Iron Age fogou: *Park an Pascoes* 1649, 'field of the grazing', C. *park an peskys.*

Pistol Ogo (SW 6911): 'waterfall cave', C. *ogo hystyl* (now in E. word order).

Plain-an-Gwarry (SW 6942): 'playing place, arena', C. *plen an gwary.*

Polbream Cove (SW 7011): 'putrid cove/pool', C. *pol breyn.*

Pol Cornick (SW 6615): *Polhorneck* 1841, 'pool/cove in an iron-producing place', C. *pol hornek.*

Polcrebo (SW 6433): *Polcrybou* 1380, 'pool by crests/ridges', C. *pol crybow.*

Poldhu Cove (SW 6619): *Porthu* 1493, 'black/dark cove', C. *porth du.*

Poldhu Point (SW 6619): *Pedn Poljew* 1876, 'head(land) at **Poldhu**', C. *pen* (LC *pedn*) *Porthdu.*

Poldowrian (SW 7416): *Bendowrian* 1250, 'foot of a watering place', C. *ben dowran.*

Poleo (SW 6536): *Polleowe* 1483, 'pool by yew-trees', C. *pol ew.*

Polgear (SW 6837): 'pool by a fort', C. *pol ger/gayr.*

Polglase (SW 6033): 'green/blue pool', C. *pol glas.*

Polgwidden (SW 7626): 'white/fair cove', C. *pol gwyn* (LC *gwidn*].

Polkanoggo (SW 7334): 'frogs'/toads' pool', C. *pol cronogow.*

Polkerth (SW 7321): 'heron's pool', C. *pol kerhyth.*

Polladras (SW 6130): 'pool with a sluice gate', C. *pol ladres*.

Polmarth (SW 7035): 'horse pool', C. *pol margh*.

Polpenwith (SW 7327): *Penreth* 1492, *Polpenryth* 1506, 'creek at Penruth (place name meaning 'red head(land)', C. *pen rudh*).

Polpeor Cove (SW 6911): *Porth Peer* 1699, 'clean cove', C. *porth pur*.

Polstangey Bridge (SW 7116): *Ponstangey* 1690, 'Tangye's bridge' (from a Celtic surname found in Cornwall and Brittany meaning 'firedog'), C. *pons Tangy*.

Polstrong (SW 6239): *Polstronk* 1302, 'fithy pool', C. *pol stronk*.

Poltesco (SW 7215): *Poltuske* c1300, 'moss-bed pool', C. *pol tuska*.

Poltesco Stream: place names along the course of this stream (see **Corgerrick** and **Kuggar**) suggest that this was C. *coger*, 'winding (stream)'.

Polurrian Cove (SW 6618): *Boloryan* 1580, apparently C. *beleryon*, 'cress-beds' + E. 'cove'.

Polwheveral (SW 7328): *Polwhefrer* 1298, 'lively creek', C. *pol whevrer*.

Ponjeverah (SW 7329): *Ponsaravith* 1591, C. *pons*, 'bridge' + unknown word(s). Traditionally pron. 'ponzer-ai'va'.

Ponsanooth (SW 7537): *Ponsonwoth* 1613, 'bridge at the stream', C. *pons an wodh*.

Ponsmedda (SW 7016): *Ponsmerther* 1325, 'bridge at **Ruan Major**', C. *pons Merther*.

Ponsongath (SW 7517): 'the cat's bridge', C. *pons an gath*.

Ponsonjoppa (SW 6917): 'bridge at the workshop', C. *pons an shoppa*.

Ponsontuel (SW 7025): 'bridge at the conduit', C. *pons an tewel*.

Pool (SW 6471): C18 E. 'pool'.

Porkellis (SW 6933): *Porthkelles* 1286, 'hidden gateway', C. *porth kelys*.

Porthallack (SW 7826): 'willows cove', C. *porth helyk*.

Porthallow (SW 7923): pron. 'per-a'la', C. *porth*, 'cove/landing place' + C. *alow*, 'water-lilies' here probably the name of the stream.

Porth-Cadjack Cove (SW 6444): *Boscadjack Cove* 1760, E. 'cove at Boscadjack (C. *bos Casek/Cajek*, 'Cadoc's dwelling'). Also known as *Polscatho* c1840, 'boats cove/pool', C. *pol scathow*.

Porthcew (SW 5296): 'cove at an enclosure/hollow', C. *porth kew*.

Porthkerris (SW 8022): *Porthkersis* 1291, 'reedy cove', C. *porth kersys*.

Porthleven (SW 6225): C. *porth*, 'cove/landing place' + C. *leven*, 'smooth', probably the former name of the stream here. No known historic form yet supports the notion that this might be 'St Elvan's Cove'.

Porth Navas (SW 7527): *Porhanavas* 1649, *Porranavas* 1649, C. *porth*, 'cove/landing place' + uncertain word(s): C. *an davas*, 'of the sheep (singular)' and C. *kynyavos* 'autumn dwelling' have been unconvincing suggestions, although *an navas* (for *an davas*) is possible by analogy with *an nor*, 'the ground', for *an dor*. Possibilities might lie in C. *an neves*, 'at the sacred grove' if it were not for the first vowel of the final word consistently appearing as –a-, and C. *an havos*, 'at the shieling/summer grazing'.

Porthoustock (SW 8021): pron. 'prow'stek', *Portheustek* 1360, 'Usticke's cove', C. *porth Ustek* (C. surname meaning 'of St Just').

Porth Saxon (SW 7827): pron. 'per-saw'zen', *Porth Zawsen* 1866, 'Saxon's cove', C. *porth Sawsen*.

Portreath (SW 6545): 'cove/landing place with sand', C. *porth treth*.

Praa Sands (SW 5727), pron 'pray', never 'prah', *Polwragh* 1331, 'hag's pool/cove', C. *pol wragh* (although the wrasse, also C. *gwragh*, may be referred to here).

Praze (SW 6327): 'meadow', C. *pras*.

Praze-an-Beeble (SW 6335): 'meadow of the conduit/pipe', C. *pras an bybel*.

Predannack (SW 6616): C. *Predennek*, 'British' (from Br. *predanniko-s*) and still retaining the ancient P initial. This may one of Britain's oldest surviving place names and may once have applied to the Lizard itself. It now names a farm and **Predannack Wollas** nearby is C. *Predennek woles*, 'lower Predannack'.

Predannack Head (SW 6616): *Pedn Predannack* 1841, 'headland at Predannack', C. *pen* (LC *pedn*) *Predennek*.

Prospidnick (SW 6431): *Pryspinik* 1284, 'pine copse', C. *prys pynnek*.

Quillets (SW 7620): E. dialect, 'small paddocks'.

Race (SW 6341): 'watercourse', C. *reys*.

Radnor (SW 7044): E., after the Earls of Radnor (Robartes of Lanhydrock).

Rame (SW 7233): named after the C17 Rame family.

Red River: now E. 'red river', from the former discoloration due to intensive tin mining on its upper course. Its C. name was *Dour Conor* c1540, 'fury water', *dowr connar*.

Redruth (SW 6942): pron. 'r'drooth' or 'drooth'. *Unyredreth* 1563. C. *Ewny*, 'St Euny' + C. *red rudh*, 'red ford', the hard ending of OC *red, ret*, 'ford', being retained due to the following R initial.

Releath (SW 6633): *Redlegh* 1270, 'slab ford', C. *res legh*.

Reskadinnick (SW 6341): *Roscadethek* 1284, 'Cadedoc's roughland', C. *ros Cadedhek*.

Reskajeage (SW 5941): *Roskadaek* 1317, 'Cadoc's hillspur', C. *ros Cajek*.

Retallack (SW 7330): *Reystalek* 1390, 'roach stream', C. *reys talek*.

Retanna (SW 7132): *Retanow* 1327, 'narrow/thin ford', C. *res tanow*.

Rill, The (SW 6713): 'cleft', C. *ryll*.

Rinsey (SW 6028): *Rynsi* 1333, 'promontory house', C. *ryn-jy*.

Rinyard. The (SW 6617): 'promontory ridge', C. *ryn-yarth*.

Roscarnon (SW 7721): 'hillspur with a cairn', C. *ros carnen*.

Roscarrock (SW 7831): *Roscadok* 1327, 'Cadoc's roughland', C. *ros Cadek* (personal name retaining its OC form, rather than softening to *Casek/Cajek*).

Roscroggan (SW 6542): 'shell/skull roughland', C. *ros crogen*.

Roscrowgey (SW 7420): 'uncultivated valley with a hut', C. *ros crowjy*.

Roseladdon (SW 6227): *Resledan* 1284, 'wide ford', C. *res ledan*.

Rosemanowas (SW 7335): 'awl-shaped hillspur', C *ros menawes*.

Rosemerryn (SW 7830): *Rosmeren* 1414, 'Meren's hillspur', C. *ros Meren*.

Rosemullion (SW 7927): *Rosmylian* 1318, *Rosmylyan* 1334, 'Milyan's promontory', C. *ros Mylyan* (C. *mullyon*, 'clover' is not involved in this name, as often thought). The farm is named after the nearby headland, **Rosemullion Head**.

Rosenithon (SW 8021): probably 'Nechtan's uncultivated valley', C. *ros Neythan*, rather than 'uncultivated valley at the furze', C. *ros an eythyn*.

Rosewarne (SW 6441): *Roswern* 1380, 'roughland with alder-trees', C. *ros wern*.

Roskear (SW 6541): *Resker* 1283, 'ford by a fort', C. *res ker/cayr*.

Roskorwell (SW 7923): *Roscurvyl* c1300, 'Cyrfyl's uncultivated valley', C. *ros Kervyl*.

Roskrow (SW 7636): 'roughland with a hut', C. *ros crow*.

Roskruge (SW 7723): *Roscruc* 1303, 'roughland with a barrow/tumulus', C. *ros crug*.

Roskymer (SW 6924): *Reskemer* c1200, 'ford at a meeting of streams', C. *res kemper*.

Rosuic (SW 7420): 'hind's roughland', C. *ros ewyk*.

St Ruan (SW 7115): after St Rumon.

Ruan Major (SW 7114): E. 'great St Ruan', formerly *Merther* 1329, 'saint's grave/reliquary', C. *merther*.

Ruan Minor (SW 7215): *Ruan Vean* 1569, 'little Ruan', C. *Rumon vyan* (after St Rumon). The site was also called *Ruan in Woone* 1727, 'St Rumon in the downs', C. *Rumon y'n wun*.

Ruthdower (SW 6131): 'red stream', C. *rudh-dowr*.

Samphire Island (SW 6344): mod. E. 'island where samphire grows'.

Scorrier (SW 7244): *Scorya* 1350, 'mine waste', from Lat. *scoria*, here adopted into Cornish.

Seaureaugh (SW 7337): *Syuwragh* 1356, C. *(g)wragh*, 'hag, crone', preceded by an unknown word, perhaps C. *resyow*, 'fords'.

Sellegan (SW 6940): *Reshelegen* 1291, 'willow-tree ford', C. *res helygen*.

Seworgan (SW 7031): *Reswoethgen* 1302, 'Goethgen's ford', C. *res Wodhgen*.

Shark's Fin (SW 8121): now E. 'shark's fin' but *Carclaze Rock* 1851, 'green/grey rock', C. *carrek glas*.

Sinns (SW 6944): *Syns* 1456, '(place of) saints/holy men', C. *syns*.

Sithney (SW 6328): *Merthersythny* 1320, 'St Sythni's grave/reliquary', C. *merther Sydhny* (this name survives as **Marsinney**). Also called *Egloseynney* 1623, 'St Sythni's church', C.*eglos Sydhny*.

Skewes (SW 6333): 'place of elder trees', C. *skewys*.

Skyburriowe (SW 6922): 'barns', C. *skyberyow*.

Spargo (SW 7532): *Spergor* 1208, 'thorn hedge', C. *spern-gor*.

Sparnon Gate (SW 6843): E. 'gate to Sparnon'. Sparnon is 'thorn-tree', C. *spernen*.

Spernic Cove (SW 7516): C. *spernek*, 'thorny' + E. 'cove'.

Stithians (SW 7336): *S. Stethyane* 1268, after St Stethyan, a female saint.

Sworne (SW 7424): *Sowrne* 1571, 'nook, corner', C. *sorn*.

Sydney Cove (SW 5728): E., after Sir Sydney Godolphin 1645–1712, statesman and landowner.

Tehidy (SW 6443): *Tihidin* c1170, C. *ty*, 'manorial centre' + probable personal name **Hidin*. *Ty*, the OC form of *chy*, 'house', was retained exclusively for the names of major manorial centres such as Tywarnhayle, Degembris, Tywardreath, etc.

Tenderra (SW 7825): *Tyndere* 1302, 'rounded hill with oaks', C. *tyn derow*.

Tolcarne (SW 6538): *Talcarn* 1340, 'brow tor', C. *tal-carn*.

Tolcarne (SW 6834): *Talkarn* 1325, 'brow tor', C. *tal-carn*.

Toldhu (SW 6617): *Tol Du* 1876, 'black/dark hole', C. *toll du*.

Tolgullow (SW 7343): *Talgolou* 1284, 'hillbrow of light', C. *tal golow*.

Tolgus (SW 6842): *Tolgoys* c1280, 'wood in a hollow', C. *toll-gos* (literally 'hole-wood').

Tolskithy (SW 6742): *Tolskethie* 1682, 'brow of a shady place', C. *tal scuesy*. An earlier name was *Rosewithan* 1655, 'roughland with a tree', C. *ros wedhen*.

Tolvaddon (SW 6542): *Talvan* c1200, 'brow of a height', C. *tal-van* (LC *vadn*).

Tolvan (SW 7027): 'hole-stone', C. *toll-ven*, the site of a famous Bronze Age holed stone.

Torleven (SW 6326): *Treleven* 1660, 'farm by the stream called Leven ('smooth')', C. *tre Leven* (see **Porthleven**).

Townshend (SW 5932): *Townsend* 1867, C19 E., after a St Aubyn-Townsend marriage in 1856, the St Aubyns being the then landowners.

Traboe (SW 7421): *Trefwurabo* 977, *Treuarabo* 1284, 'Gorabo's farm', C. *tre Worabo*.

Trannack (SW 6630): *Trewethenek* 1406, 'Guethenoc's farm', C. *tre Wedhenek*.

Transingove (SW 6722): *Tanewancoys* 1287, 'side-wood', C. *tenewan-gos*.

Treath (SW 7626): 'ferry', C. *treth*, rather than 'beach, strand' (also C. *treth*).

Trebah (SW 7627): traditionally pron. 'treb'a', *Treverybow* 1316, 'Gorabo's farm', C. *tre Worabo*.

Trebarvah (SW 7030): *Treberveth* 1302, 'middle/inner farm', C. *tre berveth*.

Trebarveth (SW 7919): 'middle/inner farm', C. *tre berveth*.

Tredawargh (SW 7423): *Tredowargh* 1332, 'peat/turf farm', C. *tre dowargh*.

Tredinnick (SW 7922): *Treredenek* 1311, 'fern-brake farm', C. *tre redenek*.

Trefula (SW 7142): 'owl's farm', C. *tref ula*.

Tregadjack (SW 7023): *Tregarasek* 1321, 'Caradoc's farm', C. *tre Garajek*.

Tregajorran (SW 6240): *Tregasworon* 1321, 'Cadworon's farm', C. *tre Gasworon*.

Tregarne (SW 7822): 'tor farm', C. *tre garn*.

Tregea (SW 6544): *Trege* c1250, 'farm by a hedge', C. *tre ge*.

Tregidden (SW 7522): *Tregudyn* c1190–1331, possibly 'wood-pigeon farm', C. *tre gudhon* (OC *cudin*).

Tregonhaye (SW 7733): *Tregenhay* 1350, 'Cynhi's farm', C. *tre Genhy*.

Tregonning (SW 6030): *Tregonan* 1341, 'Conan's farm', C. *tre Gonan*.

Tregonning Hill (SW 6029): now E. 'hill at Tregonning'; formerly *Pencair* C12, 'fort top', C. *pen ker/cayr*.

Tregowris (SW 7722): *Tregeures* 1327, 'hollow-ford farm', C. *tre gew-res*.

Tregullow (SW 7245): 'farm of light', C. *tre golow*.

Trelan (SW 7418): apparently C. *tre lan*, 'farm by an early church enclosure', except that no such site is known (although an Iron Age Celtic cemetery was found nearby). C. *glan*, 'bank', usually 'riverbank', does not seem to apply here.

Treleague (SW 7821): *Trelaek* c1300, 'Laoc's farm', C. *tre Laeg*.

Trelease (SW 7621): *Trelys* 1374, 'farm by a ruin', C.*tre lys*.

Treleigh (SW 7043): *Trelegh* 1402, 'farm by a stone slab', C. *tre legh*.

Treliever (SW 7635): *Trelyver* 1327, 'Lifr's farm', C. *tre Lyver*.

Trelill (SW 6728): *Trelulle* 1303, 'Lulla's farm', C. *tre Lulla*.

Treloar (SW 6930): *Trelowarth* 1527, 'garden farm', C. *tre lowarth*.

Trelowarren (SW 7223): *Trelewarent* 1227, C. *tre*, 'farm' + an apparent personal name **Leuarent*. C. *lowarn* (pl. *lewern*), 'fox' does not seem to be involved.

Treluswell (SW 7736): *Tredutual* 1296, 'Tudwal's farm', C. *tre Duswal* (personal name from Br. *toto-ualo-s*, 'worthy of the people').

Tremayne (SW 6435): 'farm by stones',C. *tre meyn*.

Tremenheere (SW 6728): *Tremynhir* c1530, 'standing stone farm', C. *tre menhyr*.

Tremenhere (SW 7436): 'standing stone farm', C. *tre menhyr*.

Tremenhere (SW 7720): 'standing stone farm', C. *tre menhyr*.

Tremough (SW 7634): *Tremogh* 1366–1590, 'pigs' farm', C. *tre mogh*.

Trenance (SW 6718): 'valley farm', C. *tre nans*.

Trenance (SW 8022): 'valley farm', C. *tre nans*.

Trenarth (SW 7528): *Trenerth* 1262, 'Nerth's farm', C. *tre Nerth* (personal name meaning 'strength').

Trenear (SW 6831): 'farm of the hens', C. *tre'n yer*.

Trenethick (SW 6829): *Trevenethek* 1314, 'hilly farm', C. *tre venedhek*.

Trengilly (SW 7228): 'farm at the grove', C. *tre'n gelly*. Nearby Trengilly Wartha is 'higher Trengilly', C. *Tre'ngelly wartha*.

Trengove (SW 6644): *Trengof* 1303, 'the smith's farm', C. *tre'n gof*.

Trenoweth (SW 6522): 'new farm', C. *tre noweth*.

Trenoweth (SW 7533): 'new farm', C. *tre noweth*.

Trenoweth (SW 7921): 'new farm', C. *tre noweth*

Trenwheal (SW 6132): *Trenuwal* 1283, C. *tre*, 'farm' + unknown word or name.

Tresaddern (SW 7116): *Tresoudorn* 1393, 'Soudorn's farm', C. *tre Soudorn*.

Tresavean (SW 7239): *Treyusow vyan* 1608, 'little Treyusow'. Treyusow is 'Iudhou's farm', C. *tre Yusow*.

Trescowe (SW 5730): 'elder-trees farm', C. *tre scaw*.

Tresevern (SW 7137): 'Saefern's farm', C. *tre Severn*. Nearby Tresevern Croft is 'enclosed rough grazing (C. *croft*) at Tresevern', now in E. word order.

Treskillard (SW 6739): *Treskeulard* 1490, 'kite's height farm', OC. *tre scoul-ard.*

Treslothan (SW 6537): *Tresulwethan* 1319, 'Sulwethan's farm', C. *tre Sulwedhan.*

Tresowes (SW 5929): *Tresewys* 1327, 'stitcher's/seamster's farm', C. *tre sewyas.*

Tresprison (SW 6727): 'ghosts'/spirits' farm', C. *tre sperysyon.*

Tresprisson (SW 6818): 'ghosts'/spirits' farm', C. *tre sperysyon.*

Treswithian (SW 6340): *Trevaswethen* 1302, probably C. *tre Vaswedhen,* 'Matguethen's farm', rather than C. *tref ys wedhen,* 'farm below a tree'.

Tretharrup (SW 7422): *Trewortharap* 1334, 'very pleasant farm', C. *tre wortharap.*

Tretheague (SW 7236): *Trethaec* 1213, 'pretty farm', C. *tre theg.*

Trevales (SW 7435): *Trevatheles* 1356, 'aspens farm', C. *tref edheles.*

Trevarth (SW 7240): *Trevargh* 1277-1422, probably 'March's farm', C. *tre Vargh,* rather than 'horse's farm', C. *tre vargh.*

Trevenen (SW 6829): *Trevaenwyn* 1310, 'white-stone farm', C. *tre ven-wyn.*

Treverva (SW 7531): *Trefurvo* 1358, 'Urvo's farm', C. *tref Urvo.*

Trevethan (SW 7241): *Trefuthyn* c.1516, 'meadow farm', C. *tre vuthyn.*

Trevone (SW 7432): *Trevouhan* 1343, 'oxen farm', C. *tref ohen.*

Trew (SW 6129): *Treuf* c1250, 'Yuf's farm', C. *tre Yuf.*

Trewardreva (SW 7230): *Trewodreve* 1303, 'homesteads farm', C. *tre wodrevy.*

Trewarnevas (SW 7824): *Treworneves* 1302, 'Gornevet's farm', C. *tre Worneves* (personal name from Br. *uor-nemeto-s,* 'very holy').

Trewavas (SW 5926): 'farm at a winter dwelling', C. *tre wavos.*

Trewennack (SW 6728): *Trewethenek* 1296, 'Guethenoc's farm', C. *tre Wedhenek.*

Trewirgie (SW 6939): *Trewythgi* 1326, 'Gwithgi's farm', C. *tre Wydhgy.*

Treworgan (SW 7828): *Trewothgen* 1315, 'Goethgen's farm', C. *tre Wodhgen.*

Treworgie (SW 7629): *Treworgy* 1323, 'Wurci's farm', C. *tre Worgy.*

Troon (SW 6638): *Trewoen* 1327, 'downs farm', C. *tre wun.*

Truthall (SW 6530): *Treuthal* 1281, 'Iudhael's farm', C. *tre Yudhal.*

Truthwall (SW 5934): *Trewothwal* 1356, 'Gudual's farm', C.*tre Wodhwal.*

Trythance (SW7920): *Treyuthgans* 1330, 'Iudcant's farm', C. *tre Yuthgans.*

Tuckingmill (SW 6232): E. 'tucking mill, fulling mill'. This was *Talgarrek Fulling Mill* 1260, E. 'fulling mill at **Tolgarrick**', this being 'brow tor', C. *tal garrek.*

Tucoyse (SW 7129): 'side-wood', C. *tu-cos.*

Velanewson (SW 6632): *Vellanusen* 1748, 'chaff mill', C. *melyn usyon.*

Vellynsaundry (SW 6438): 'Sandry's mill', C. *melyn Sandry,* after C16 Sandrye family.

Venton Ariance (SW 6819): 'silver spring', C. *fenten arhans.*

Ventonear (SW 6538): 'St Ia's spring', C. *fenten Ya.*

Ventonraze (SW 6743): *Fyntenras* 1388, 'grace spring', C. *fenten ras.*

Venton Vedna (SW 6426): 'overflowing spring', C.*fenten fenna* (LC *fedna*).

Viscar (SW 7133): *Fursgore* 1290, E. furze corner', OE *fyrs gara.*

Vogue (SW 7242): *Voss* 1603, *Vose* 1664, 'wall, dyke', C. *fos.*

Vogue Beloth (SW 6743): *Vogue Bellow* 1945, 'further **Vogue**', C. *Fos pella*.

Vro, The (SW 6617): 'the badger', C. *an vrogh* (although lenition of B to V should not occur here).

Water-ma-Trout (SW 6628): E. 'wet my throat', for a dry field or one that is difficult to work.

Weeth (SW 6527): *The Weath* 1677, 'the trees', C. *an wedh*.

Wendron (SW 6731): *Egloswendron* 1513, 'church of St Gwendern', C. *eglos Wendern*. An earlier name was *Eglosiga* 1208, 'Siga's church', C. *eglos Syga*.

Wheal Buller (SW 6939): C. *whel*, 'mine, workings' + E. family surname.

Wheal Vor (SW 6230): 'mine by a road', C. *whel fordh*.

Winnianton (SW 6520): *Winnentona* 1086, *Gwynyon* 1439, C. *gwyn-an*, 'white/fair place' + addition of OE *tun*, 'farm, settlement'.

Zawn Vinoc (SW 7516): 'stony cliff-chasm', C. *sawan veynek*.

Zoar (SW 7519): C18/19 Methodist Biblical name, after the village of Zoar near Sodom and Gomorrah.

Kerrier: lych gate at Mawnan church

District of NORTH CORNWALL
Randyr an TYRETH UHEL

KILKHAMPTON
Kelgh

BUDE
Porth Bued

R. Tamar
Dowr Tamer

R. Ottery
Otery

Tintagel Castle   BOSCASTLE
Dyn Kernowyon   Castel Boterel

Brown Willy   LAUNCESTO
Bron Wennyly   Lan Stefan

POLZEATH   CAMELFORD
Pol Segh   ST BREWARD   LEWANNICK
Bruered   Lan Wenek

ST KEW
Lan Doho
PADSTOW   Bodmin   Moor
Lan Wedhenek   Gun   Bren   Kilmar Tor
Kyl Margh

BODMIN
Bos Menehy   R. Fowey   CARADON
Fawy

N

RESTORMEL   0   5

miles

Place Names of the District of
NORTH CORNWALL

Henwyn Plasow an Randyr
Tyreth Uhel

Advent (SX 1282): *Adwyn* 1327, from St Adwin, a male saint whose name derives from Br. *ato-uindo-s*, 'very white/fair/holy'.

Allen (river): *Layne* 1466. Layne is of unknown meaning and was mistakenly renamed Allen (formerly the name of the lower reaches of the **Camel** river) by the Ordnance Survey in 1888.

Altarnun (SX 2281): *Alternon* c1224, 'altar of St Non', C.*alter Non.*

Amble (river): *Amal* 1086, 'edge, boundary, slope', C. *amal.*

Badgall (SX 2386): *Bodgalla* c1200, 'Calla's dwelling', OC *bod Galla.*

Badharlick (SX 2686): *Bodharlek* 1432, 'Haerlec's dwelling', OC *bod Harlek.*

Barlendew (SX 1072): *Barlendu* 1304, 'dark-pool summit', C. *bar lyn-du.*

Barras Nose (SX 0589): *Burrows* c1840, E. 'nose' (i.e. headland) with barrows/tumuli'.

Bathpool (SX 2874): *Bathpole* 1474, E. 'pool for bathing'.

Beals Mill (SX 3576): E. 'Bile's mill' after Roger Bile 1338.

Bearah (SW 2874): *Beare* 1334, 'at the grove', ME *atte beare.*

Bedruthan (SW 8569): *Bodruthyn* 1335, 'Ruthyn's dwelling', OC *bod Rudhyn.* Nearby **Bedruthan Steps** is C19 E. 'steps at Bedruthan'.

Beeny (SX 1192): *Bideney* 1210, 'hollow stream', OE *byden ea.*

Bennacott (SX 2992): *Bynnacote* 1331, 'Binna's cottage', OE *Binnan cot.*

Berriow (SX 2775): *Byreyo* 1474, 'fort river', OE *byrig ea.*

Billacott (SX 2590): *Byllyngcote* 1330, 'cottage of Billa's people', OE *Billinga cot.*

Blable (SW 9470): *Bleythpol* 1302, 'wolf-pit', C. *bleyth-bol.*

Blisland (SX 1073): *Glustona* 1086, *Bloistun* 1177, a very difficult name to unravel despite a wealth of early forms. There is an outside chance that it may originally have been C. *glas*, 'green', with the addition of OE *tun*, 'farm, settlement' or even C. *glastan*, 'holm-oaks', with the last syllable mistaken by the Domesday scribes for OE *tun*. The E. 'land' of the present name refers to the estate lands of the Norman period manor.

Bodieve (SW 9973): *Bodyuf* 1323, 'Yuf's dwelling', OC *bod Yuf.*

Bodiniel (SX 0567): *Bodynyel* 1284, 'dwelling at a fortified place', OC *bod dyn-yel.*

Bodmin (SX 0667): *Botmenei* C9, *Bodminie* 1312, *Bosvena* C18, 'dwelling on church land', C. *bos venehy.*

Bodmin Moor: *Goen Bren* C12, *Fawymore* 1274, originally 'hill downs', C. *gun bren*; then E. 'Fowey moor', i.e. where the river Fowey rises (compare Dartmoor and Exmoor). The present name is an inexplicable Ordnance Survey invention of 1813.

Bodrigan (SX 0773): *Bodrygan* 1284, 'Rigan's dwelling', OC *bod Rygan*.

Bodwen (SX 0771): *Bossewoen* 1302, 'downland dwelling', C. *bos wun*.

Bogee (SW 9069): *Bosyuf* 1340, 'Yuf's dwelling', C. *bos Yuf.*

Bokiddick (SX 0562): *Boskedek* 1278, *Bodcadek* 1284, 'Cadoc's dwelling', C *bos Cadek* (with the personal name retaining its OC form).

Bolventor (SX 1876): *Boldventure* 1844, C19 E. 'bold venture', from attempt to break in moorland for farming.

Boscarne (SX 0467): *Bodcarn* 1402, 'dwelling by a tor', C. *bos carn*.

Boscastle (SX 0990): *Castelboterel* 1334, 'castle of the Boterel family', C. *castel Boterel.*

Bossiney (SX 0688): *Boscyny* 1302, 'Cyni's dwelling', C. *bos Kyny.*

Botathen (SX 2981): *Botadon* 1584, perhaps 'Tadon's dwelling', OC. *bod Tadhon.*

Botternell (SX 2774): *Botornel* c1320, 'Dornel's dwelling', OC *bod Dornel.*

Bowda (SX 2477): *Bowode* 1474, 'wood where bows are cut', OE *boghe wudu.*

Bowithick (SX 1882): *Bodwydek* 1284, dwelling in a place of trees', OC *bod wedhek.*

Box's Shop (SS 2101): E. 'Box's workshop', from C18 family.

Boyton (SX 3291): *Boiatona* 1086, 'Boia's farm', OE *Boia tun.*

Brazacott (SX 2691): *Brasyngacote* 1333, 'cottage of Bras's people', OE *Brasinga cot* (personal name Bras is C. *bras*, 'big man').

St Breock (SW 9771): *S. Brioc* 1298, after St Brioc. The alternative name was *Nansant* 1288, C. *nans*, 'valley', + OC *sant*, 'holy, sacred'.

St Breward (SX 0977): *S. Brueredus* c1180, after St Bruered, of which the popular alternative 'Simonward' is merely a corruption.

Brockabarrow (SX 1575): *Brocka barrow* 1732, 'badger's barrow/tumulus', OE *broccan beorg.*

Brocton (SX 0168): 'brook farm', OE *broc tun.*

Brown Willy (SX 1679): *Bronwenely* 1280, 'swallows' hill', C. *bron wennyly.*

Bude (SS 2006): *Bude* 1400, *Beed Haven* 1727, probably from river name which may be early Celtic **budr*, 'dirty'.

Bude River: *The Bedewater* 1577. An early Celtic name, apparently cognate with W. *budr*, 'dirty' (compare with its tributary, the river **Neet**).

Burlawne (SW 9970): *Bodlowen* 1277, 'happy dwelling', OC *bod lowen.*

Burlorne (SX 0169): *Bodlowen* 1277, 'happy dwelling', OC *bod lowen.*

Callywith (SX 0867): *Kellegwyth* 1276, 'grove of trees', C. *kelly wedh.*

Cambeak (SX 1276): 'crooked beak', C. *cam-byg.*

Camel (river): In terms of its historic names, this river should be divided into three parts:

1. **Source to Trecarne** (SW 0980): this was *Camle* 1256, *Camel* 1284, 'crooked/curved one', C. *cam-el.*

2. **Trecarne to Wadebridge**: this was the stretch known as the Allen (*Alan* 1199, *Aleyn* 1298) until 1884 when the name was wrongly transferred to the Layne river by the Ordnance Survey. Br. *alaunos*, perhaps 'brilliant, shining'. Place names such as **Pendavy** show that this stretch was also known as the Dewey, 'dark river', C. *du-y*.

3. **The estuary**: this has only been referred to as the Camel since C18. Before then it was *Heyl* 1284, 'estuary with tidal flats', C. *heyl*, this name being preserved by those of **Hayle Bay** and **Egloshayle**.

Camelford (SX 1083): *Camelford* c1200, E. 'ford across the river Camel'.

Canaglaze (SX 1981): *Caringlaze* 1671, 'green tor', C. *carn glas*.

Cannalidgey (SW 9369): *Canelysy* 1308, 'St Idi's channel', C. *canel Ysy*.

Cant Hill (SW 9474): E. 'hill at Cant'. The settlement name is OC *cant-a*, 'white/fair place'.

Canworthy (SX 2292): *Carneworthy* 1327, C. *carn*, 'tor' with addition of OE *worthig*, 'holding'.

Carbilly Tor (SX 1275): E. 'tor at Carbilly'. Carbilly is 'Bili's fort', C. *ker/cayr Byly*.

Cardew (SX 0988): *Cartheu* 1327, 'black/dark fort', C. *ker/cayr dhu*.

Cardew (SX 1891): *Carthu* 1334, 'black/dark fort', C. *ker/cayr dhu*.

Cardinham (SX 1268): *Cardinan* c1180, apparently tautologous as C. *ker/cayr* and C. *dynan* both mean 'fort', unless **Dynan* is a personal name, in which case the place name would be 'Dinan's fort'.

Cardinham River: the present name, E. 'river at Cardinham', has only been in use since C18. Its C. name was *Devioch* c1260, *Deviek* 1311, 'cultivated', C. *an devyek*.

Cargelley (SX 1078): *Cargelly* 1332, 'fort at a grove', C. *ker/cayr gelly*.

Cargentle (SX 2887): *Cargyntell* 1287, 'fort of meeting/gathering', C. *ker/cayr guntell*.

Carhart (SW 9573): *Kaerhorta* c1250, C. *ker/cayr*, 'fort' + an archaic plural of C. *hordh*, 'ram'.

Carne, South & West (SX 2082): 'tor', C. *carn*.

Carneglos Tor (SX 1977): 'church tor', C. *carn eglos*, presumably from shape of outcrop as no church or chapel site is known here + unnecessary addition of E. 'tor'.

Carnevas (SW 8672): *Crucneves* c1250, *Crugnyves* 1320, 'barrow/tumulus at a sacred grove', C. *crug neves*.

Carnewas (SW 8569): *Carneues* 1306, *Canhewas* 1748, 'crag at a shieling/summer grazing', C. *carn havos*.

Caroe (SX 1691): *Cayrou* 1327, 'forts', C. *kerrow/cayrow*.

Carwen (SX 1178): *Carwen* 1327, 'white/fair fort', C. *ker/cayr wen* (fem. form of *(g)wyn*).

Carwithan (SX 1592): *Caerwytha* 1284, 'guarding/protecting fort', C. *ker/cayr wytha*.

Castle Canyke (SX 0866): *Castel Keynok* 1478, 'ridge-place castle', C. *castel keynek*.

Castledewey (SX 1670): *Castelduy* 1327, 'castle on the **Dewey** river', C. *castel Duy*.

Castle Goff (SX 0882): *Castelgof* 1357, 'smith's castle', C. *castel gof*.

Castle Killibury (SX 0173): *Killiburgh* 1215, C. *kelly*, 'grove' + OE *burh*, 'fort'. Also called Kelly Rounds.

Cataclews Point (SW 8776): *carreg loos* (undated), 'grey rock', C. *carrek los*.

Chapel Amble (SW 9975): *Amaleglos* 1284, 'church on the river **Amble**', C. *Amaleglos*.

Clann (SX 0363): *Kellilan* 1309, 'grove at a church enclosure', C. *kelly-lan*.

Cleave (SS 2012): *Cliffe* 1480, 'cliff', OE *clyf*.

St Clether (SX 2084): *S. Cleder* 1259, after St Cleder.

Clubworthy (SX 2792): *Clobiry* 1322, 'ravine fort', OE *cloh byrig*.

Coad's Green (SX 2976): E. 'Coade's green' after C18 family.

Codda (SX 1778): *Stumcodda* 1280, probably 'Codde's bend', C *stum*, 'bend' + OE personal name.

Cold Northcott (SX 2086): *Northcott* 1608, 'northern cottage', OE *north cot*, with late addition of E. 'cold' from its exposed position.

Colesloggett (SX 1065): *Castle Loggett* 1733, 'castle of mice', OC *castel logot*.

Colvannick Tor (SX 1271): now E. 'crag at Colvannick'. The settlement name, *Calvannek* 1327, is descriptive of the hill itself, 'pointed hill', C. *cal vannek* (literally 'penis-peaked').

Condolden (SX 0986): *Goyndolvan* 1302, 'dolmen/holed-stone downs', C. *gun doll-ven*.

Congdon's Shop (SX 2878): E. 'Congden's workshop', from C18 family.

Constantine Bay (SW 8574): *Egloscontantyne* c1535, 'St Constantine's church', C. *eglos Costentyn*.

Coombe (SX 2011): 'valley', OE *cumb* (itself borrowed from C. *com*, 'valley').

Coppathorne (SS 2000): *Cobbethorne* 1360, 'pollarded thorn tree', OE *coppodan thorn*.

Costislost (SX 0270): E. 'cost is lost', from poor or unprofitable land.

Crackington Haven (SX 1496): E. 'haven at Crackington'. The settlement name was *Crakenton* 1181, C. *craken*, 'little crag' with addition of OE *tun*, 'farm, settlement'.

Crimp (SS 2515): *Crympe* 1568, 'crooked', OE *crump*.

Croanford (SX 0271): E. 'ford at Croan'. The settlement name was *Crowen* 1302, C. *crowyn*, 'little hut'.

Crowdy (SX 1483): 'hut, hovel', OC *crowdy*.

Crugmeer (SW 9076): *Crucmur* 1339, 'great barrow/tumulus', C. *crug muer*.

Curry, East & West (SW 28/2993): *Cory* C14, from a Celtic river name of unknown meaning.

Cutmadoc (SX 0963): *Coysmadok* 1320, 'Madoc's wood', C. *cos Madek* (the personal name retaining its OC form).

Davidstow (SX 1587): *S. David* 1269, *Dewystowe* 1395, C. *Dewy*, '(St) David' + OE *stow*, 'holy place'.

Davidstow Moor (SX 1583): now E. 'moor at Davidstow' but formerly *Halmur* 1296, 'great moor/marsh', C. *hal muer*.

Daw's House (SX 3182): E. 'Dawe's house', from C17 family.

Daymer Bay (SX 3182): C19 E. 'daymark bay', as it faces the daymark tower on Stepper Point.

Delabole (SX 0784): 'pit at Deli', C. *Delyow-bol*. The central settlement name (**Deli** at SX 0884) was *Deliou* 1086, '(place of) leaves', C. *delyow*.

Delamere (SX 0683): *Delyoumur* 1284, 'great Deli' (see **Delabole**), C. *Delyow muer*.

De Lank (SX 1275): *Dynlonk* C16, 'ravine fort', C. *dyn lonk*.

De Lank River: *Dynlonk* C16, 'fort at a ravine', C. *dyn lonk*.

Delinuth (SX 0782): *Delyownewyth* 1296, 'new Deli' (see **Delabole**), C. *Delyow noweth*.

Dewey (river): *Duy* 1230, this Dewey being a tributary of the **Warleggan** river. 'dark river', C. *du-y*.

Dinas Head (SW 8476): C. *dynas*, 'fort' + E. 'head(land)'.

Dizzard Point (SX 1698): E. 'headland at Dizzard'. The settlement of Dizzard, perhaps named after the headland itself, was *Dysert* 1238, 'very steep, precipitous', OC *dysert*.

Drinnick (SX 3079): *Dreynek* 1582, 'thorny', C. *dreynek*.

Dunheved (SX 3384): *Dunhevet* 1086–1584, generally assumed to be 'end of a hill', OE *dun heafod*, but could also be 'fort at a shieling/summer grazing', OC *dyn havod*. However the C11 form *Dounhed* favours the former.

Dunmere (SX 0467): *Dynmur* 1220, 'great fort', C. *dyn muer*.

Durfold (SX 1173): *Dyrfold* c1580, 'deer fold', OE *deor fold*.

Dutson (SX 3485): *Dodeston* 1281, 'Doda's farm', OE *Dodas tun*.

Eastcott (SS 2515): *Estcote* 1314, 'eastern cottage', OE *east cot*.

Egloshayle (SX 0071): *Eglosheyl* 1197, 'church on the **Camel** estuary', C. *eglos Heyl* (*Heyl* being the former name of the Camel estuary).

Egloskerry (SX 2786): *Egloskery* c1145–1474, 'St Keri's church', C. *eglos Kery*, after a male saint.

Emblance Downs (SX 1277): *Emlands* c1580, 'flat-topped land', OE *emn land*.

St Endellion (SW 9978): *Endelient* 1439, *Endelyn* 1522, after St Endelient, a female saint.

Engollan (SW 8669): *Hengollen* 1418, 'old hazel tree', C. *hen-gollen*.

St Enodoc (SW 9377): *S. Guinedoc* 1434, *Guenedouce* 1613, after St Guinedoc. The nickname 'Sinking Neddy' is not a reference to the church being engulfed by advancing sand dunes but, as *Sinkininny* C19, a corruption of 'St Guinedoc'.

St Ervan (SW 8970): *S. Ermete* 1208, *Ermet* 1327, after St Hermet (see also **St Erme**, Carrick).

St Eval (SW 8769): *S. Uvele* 1260, after St Uvel.

Fentonadle (SX 0878): *Fentonadwen* C13, 'St Adwyn's spring', C. *fenten Adwyn*.

Fentonluna (SW 9175): *Fenten-leno* 1552, 'pools spring', C. *fenten lynnow*.

Five Lanes (SX 2280): C18 E. 'where five lanes meet'.

Fletcher's Bridge (SX 1065): *Flatches Bridge* 1748, 'Flegard's bridge', after the Flegard family.

Flexbury (SS 2107): *Flexberi* 1201, 'fort by flax-land', OE *fleax byrig*.

Fonston (SX 2191): *Faunteston* 1248, 'Faunte's farm', MF personal name + ME *tone*, 'farm, settlement'.

Forda (SS 2711): *Forde* 1442, 'at the ford', ME *atte forde*.

Forrabury (SX 0990): *Forbiri* 1189, 'outworks of a fort', ME *fore byry*.

Fowey (river): *Fawe* c1210–1306, *Fawi* 1241, *Fawy* 1241–1339, 'beech-trees river', C. *faw-y*. Some modern sources give **Fawydh* but this is not borne out by historical references except the late *Foath* c1600 and the reference to its source (below). Its source, high on Bodmin Moor and now called Fowey Well, was *Venton Foath* c1680, 'spring of the Fowey river', C. *fenten Fawy*.

Garrow Tor (SX 1478): E. 'crag at Garrow'. The settlement name, *Garros* 1640, is 'rough hillspur', C. *gar'ros* (contraction of *garow-ros*).

St Gennys (SX 1597): *Sanguinas* 1086, after St Guinas.

Glynn (SX 1164): *Glyn* 1351, 'deep valley', C. *glyn*.

Gonvena (SW 9972): *Gwynveneth* 1286, 'white/fair hillside', C. *gwyn-venedh*.

Gooseham (SS 2216): *Gosham* 1201, 'river-meadow frequented by geese', OE *gosa hamm*.

Goscott (SX 2396): *Godescot* 1238, 'Goda's cottage', OE *Godas cot*.

Greystone Bridge (SX 3680): E. 'bridge at Greystone'. The settlement name was *Greyston* 1310, 'badger's stone', OE *graeg stan*.

Grimscott (SS 2606): *Grymescote* 1284, 'Grim's cottage', OE *Grimes cot*.

Gulland Rock (SW 8778): *Gullond rok* 1545, probably E. 'gull land', although it might derive from C. *gwylan*, 'gull'.

Gunvenna (SW 9678): *Goenfynou* 1275, 'boundaries' downs', C. *gun fynnow*.

Gunver Head (SW 8977): perhaps 'white sea', C. *gwyn-vor*.

Gwennymoor (SW 9967): E. 'Gwynnow's marsh', from a C16 family.

Halgabron (SX 0788): *Halgybran* 1302, 'carrion-crow's marsh', C. *hal gygbran*.

Halgavar Moor (SX 0765): *Halgaver* 1447, 'goat's marsh', C. *hal gavar*.

Hallworthy (SX 1887): *Halworgy* 1439, 'Wurci's marsh', C. *hal Worgy*. An alternative name, Halldrunkard, was *Haldronket* 1415, 'marsh at a hill-spur wood', OC *hal dron-cuyt*.

Halvana (SW 2178): *Hyrmene* 1194, 'long hillside', C. *hyr-venedh*.

Halwyn (SW 9373): *Helwyn* 1259, 'white/fair hall', C. *hel wyn*.

Hampt (SX 3874): *Havet* 1338, 'shieling/summer grazing', OC *havod*.

Hantergantick (SX 1075): *Hendregantek* 1296, 'home farm on borderland', C. *hendre gantek*.

Harlyn Bay (SW 8775): now E. 'bay at Harlyn'. The settlement name was *Arlyn* 1334, 'facing a pool', C. *ar-lyn*. The bay was *Perleze Bay* c1830, apparently 'cove/landing place by a ruin', C. *porth lys*.

Harrowbridge (SX 2074): *Horebregge* 1220, 'grey bridge', OE *har brycg*.

Hawk's Tor (SX 1475): *Hawkstorr* c1530, E. 'hawk's crag'.

Hayle Bay (SW 9379): E. 'bay by the **Camel** estuary (formerly *Heyl*)'.

Hele (SS 2104): *La Heyle* 1250, 'inlet with tidal flats', C. *heyl*.

Hele (SS 2197): *Hele* 1196, 'nook, corner of land', OE *healh*.

Helland (SX 0771): 'disused church enclosure', C. *hen-lan*.

Hellescott (SX 2888): *Hilscote* 1330, 'holly cottage', OE *hyles cot*.

Helsbury Castle (SX 0879): *Hellesbiri* 1279, C. *hen-lys*, 'old ruin' + addition of OE *byrig*, 'fort'.

Helstone (SX 0881): *Henliston* 1086, C. *hen-lys*, 'old ruin/administrative centre', with addition of OE *tun*, 'farm, settlement'.

Hendra (SX 0280): 'old farm, home farm', C. *hen-dre*.

Hendraburnick (SX 1287): *Hendrebrunnek* 1296, 'home farm by a rush-bed', C. *hendre bronnek*.

Hersham (SS 2507): *Hesham* 1355, 'brushwood enclosure', OE *haes hamm*.

Hingston Down (SX 4071): *Hengesdon'* 1297, apparently 'stallion's hill', OE *hengest dun* (although *Hengest* may also have been a personal name). There is no evidence to support the assumption that this was the site of the battle of *Hengestesdun* cited in the Anglo-Saxon Chronicle between an allied Cornish-Danish force and Egberht of Wessex in 838 AD (this may well have been Hingston Down near Moretonhampstead, Devon), and no such place name appears to be attached to the site before 1297.

Horsebridge (SX 3974): *Hautes Brygge* 1437, ME *brigge*, 'bridge', preceded by either a F. personal name or F. *haut*, 'high'.

Hustyn (SX 0068): *Husting* 1243, 'assembly house', ME *husting*.

Illand (SX 2875): *Eyllalande* 1284, 'Illa's land', OE *Illa land*.

St Ingunger (SX 0563): *Stymgongar* 1283, 'Congar's bend', C. *stum Gongar*.

Inney (river): *Aeni* 1044, *Eny* c1160–1328. Probably 'ash-trees river', C. *en-y*.

St Issey (SW 9271): *S. Ydi* 1195, after St Idi. The alternative name was *Egloscrug* 1345, 'church at a barrow/tumulus', C. *eglos crug*.

Jacobstow (SX 1995): *Jacobestowe* 1270, 'St James's holy place', ME *Jacobes stow*.

St Jidgey (SW 9369): *S. Idi* 1169, after St Idi.

Kelly (SX 0173): *Kelly* c1260, 'grove', C. *kelly*.

Kellygreen (SX 0475): *Keligren* 1258, 'aspen grove', C. *kelly gren*.

Kennacott (SX 2989): *Hennacote* c1840, either 'hen's cottage', OE *hena cot*; or 'Henna's cottage', OE *Henna cot*.

Kennard's House (SX 2882): E. 'house of the Kennard family'.

Kensey (river): *Kyensi, Kensi, Kynsy* 1229. Both the language and meaning of this name are unknown. It may be a Cornish name with the –*y* river name suffix, or perhaps 'king's water', OE *cyninges ea*.

St Kew (SX 0276): *S. Cywa* c962, *Kua* c1317, after St Kywa, apparently a female saint. The C. name was *Landochou* 1179, 'Docho's church enclosure', from an earlier saint, C. *lan Doho*.

Keybridge (SX 0873): *Key Bridge* 1799, 'cow's bridge', OE *cu* (genitive *cy*) *brycg*.

Keyrse (SX 2186): *Keuros* c1150, 'hollow-roughland', C. *kew-ros*.

Kilkhampton (SS 2511): *Kelk* c839, *Kilcton* c1175, C. *kelgh*, 'circle', with addition of OE *tun*, 'farm'. Further expansion to the present name results from the form *Kilchetona* 1086, where the originally silent –*e*- vowel became voiced.

Kilmar Tor (SX 2574): *Kilmarhe rock* 1584, 'horse's back', C. *kyl margh*.

Kingston (SX 3675): *Kyenestone* 1317, 'Cyne's farm', OE *Cynes tun*.

Kirland (SX 0665): *Crellen* 1302, 'aspens pool', C. *cren-lyn*.

Kit Hill (SX 3771): 'kite's hill', OE *cyta hyll*.

Ladycross (SX 3288): E. 'Our Lady's cross'.

Lamorick (SX 0364): *Lammorek* 1327, probably 'Moroc's church enclosure', C. *lan Morek*.

Landue (SX 3580): *Landu* c1210, probably 'dark valley', OC *nant du*.

Laneast (SX 2283): *Lanast* 1076, *Lanayst* c1226, C. *lan* 'early church enclosure' + a personal name of unknown form.

Langdon (SX 3092): *Langedon* 1201, 'long hill', OE *langan dun*.

Langford (SS 2301): *Langeford* 1321, 'long ford', OE *langan ford*.

Langore (SX 2986): *Langover* 1431, 'stream valley', OC *nant gover*.

Lanhydrock (SX 0863): *Lanhydrek* 1327, 'Hidroc's church enclosure', C. *lan Hydrek*.

Lanivet (SX 0364): *Lannived* 1268, *Lanneves* 1301, 'church enclosure at a sacred grove', C. *lan neves*.

Lanjew (SW 9864): *Lendu* 1356, 'black/dark pool', C. *lyn du*.

Lank (SX 0875): *Lonk* 1302, 'gully, ravine', C. *lonk*.

Lanlavery Rock (SX 1582): *Lamlavera* 1440, 'striving leap', C. *lam lafurya*.

Lanseague (SX 0477): *Lanseuegy* 1302, *Nansceuguy* 1321, 'hinds' valley', C. *nans ewygy*.

Larrick (SX 3280): *Lanrek* 1327, 'clearing', C. *lanergh*.

Latchley (SX 4073): *Lacchislegh* 1318, 'clearing by a boggy stream', OE *laecc leah*.

Launcells (SS 2405): *Lanceles* 1204, 'Seled's church enclosure', C. *lan Seles*.

Launceston (SX 3384): *Lansteventon* 1189, 'St Stephen's church enclosure', C. *lan Stefan*, with addition of OE *tun*, 'settlement'.

Lavethan (SX 0973): *Lavedewen* 1330, 'birch-tree valley', OC *nant bedewen*.

Lawhitton (SX 3582): *Lanwithan* 905, 'valley with a tree', OC *nant medhen*.

St Lawrence (SX 0466): *Seynt Laurens* 1380, after St Lawrence, patron of lepers and the sick.. An alternative name was *Ponteboys* 1476, 'wooden bridge', F. *pont bois*.

Leaze (SX 1376): *Layes* c1580, 'pasture meadows', OE *laes*.

Lelizzick (SW 9077): *Lanwoledic* 1284, 'Woledic's church enclosure', C. *lan Wolesyk*.

Leskernick (SX 1879): *Leskernycke* 1568, 'old ruin in a corner', C. *lys kernyk*.

Lesnewth (SX 1290): *Lysnewyth* 1238, 'new court/administrative centre', C. *lys noweth*.

Lesquite (SX 0662): *Lostcoys* 1320, 'tail of a wood', C. *lost cos*.

Lewannick (SX 2780): *Languenec* 1150, 'Guenoc's church enclosure', C.*lan Wenek*.

Lezant (SX 3379): *Lansant* c1175–1352, 'holy church enclosure', OC *lan sant*.

Lidwell (SX 3774): *Lydewelle* 1357, 'source of a noisy stream', OE *hlyde wielle*.

Little Petherick (SW 9272): *St Petrocus Minor* 1327, Lat. 'St Petroc's lesser church'. The alternative C.name was *Nansfunten* 1264, 'valley with a spring', C. *nans fenten*.

Longstone (SX 0673): *Langestone* 1327, E. 'longstone, standing stone'.

Lynstone (SS 2005): *Lulleston* 1262, 'Lulla's farm', OE *Lullas tun*.

St Mabyn (SX 0473): *Seynt Mabon* 1441, after St Mabon.

Maer (SS 2007): *Mere* 1699, 'pool', OE *mere*.

Maidenwell (SX 1470): *Medenawille* 1345, 'maids' spring/stream', OE *maegden wielle*.

Marhamchurch (SS 2203): *Marona* c1085, *Marwenechurche* 1284, E. 'St Maerwyn's church'.

Marshgate (SX 1591): C18 E. 'marsh gate'.

Marsland Mouth (SS 2017): E. 'valley mouth at marsland'. The settlement name was *Maddockeslonde* 1288, E. 'Madoc's land', though with a Celtic personal name.

Maxworthy (SX 2593): probably 'Macca's holding/enclosed farm', OE *Maccas worthig*.

Mellingey (SW 9271): *Melynsy* 1302, 'mill-house', C.*melynjy*.

St Merryn (SW 8874): *S. Marina* 1259–1448, *Seynt Meryn* 1379, after St Marina.

Michaelstow (SX 0778): *Mihelstou* 1311, *S. Michael* 1338, 'St Michael's holy place', OE *Miheles stow*.

Middlewood (SX 2775): 'middle wood', ME *mydel wode*.

Millook (SX 1899): *Mellek* 1349, 'honeyed', probably a stream name, C.*melek*.

Millook Haven (SX 1800), now E. 'haven at Millook' but formerly *Porthoy* 1481, presumably 'cove/landing place with an egg (-shaped boulder)', C. *porth oy*.

Millook Stream: probably originally C. *melek*, 'honeyed' (see **Millook** above) but was called *water of Porthoy* C13, 'stream of Millook Haven'.

Minster (SX 1090): *Mynster* 1296, 'endowed church', C. *mynster*. It was also called *Talcarn* 1483, 'brow-tor', C. *tal-carn*.

St Minver (SW 9677): *S. Menfreda* 1256, *Menfre* 1444, after St Menfreda.

Morwenstow (SS 2015): *Morwennestouwe* 1284, Celtic female saint's name *Morwena* + OE *stow*, 'holy place'.

Mother Ivey's Bay (SW 8676): *Mother Ive's Bay* 1870, C19 E. after a local character. The C. name was *Polventon Bay* c1810, 'pool/cove by a spring', C. *pol fenten*.

Mouls, The (SW 9381): 'wether sheep', C.*mols*. Many Cornish coastal features are named after animals.

Nanstallon (SX 0367): *Lantalan* 1201, *Nanstalen* 1392, probably 'valley of the river Allen' (see **Camel** river), C *nans Alan* (OC *nant Alan*).

St Nectan's Kieve (SX 0788), not named after St Nechtan, as popularly believed but was *Nathan's Cave* 1799, from a local character, either Nathan Williams or Nathan Cock, both of whom died in C18, + C. *cuva*, 'tub', from the rock formation at the foot of the waterfall.

Neet (river): *Nehet, Neth* c1250, probably OC *neth*, 'clean, pure' (with an Irish cognate *necht*). Also called the river Strat, a modern back-formation from the village (and Hundred) of **Stratton**, of which this element is OC *strad*, 'flat-bottomed valley'.

Newland Rock (SW 9181): *Lueland* 1694, probably 'fleet pool', C. *lu-lyn*.

Newtown (SX 2978): *Newton* 1503, E. 'new farm'.

North Hill (SX 2776): *Henle* 1238, 'high clearing', OE *hean leah*, with addition of E. 'north' to differentiate it from **South Hill** (Caradon).

North Tamerton (SX 3197): *Tamertuna* c1150, Celtic river name **Tamar** + addition of OE *tun*, 'farm, settlement' and E. 'north' (although there is no South Tamerton). [**Tamar**]

Otterham (SX 1690): *Oterham* 1231, 'river meadow on the **Ottery** river', OE *oter-ea hamm*.

Ottery (river): *Oter, Otery* 1284, 'otter river', OE *oter ea*.

Padstow (SW 9175): The present name is a contraction of *Petrocystowe* 1358, from Celtic saint's name *Petroc* + OE *stow*, 'holy place'. An alternative E. name, in use between 1201 and 1580 was *Aldestowe* 1249, OE *eald stow*, 'old holy place'. The C. name was *Lanwethenek* 1350, 'Guethenoc's church enclosure', C. *lan Wedhenek*.

Park Head (SW 8370): now E. 'park headland' since C19. In 1210, it was *Pentir*, 'promontory', C. *pentyr*; and in C17/18 *Pencarne Point*, 'crag head(land)', C. *pen carn* + E. 'point'.

Pawton (SW 9570): *Polltun* 905, 980, C. *pol*, 'pool' + addition of OE *tun*, 'farm, settlement'.

Pencarrow (SX 0471): *Pencarw* c1290, 'stag's head/top', C. *pen carow*.

Pencarrow (SX 1082): *Pencayrou* 1327, 'end/top with forts', C. *pen kerrow/ cayrow*.

Pendavy (SX 0977): *Penduwy* 1423, 'head of the river Dewey' (see **Camel** river), C. *pen Duy*.

Pendewey (SX 0467): *Bendewy* 1310, 'foot of the river **Dewey**', C. *ben Duy*.

Pendoggett (SX 0279): *Pendewegoys* 1302, 'top of two woods', C. *pen dew-gos*.

Pendrift (SX 1074): *Pendref* 1318, 'principal farm', C. *pen-dref*.

Penfound (SX 2299): *Penfoune* c1300, 'hilltop with a beech tree', C. *pen fawen*.

Pengelly (SX 0783): 'end/top of a grove', C. *pen gelly*.

Penhallym (SX 2197): *Penalun* 1244, 'head of the stream called Alan', a common river and stream name throughout Celtic Britain, C. *pen Alan*.

Penhargard (SX 0669): *Penghirgarth* 1281, 'end of a long ridge', C. *pen hyr-yarth*.

Penmayne (SW 9476): *Penmayn* 1227, 'end of stones', C. *pen meyn*.

Pennant (SW 9979): 'top of a valley', OC *pen-nant*.

Pennygillam (SX 3283): *Pennaguinuall* 1311, 'end of a desolate gap', C. *pen ajy-ynyal*.

Pennytinney (SX 0177): *Penventinew* 1718, 'spring-heads', C. *pen-fentynyow*.

Penpont (SX 0974): 'bridge end', OC *pen-pont*.

Penpont (SW 9975): 'bridge end', OC *pen-pont*.

Penquite (SX 0976): 'top of a wood', OC *pen-cuyt*.

Penrose (SW 8770): *Penros* 1286, 'top of a hillspur', C. *pen-ros*.

Penstowe (SS 2411): mod. (C19) hybrid name for a house built on the site of **Stowe** adding C. *pen*, 'head, top, end' to the original E. name.

Pentire (SW 8570): *Pentyr* 1327, 'promontory', C. *pentyr*.

Pentire Point (SW 9280): *Pentyr* 1284, 'promontory', C. *pentyr*.

Pentireglaze (SW 9479): *Pentireglas* 1586, 'green Pentire', C. *Pentyr glas*.

Penvose (SX 0577): *Penfos* 1284, 'end of a wall/bank', C. *pen fos*.

Petherwin, North (SX 2889): *S. Paternus* 1171, *North Piderwine* 1259, 'white/holy St Padarn', C. *Padarn wyn*, with addition of E. 'north'.

Petherwin, South (SX 3081): *Pidrewyn* c1147, *Suthpydrewyn* 1269, 'white/holy St Padarn', C. *Padarn wyn* + E. 'south'.

Piper's Pool (SX 2584): E. 'Piper's pool', from C16 family.

Pityme (SW 9576): C18 E. nickname for poor dwelling or land.

Plusha (SX 2580): *Plesha* 1584, 'marshy place', OE *plysc*.

Polapit Tamar (SX 3389): *Poolapit Tamer* 1625, probably E. 'bullpit near the river Tamar' from nearby place name Bullapit (SX 3289), *Bulapit* 1149, 'bull pit', OE *bula pytt*.

Polbrock (SX 0169): *Polbrogh* 1321, 'badger's pool', C. *pol brogh*.

Poley's Bridge (SX 0874): E. 'Pawley's bridge' from C16 family.

Polglaze (SX 0574): *Polglas* 1302, 'blue/green pool', C. *pol glas*.

Polmorla (SW 9871): *Polmorva* 1208, 'marsh pool', C. *pol morva*.

Polyphant (SX 2681): *Polefant* c1170, 'frog/toad pool', OC *pol lefant*.

Polzeath (SW 9378): *Polsegh* 1311, 'dry pool', C. *pol segh*.

Port Gaverne (SX 0080): *Porcaveran* 1337, C. *porth*. 'cove/landing place' + a possible stream name, meaning uncertain.

Porthcothan (SW 8642): *Portgohedon* c1250, *Porthkehothan* 1296, 'cove/landing place at a small barley plot', C. *porth go-hedhen*.

Porthilly (SW 9375): 'salt water cove/landing place', C. *porth hyly*.

Port Isaac (SW 9980): *Portusek* 1337, *Portissek* c1540, probably 'corn-rich cove/landing place', C. *porth ysek*.

Portquin (SW 9780): *Porthguyn* 1297, 'white/fair cove', C. *porth gwyn*.

Poughill (SS 2207): *Pochewelle* 1227, 'frog stream/spring', OE *pocce wielle*.

Poundstock (SX 2099): *Pundestok* 1201, 'settlement with a stock pound', OE *pund stoc*.

Prideaux Place (SW 9175): now named after the Prideaux-Brune family, builders of the house in 1588. It was previously *Gwarthendrea* (undated), 'top of the town', C. *gwarth an dre*.

Quies, The (SW 8376): 'sow (female pig)', C. *gwys*.

Redevallen (SX 0988): *Redevallan* 1306, *Rosavallen* 1359, 'apple-tree ford', C. *res avallen*.

Red Post (SS 2605): now E. 'red post'; earlier *Redderise* c1170, 'ford by ploughland', OC *ret erys*.

Reperry Cross (SX 0463): *Respery* 1300, 'kite's ford', C. *res pery* + E. 'cross' (for 'crossroads').

Retire (SX 0064): *Redhyr* 1284, *Restyr* 1302, 'long ford', C. *res hyr*.

Rezare (SX 3677): *Riscer* 1307, 'ford at a fort', C. *res ker/cayr*.

Rock (SW 9375): contraction of E. *Black Rock* 1748, *Blaketorre* 1337, 'black rock, black crag'. The C. name was *Penmayn* 1303, 'end of stones', C. *pen meyn*.

Roscarrock (SW 9880): *Roscarrec mur* 1249, 'great Roscarrock', C. *Roscarrek muer*. Roscarrock is 'roughland with a rock', C. *ros carrek*. (see **Scarrabine**).

Rosecare (SX 1695): *Resker* 1306, 'ford by a fort', C. *res ker/cayr*.

Rough Tor (SX 1480): *Roghetorr* 1284, 'rough crag', OE *ruh torr*.

Row (SX 0975): C19 E. 'row (of houses)'.

Rumford (SW 8970): 'wide ford', OE *rum ford*.

Rumps, The (SW 9381): now C19 E. 'the rumps', from double-peaked shape of the headland. Earlier *Pentyre forte* 1584, from the Iron Age cliff castle here, E. 'fort at **Pentire**'.

Rushyford Gate (SX 2276): E. 'gate to a rushy ford'.

Ruthern (river): *Roythan* 1296, *Ruthen* 1412, *Rothyn* 1494, perhaps 'little red one', C. *rudhyn*.

Scarrabine (SW 9879): *Roscarrec bian* 1249, 'little Roscarrock', C. *Roscarrek byan* (see **Roscarrock**).

Sharpnose Point (SS 1912/14): 'sharp nose (promontory)', OE *scearp naess*.

Shop (SW 8773): *Parkens Shop* 1748, E. 'Parkyn's workshop' from C16 family.

Shop (SS 2214): C19 E. 'shop, workshop'.

Slades (SX 1580): 'valley', OE *slaed*.

Sladesbridge (SX 0171): *Layne Bridge* 1470, E. 'bridge over the river **Layne**'.

Slipperhill (SX 2586): *Sleperhille* 1529, 'muddy slope', OE *slipa hyll*.

Splatt (SW 9476): E. dialect *splat* (adopted into C.), 'plot of land'.

Stannon (SX 1280): *Standon* C15, 'stone hill', OE *stan dun*.

Start Point (SX 0485): *Start* 1841, 'tail of land, promontory', OE *steort*, with unnecessary addition of mod. E. 'point'.

Steeple Point (SS 1911), 'steep place', OE *stepel*, + mod. E. 'point'.

Stephengelly (SX 0565): *Stymguelli* c1300, 'bend of a grove', C. *stum gelly*.

Stepper Point (SW 9178): *Stuppert poynte* 1584, uncertain derivation, possibly OE *stod port*, 'horse market'.

Stibb (SS 2210): 'tree-stump', OE *stybb*.

Stoptide (SW 9375): E. 'stop-tide', for the tidal limit of the Camel estuary.

Stowe (SS 2111): 'holy place', OE *stow*.

Stratton (SS 2306): *Straetneat* c880, 'flat-bottomed valley of the river Neth', OC *strad Neth*.

Street (SX 2797): 'road', OE *straet*.

Sweets (SX 1595): *Sweets Tenement* (undated), E. 'land held by the Sweet family'.

Tamar (river): *Tamar, Tamaros* C2, *Tamer* 997–1870. An early Celtic name with common element *tam-*, possibly 'flowing' (as also in Thames, Thame, Tame etc.) with the *-ar, -er* suffix also found in the river **Lynher** (Caradon).

Tamsquite (SX 0575): *Stymcoyt, Stymguyt* 1327, 'bend of a wood', OC *stum guyt*.

St Teath (SX 0680): *Egglostetha* c1190, 'church of St Tetha', C. *eglos Tetha*.

Temple (SX 1473): *Templies* c1200, 'temple', Lat. *templus*, for church founded by the Knights Templar.

Thorne (SS 2510): 'thorn tree', OE *thorn*.

Tintagel (village) (SX 0588): *Trewarvene* 1259, 'farm/settlement on a hillside', C. *tre war venedh*.

Tintagel Castle (SX 0488): *Purocoronavis* (for *Durocornovio*) c400 (c700), 'fort of the Cornish people', Br. *duro Cornouio-n*.

Tintagel Head (SX 0488): *Tintagol* c1145. As this name is not recorded prior to Geoffrey of Monmouth (c1138), it is considered to be of NF origin: *tente d'agel*, 'the devil's stronghold' (compare Tintageu, earlier Tente d'Agel, Sark). An offered C. derivation 'fort of the constriction', *dyn tagell*, is not accepted here for several reasons.

Tinten (SX 0675): *Tynten, Tynteyn* 1240, perhaps 'fort on a rounded hill', C. *dyn tyn*.

Titson (SS 2401): *Tetyanston* 1313, 'lookout stone', OE *totan stan*.

Tonacombe (SS 2014): *Tunnecombe* 1302, E. 'valley of the stream called Tunna'. Tunna is a Celtic river name of uncertain meaning.

Towan (SW 8774): *Tewyn* 1277, 'sand dunes', C. *tewyn*.

Treator (SW 9075): *Tryetor* 1327, *Treytard* 1350, C. *try*, 'three' + perhaps C. *tardh*, 'burst' i.e. 'three rushing streams'.

Trebartha (SX 2677): *Tribertham* 1086, possibly 'farm in a bushy place', C. *tre berth-an*.

Trebarwith (SX 0586): *Treberveth* 1296, 'middle farm', C. *tre berveth*.

Trebeath (SX 2587): *Trebigh* 1583, 'small farm', C. *tre bygh*.

Trebetherick (SW 9378): *Trebedrek* 1302, 'St Petroc's farm', C. *tre Bedrek*.

Trebullett (SX 3278): *Trebalvet* 1383, C. *tre*, 'farm, settlement' + unknown word or name, apparently of the form OC **palvet*.

Treburgett (SX 0579): *Trebridoc* C12, *Trebruthek* 1283, C. *tre*, 'farm, settlement' + C. *brythek*, 'dappled one, dappled place', perhaps a stream name.

Treburley (SX 3477): 'farm of the Borlay family', from a family recorded in 1327, C. *tre Borlay*.

Treburrick (SW 8670): *Trebruthek* 1327, C, tre, 'farm, settlement' + C. *brythek*, 'dappled one/place', possibly a stream name.

Trebursye (SX 3083): *Trebursi* 1199, 'Beorhtsige's farm', C. *tre*, 'farm, settlement' + OE personal name.

Trebyan (SX 0763): *Trebyhan* 1249, 'small farm', C. *tre byan*.

Trecarne (SX 0585): *Talcarn* 1309, 'brow tor', C. *tal carn*.

Trecarne (SX 1090): *Trecarne* 1338, 'farm by a tor', C. *tre carn*.

Trecarrel (SX 3178): *Trecarl* 1202, 'Carl's farm', C. *tre Carl*.

Trecrogo (SX 3080): *Trecrugow* 1397, 'farm at barrows/tumuli', C. *tre crugow*.

Tredarrup (SX 0779): *Tretharap* 1298, 'very pleasant farm', C. *tre wortharap*.

Tredarrup (SX 1990): *Tretharap* 1411, 'very pleasant farm', C. *tre wortharap*.

Tredaule (SX 2381): *Tredaual* 1086, 'quiet farm', C. *tre dawel*.

Tredenham (SX 0463): *Tredynan* 1428, 'farm by a fort', C. *tre dynan*.

Tredethy (SX 0671): *Tredethy* 1350, perhaps 'Tetha's farm', C. *tre Detha*.

Tredinnick (SX 0762): *Tredenek* 1518, probably 'fern-brake farm', C. *tre redenek*.

Tredinnick (SW 9270): *Treredenek* 1286, 'fern-brake farm', C. *tre redenek*.

Tredrizzick (SW 9568): *Trethreysek* 1284, 'brambly farm', C. *tre dhreysek*.

Tredrustan (SW 9671): *Tredrysten* 1549, 'Tristan's farm', C. *tre Drystan*.

Treffry (SX 0763): *Trefry* 1356, 'Fri's farm', C. *tre Fry* (Celtic personal name meaning 'nose').

Trefreock (SW 9979): *Trefryek* 1284, 'Frioc's farm', C. *tre Fryek* (Celtic personal name meaning 'big-nosed').

Trefrew (SX 1084): 'farm at a slope', C. *tref rew*.

Tregada (SX 3481): *Tregadou* 1321, 'Cado's farm', OC. *tre Gado*.

Tregaddick (SX 0873): *Tregadek* 1305, 'Cadoc's farm', OC. *tre Gadek*.

Tregadillett (SX 2983): *Tregadylet* 1076, 'Cadylet's farm', OC *tre Gadylet*.

Tregardock (SX 0483): *Tregaradoc* 1196, 'Caradoc's farm', OC *tre Garadek*.

Tregatta (SX 0587): *Tregata* 1284, 'Cata's farm', OC *tre Gata*.

Tregaverne (SX 0180): *Tregaveren* 1284, 'farm on the stream named Caveran (meaning unknown)', C. *tre Gaveran*. **See Port Gaverne.**

Tregear (SX 0367): *Cayr* 1444, 'at the fort'. ME *atte*, 'at the' + C. *ker/cayr*, 'fort', here referring to a short-lived Roman fort.

Tregeare (SX 0379): *Tregayr* 1416, 'farm by a fort', C. *tre ger/gayr*.

Tregeare (SX 2486): *Treger* c1150, 'farm by a fort', C. *tre ger/gayr*.

Tregelles (SX 0177): *Tregelest* 1311, 'Celest's farm'. C. *tre Gelest*.

Treglennick (SW 8970): *Tregelennek* 1359, 'farm at a holly grove', C. *tre gelynek*.

Tregolds (SW 9171): *Tregathlos* 1392, perhaps 'Catlod's farm', C. *tre Gathlos*.

Tregole (SX 1998): *Tregewal* 1306, 'enclosed farm', C. *tre gewel*.

Tregonce (SW 9273): *Tregendros* 1201, 'Cyndrod's farm', C. *tre Gendros.*
Tregonger (SX 1884): *Tregongar* 1453, 'Congar's farm', C. *tre Gongar.*
Tregoodwell (SX 1183): *Tregothwal* 1298, 'Gudual's farm', C. *tre Godhwal.*
Tregulland (SX 1985): *Tregolan* 1302, probably 'Coloin's farm', C. *tre Golan,* rather than 'hazel-tree farm', C. *tre gollen.*
Tregunna (SW 9673): *Tregonhou* c1300, 'Conhou's farm', C. *tre Gonhow.*
Tregunnon (SX 2283): *Gunan* 1189, 'downland place', C. *gun-an,* later preceded by ME *atte,* 'at the'.
Trehudreth (SX 1172): *Treiudret* 1201, 'Iudret's farm', C. *tre Yudreth.*
Trekelland (SX 2979): *Trekelryn* c1400, 'farm at a sheltering spur', C. *tre kel-ryn.*
Trekelland (SX 3480): *Trekynmond* 1397, 'Cynemund's farm', C. *tre,* 'farm, settlement' + OE personal name.
Trekenner (SX 3478): *Trekyner* 1284, 'Cynor's farm', C. *tre Kyner.*
Treknow (SX 0586): *Tretdeno* 1086, *Trenow* c1250, 'farm at a tributary valley', C. *tre denow.*
Trelash (SX 1890): *Trellosk* 1284, 'burnt/swaled farm', C. *tre losk.*
Trelawny (SX 2182): *Treleuny* 1175, perhaps 'farm on the stream called Lueny', C. *tre Lueny* (the stream name would be C. *luen-y,* 'full stream').
Trelights (SW 9969): *Treleghtres* 1426, possibly 'pavement farm', C. *tre legh-treys* (*legh-treys* literally meaning 'feet-slab').
Trelill (SX 0478): *Trelulla* 1262, 'Lulla's farm', C. *tre Lulla.*
Trelow (SW 9269): *Trelewyth* 1327, 'Leuit's farm', C. *tre Lewyth* (C. personal name meaning 'steersman, pilot').
Tremabyn (SX 0564): *Tremaban* 1327, 'Mabon's farm', C. *tre Mabon.*
Tremail (SX 1686): *Tremayl* 1284, 'Mael's farm', C. *tre Mayl.*
Tremaine (SX 2388): *Tremen* c1230, 'stone farm', C. *tre men.*
Tremeer (SX 0676): *Tremuer* 1332, 'great farm', C. *tre muer.*
Tremollett (SX 2975): *Tremollou* 1350, C. *tre,* 'farm, settlement' + unknown word or name.
Tremollett Down (SX 3375): *Molotedoune* 1337, 'at the rowel-shaped hill', ME *atte molet doun.*
Tremore (SX 0164): *Tremhor* 1086, perhaps 'the ram's farm', C. *tre'n hordh.*
Trenance (SW 9270): 'valley farm', C. *tre nans.*
Treneague (SW 9871): *Trenahek* 1333, C. *tre,* 'farm, settlement' + unknown word or name.
Treneglos (SX 2088): 'farm by the church', C. *tre'n eglos.*
Trenewth (SX 0878): *Trenewyth* 1296, 'new farm', C. *tre noweth.*
Trengune (SX 1893): *Trengun* 1356, 'farm at the downs', C. *tre'n gun.*
Trentinney (SX 0077): *Treventenyu* 1345, 'farm by spring-heads', C. *tre fentynyow.*
Treore (SX 0280): *Treworou* 1281, 'Goreu's farm', C. *tre Worow.*
Trequite (SX 0276): *Tregoyt* 1331, 'farm at a wood', OC *tre guyt.*
Treskinnick (SX 2098): *Treskeynek* 1442, 'at the ridged roughland', ME *atte* + C. *ros keynek.*

Treslay (SX 1388): *Roslegh* 1338, 'roughland with a stone slab', C. *ros legh*.

Tresmeer (SX 2387): *Trewasmur* 1185, 'Gwasmuer's farm', C. *tre Wasmuer* (C. personal name meaning 'great fellow').

Tresparrett (SX 1491): *Rospervet* 1086, 'middle roughland', OC *ros pervet*.

Trespearne (SX 2384): *Trespernan* c1200, 'thorn-tree farm', C. *tre spernen*.

Trethevy (SX 0789): *Tredewi* 1196, 'Dewi's farm', C. *tre Dhewy*.

Trethewey (SW 9072): *Tredewi* 1208, 'Dewi's farm', C. *tre Dhewy*.

Trevalga (SX 0889): *Trevalga* 1238, 'Maelga's farm', C. *tre Valga*. Also called *Menaliden* c1150, 'broad hillside', C.*menedh ledan*.

Trevance (SW 9371): *Trevantros* 1201, 'farm at a hollow hillspur'. OC *tre vant-ros*.

Trevanger (SW 9577): *Trevangar* 1284, 'Ancar's (or hermit's) farm', C. *tref Angar*.

Trevanion (SW 9871): *Trevenyon* 1326, 'Enian's farm', C. *tref Enyan*.

Trevanson (SW 9772): *Trevansun* 1259, 'Antun's farm', C. *tref Ansun*.

Treveglos (SX 0473): 'church farm, churchtown', C. *tref eglos*.

Treveighan (SX 0779): *Trevegon* 1309, *Trevygan* 1461, early forms rule against 'small farm', C. *tre vyan*. C. *tre*, 'farm, settlement' + unknown word or name.

Trevena (SX 0588): *Trewarvene* 1259, 'farm on a hillside', C. *tre war venedh*. The true name of **Tintagel** village.

Trevia (SX 0983): *Trewya* 1272, 'farm where weaving is carried out', C. *tre wya*.

Trevillador (SW 9170): *Treveleder* 1327, 'Eleder's farm', C. *tref Eleder*.

Trevillett (SX 0788): *Trevellet* 1338, 'farm where vermillion grows', OC *tre velet*.

Trevisquite (SX 0474): *Treveskoyd* 1306, 'farm below a wood', OC *tref ys cuyt*.

Trevivian (SX 1785): *Trefyuian* 1301, 'yew-tree farm', C. *tref ewen*.

Trevone (SW 8975): *Treavon* 1302, apparently 'river farm', C. *tre avon*, although **avon*, 'river' is not commonly found in C. and makes its few appearances as *awan, awen*.

Trevone Bay (SW 8876): now E. 'bay at **Trevone**' but earlier Porthmissen (*Porthmusyn* 1396), C. *porth*, 'cove, landing place' + an apparent stream name **Musyn*, of unknown meaning.

Trevorder (SW 9870): *Trewordre* 1284, 'farm on a principal estate', C. *tre wor-dre*.

Trevorrick (SW 8672): *Trevorek* 1474, 'Moroc's farm', C. *tre Vorek*.

Trevorrick (SW 8757): *Trevorec* 1291, 'Moroc's farm', C. *tre Vorek*.

Trevose (SW 8675): *Trenfos* 1302, 'farm at the wall/bank', C. *tre'n fos*.

Trevose Head (SW 8475): E. 'head(land) at **Trevose**'.

Trewalder (SX 0872): *Trewaleder* 1286, 'Gwalader's farm', C. *tre Walader*.

Trewardale (SX 1071): *Trevertal* 1201, 'farm on a hill-brow', C. *tre war dal*.

Trewarlett (SX 3380): *Trewalred* 1308, 'Gwalred's farm', OC *tre Walred*.

Trewarmett (SX 0686): *Trewerman* 1302, 'Germanus's farm', C. *tre Werman*.

Trewassa (SX 1486): *Trewasa* 1284, 'Cata's farm', C. *tre Wasa*.

Treween (SX 2282): *Trewoen* 1356, 'downs farm', C. *tre wun*.

Trewetha (SX 0080): *Treweyther* 1426, 'Gwythyr's farm', C. *tre Wyther*.

Trewethern (SX 0479): *Trewetheran* 1436, 'Guedran's farm', C. *tre Wedhran*.

North Cornwall 91

Trewince (SW 9371): *Trewyns* 1348, 'wind(y) farm', C. *tre wyns*.

Trewint (SX 1897): *Trewynt* 1300, 'wind(y) farm', OC *tre wynt*.

Trewint (SX 2180): *Trewynt* 1324, 'wind(y) farm', OC *tre wynt*.

Treworld (SX 1190): *Treworwel* 1288, 'Gorwel's farm', C. *tre Worwel*.

Trewornan (SW 9874): *Tregronan* 1303, 'grain farm', C. *tre wronen*.

Treyarnon (SW 8673): *Trearnen* c1210, 'Garnen's farm', C. *tre Arnen*.

Tuckingmill (SX 0977): C18 E. 'tucking/fulling mill'.

Trippet Stones (SX 1375): E. dialect, 'dancing stones'.

St Tudy (SX 0676): *Ecglostudic* 1086, 'St Tudic's church', OC. *eglos Tudek*.

Tutwell (SX 3975): *Tudewell* 1297, probably 'Tuda's spring/stream', OE *Tuda wielle*.

Twelve Men's Moor (SX 2575): *Twelfmanamore* c1170, E. 'twelve men's moor'. In C12/13, this area was let to twelve tenants by the landowners, the Prior and Canons of Launceston.

Upton (SS 2004): *Uppeton* 1428, 'higher farm', OE *uppe tun*.

Valency (river): 'the mill-house', C. *an velynjy*.

Valley Truckle (SX 1082): *Velyn-trukky* (undated), 'tucking/fulling mill', C. *melyn drokkya*.

Venterdon (SX 3574): *Fentyndon* 1303, seemingly 'pastureland spring', C. *fenten don*, although the second element is later (1337) represented as ME *doune*, 'hill'.

Wadebridge (SW 9072): *Wade* 1312, 'ford', OE *waed*, with ME *brigge*, 'bridge' added in C15.

Wainhouse Corner (SX 1895): *Winhouse* 1417, E. 'wine-house'.

Wanson (SS 1900): *Wansand* 1303, 'dark sand', OE *wann sand*.

Warbstow (SX 2090): *Warberstowe* 1309, 'St Waerburh's holy place', OE *Waerburhes stow*.

Washaway (SX 0369): 'hollow-way', ME *washway*.

Week St Mary (SX 2397): *Wihc* 1086, 'settlement, dairy farm', OE *wic*, St Mary being added to the name in C13.

Welltown (SX 1367): *Wylton* 1565, 'well farm', ME *wille ton*.

Wenford Bridge (SX 0875): *Wennford Bridge* 1613, E. 'bridge at the ford across the river called Wenn'. The river name is C. *gwen*, the fem. form of *gwyn*, 'white,fair'.

St Wenn (SW 9664): *S. Wenna* 1236, after the female St Wena.

Werrington (SX 3287): *Ulvredintone* 1086, 'farm of Wulfred's people', OE *Wulfredinga tun*.

Westcott (SS 2015): *Westecote* 1340, 'western cottage', OE *west cot*.

Wheatley (SX 2492): *Wyteleye* 1327, 'white/fair clearing', OE *hwit leah*.

Whiteleigh (SX 2494): *Whitelegh* 1345, 'white/fair clearing', OE *hwit leah*.

Whitstone (SX 2698): *Whytestone* 1269, 'white stone', OE *hwit stan*.

Widemouth Bay (SS 2002): *Widemuthe* 1181, 'wide break in cliffline', OE *widan mutha*, with modern addition of E. 'bay'.

Willapark (SX 0689): *Willparke* 1556, 'well paddock', ME *wille parke*.

Withey Brook (stream): *Withebrook Water* 1613, 'willow brook', OE *withig broc*.

Withiel (SW 9965): *Guythiel* 1355, 'place of trees', C. *gwedh-yel*.

Withielgoose (SX 0065): *Wythiell Goyse* 1549, 'wood at Withiel', C. *Gwedhyel gos*, apparently in E. word order.

Woodford (SS 2113): *Wodeford* 1201, 'ford at a wood', ME *wode ford*.

Woolley (SS 2516): *Wullegh* 1493, 'wolf's clearing', OE *wulfa legh*.

Worthyvale (SX 1086): *Guerdevalan* 1086, 'above an apple tree', C. *gwarth avallen*.

Yeolmbridge (SX 3137): *Yambrigge* c1250, E. 'bridge over the river Yam'. The river name, apparently Celtic, is of unknown meaning.

Yeolmouth (SS 2016): *Yulmoth* 1327, 'mouth of a chasm', OE *geol mutha*.

Youlstone (SX 1989): *Yoldeton* 1326, 'old farm', OE *eald tun*.

Youlstone (SS 2615): *Yulkesdone* 1302, 'Geoloc's hill', OE *Geoloces dun*, or 'yellow hill', OE *geoloc dun*.

North Cornwall: Tintagel Castle

District of PENWITH
Conteth PENWYTH

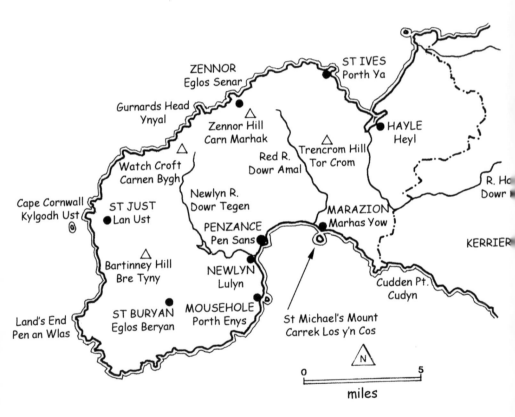

ZENNOR
Eglos Senar

ST IVES
Porth Ya

Gurnards Head
Ynyal

Zennor Hill
Carn Marhak

HAYLE
Heyl

Watch Croft
Carnen Bygh

Red R.
Dowr Amal

Trencrom Hill
Tor Crom

R. Ho
Dowr

Cape Cornwall
Kylgodh Ust

ST JUST
Lan Ust

Newlyn R.
Dowr Tegen

MARAZION
Marhas Yow

KERRIER

PENZANCE
Pen Sans

Bartinney Hill
Bre Tyny

NEWLYN
Lulyn

Cudden Pt.
Cudyn

Land's End
Pen an Wlas

ST BURYAN
Eglos Beryan

MOUSEHOLE
Porth Enys

St Michael's Mount
Carrek Los y'n Cos

N

0   5
miles

Place Names of the District of PENWITH

Henwyn Plasow an Conteth
Penwyth

Aire Point (SW 3528): *Are* 1751, 'high place', C. *ardh*.

Alsia (SW 3925): *Als* 1266, *Alsa* 1304–1640, originally 'slope', C. *als*, then 'slope-place', C. *als-a*. Pronounced 'ayl-ya'.

Amalebra (SW 4936): *Ammalebry* 1302, 'lower Amal', C. *Amal ebry*. **Amal** appears to be a river name, meaning 'edge, boundary or slope' (see **Red River**).

Amalveor (SW 4837): 'great Amal' (see **Amalebra**), C. *Amal vuer*.

Amalwhidden (SW 4837): *Ammalwyn* 1334, 'white Amal' (see **Amalebra**), C. *Amal wyn* (LC *widn*).

Angarrack (SW 5838): 'the rock', C. *an garrek*.

Anjarden (SW 4128): *Nansardon* 1692, 'valley facing pastureland', C. *nans ar don* (see **Chiverton**).

Ardensawah (SW 3723): *Arghansawyth* 1302, 'silver stream', C. *arhans-aweth*.

Armed Knight (SW 3424): E. 'armoured knight', a name transferred from a collapsed sea stack off Peal Point in C16. The C. name was *Gwyllo* 1580, apparently C. *gwel-a*, 'viewpoint, landmark'.

Avarack, The (SW 3735): 'summer fallow land' (an ironic name as this is a wave-swept rock), C. *havrek*.

Ayr (SW 5140): *Arthia* 1454, 'St Ia's height', C. *ardh Ya*.

Balleswidden (SW 3931): 'mineworkings at **Leswidden**', C. *bal Lyswyn* (LC *Leswidn*).

Barnoon (SW 5140): 'top of the downs', C. *bar'n wun*.

Bartinney (SW 3929): *Breteny* 1245, 'rump-like hill', C. *bre tyn-y*.

Beagletodn (SW 4837): 'pasture hillock', C. *begel ton* (LC *todn*).

Bellowal (SW 4326): *Bollowen* 1309, 'happy dwelling', C. *bos lowen*.

Bishop's Head and Foot (SW 4636): after former cross and base at meeting point of three parishes, including Gulval and the bishop's manor of Lanisley. Its C. name was *Meen Crowse an Especk* 1613, 'the bishop's cross stone', C. *men crows an epscop*.

Bodinnar (SW 4232): *Bodener* 1357, probably 'Dener's dwelling', C. *bos Dener*.

Bodrifty (SW 4435): *Bodrythkey* 1344, OC *bod*, 'dwelling' + personal name *Rythgi* ('red hound').

Bojewyan (SW 3934): *Bosuyan* 1302, 'Uyan's dwelling', C *bos Uyan*.

Boleigh (SW 4324): *Bolegh* 1275, 'dwelling by a stone slab', C. *bos legh*.

Bollowall (SW 3531): *Bolouhal* 1327, 'Louhal's dwelling', C. *bos Louhal*.
Bologgas/Bellogas (SW 4428): *Bollogas* 1356, 'dwelling of mice', C. *bos logos*.
Bone (SW 4632): *Boden* 1327, 'little dwelling', C. *bodyn*.
Borah (SW 4424): *Boswragh* 1302, 'hag's dwelling', C. *bos wragh*.
Bosanketh (SW 3826): 'Angawd's dwelling', C. *bos Ankodh*.
Bosavern (SW 3730): *Bosavarn* 1302, 'Afaern's dwelling', C. *bos Avarn*.
Boscaswell (SW 3834): *Boscaswal* 1310, 'Cadwal's dwelling', C. *bos Caswal*.
Boscathnoe (SW 4531): *Bethkednou* 1447, 'Cadno's grave', C. *bedh Cadhno*.
Boscawen-ros (SW 4323): 'roughland of Boscawen', C. *ros Bosscawen*, now in E.
word order. **Boscawen** is 'dwelling by an elder-tree', C. *bos scawen*.
Boscawen-un/Boscawen-noon (SW 4127): 'downs of Boscawen', C. *gun Bosscawen*, now in E. word order (see **Boscawen-ros**).
Boscawen-un stone circle (SW 4127): *Daunce Mine* c1680, 'dance of stones', C. *dons meyn*.
Boscean (SW 3632): *Bosseghan* 1302, 'dwelling at a dry place' (i.e without independent water supply), C. *bos sehen*.
Bosence (SW 4030): *Bossens* 1317, 'dwelling of saints/holy men', C. *bos syns* (with reference to the early chapel ruins nearby).
Bosence (SW 5732): *Boswyns* 1330, 'wind(y) dwelling', C. *bos wyns*.
Bosfranken (SW 3825): 'Frenchmen's/freemen's dwelling', C. *bos frynkyon*.
Bosigran (SW 4236): *Bosygarane* 1333, *Boschygarn* 1361, C.*bos*, 'dwelling' + lost place name, probably *Chygaran*, 'crane's/heron's house' or 'house of a man called Garan', C. *chy garan*.
Bosiliack (SW 4333): *Boshouliek* 1303, 'sunny dwelling', C. *bos howlek*.
Bosistow (SW 3623): *Bosestou* c1302, 'Esteu's dwelling', C. *bos Estow*.
Boskednan (SW 4434): *Boskennan* 1313, 'Cynan's dwelling', C.*bos Kenan* (LC *Kednan*).
Boskednan stone circle (SW 4335): *Mein yn dans* 1700, 'stones in a dance', C. *meyn yn dons*.
Boskenna (SW 4223): *Boskennou* 1321, 'Ceneu's dwelling', C. *bos Kenow*.
Boskennal (SW 4125): *Boskenhal* 1309, 'Cynhael's dwelling', C. *bos Kenhal*.
Boskennal (SW 5034): *Boskenhal* 1325, 'Cynhael's dwelling', C. *bos Kenhal*.
Boslow (SW 3932): *Boslowe* 1655, 'dwelling where charcoal is made', C. *bos (g)low*.
Bosoljack (SW 4532): *Bossulsek* 1334, 'Sulleisoc's dwelling', C. *bos Sulsek*.
Bosporthennis (SW 4436): 'dwelling at a gateway to **Ninnis**', C. *bos porth-Enys*.
Bostrase (SW 5730): *Bostras* c1815, 'dwelling at a flat-bottomed valley', C. *bos stras*.
Bostraze (SW 3931): *Penstras* 1300, 'head/end of a flat-bottomed valley', C. *pen stras*.
Bosullow (SW 4134): *Boschiwolow* 1301, 'dwelling at Chywolow', C. *bos*, 'dwelling' + lost place name *Chywolow*, C. *chy wolow*, 'house of light'.
Bosulval (SW 4634): *Boswolvel* 1327, 'Guolvel's dwelling', C. *bos Wolvel*.
Bosvenning (SW 4321): *Bosvaenon* 1289, 'Maenon's dwelling', C. *bos Vaynon*.

Boswarthan (SW 4433): *Bosvarghan* 1296, 'Meirchyon's dwelling', C. *bos Varghan*.

Boswarthen (SW 4128): *Bosvarghan* 1338, 'Meirchyon's dwelling', C. *bos Varghan*.

Boswarva (SW 4332): *Bosworweth* 1289, 'dwelling at a wooded slope', C. *bos worwedh*.

Boswednack (SW 4437): *Boswennek* 1327, 'Winnoc's dwelling', C. *bos Wynnek*.

Boswens (SW 4033): *Boswyns* 1329, 'wind(y) dwelling', C. *bos wyns*.

Bosworlas (SW 3730): *Bosworlosk* 1284, 'dwelling on burnt/swaled (ground)', C. *bos war losk*. Traditionally pronounced 'b'sur-lus'.

Botallack (SW 3632): 'Taloc's dwelling', C. *bos Talek* (personal name meaning 'big-browed/heavy-browed').

Botrea (SW 4030): *Bostregh* 1314, C. *bos*, 'dwelling' + *tregh*, 'cut, slice', perhaps 'cut wood'.

Bowgyheere (SW 5132): 'long cowshed', C. *bowjy hyr*.

Brane (SW 4021): *Bosvran* 1323, 'Bran's dwelling', C. *bos Vran* (personal name meaning 'crow'.

Breja (SW 4838): *Breyssa* 1580, 'outermost hill', C. *bre ussa*.

Brisons, The (SW 3431): *Bresan Insula* 1576, 'reef', F. *brisant*.

Brunnion (SW 5036): *Bronyon* 1452, 'hills', C. *bronyon*.

Burnewhall (SW 4023): *Bodenewel* 932–1327, 'dwelling in the mist', C. *bos y'n newl*.

Buryas Bridge (SW 4429): now E. 'bridge at Buryas'; formerly *Berrys* 1356, *Nans Berries* 1652, 'short-ford valley', C. *nans ber-res*.

St Buryan (SW 4025): *Egglous Boryan* 1588, 'St Beriana's church', C. *eglos Beryan*.

Bussow (SW 4938): *Bosow* 1284, 'dwellings', C. *bosow*.

Caer Bran (SW 4029): 'fort at **Brane**', C. *ker/cayr Bosvran*.

Canonstown (SW 5335): E. 'canon's town', once thought to be named after Canon John Rogers 1778–1856, but 1562 record of the place name rules this out.

Cape Cornwall (SW 3531): C16 E. 'cape of Cornwall' replacing *Kulgyth East* 1580, *The Kilguthe* 1584, 'goose-back at St Just', C. *kyl-godh Ust*.

Carbis (SW 5533): now C. *carbons*, 'paved road, causeway', but formerly *Rosmelin* 1233, 'roughland with a mill', C. *ros melyn*.

Carbis Bay (cove) (SW 5238): *Porthreptor* 1580, 'cove beside an eminence', C. *porth reb tor*.

Carbis Bay (village) (SW 5238): *Carbons* 1391, 'paved road, causeway', C. *carbons*.

Carfury (SW 4434): *Carnfuru* 1327, C. *carn*, 'tor' + uncertain word or name, perhaps C. *furow*, 'wise ones'.

Carn, The (SW 4134): *Carnmorvah* 1884, 'tor at Morvah', C. *carn Morvedh*.

Carn Barges (SW 4423): 'buzzard's crag', C. *carn bargos*.

Carn Bargus (SW 3626): 'buzzard's crag', C. *carn bargos*.

Carn Barra (SW 3522): 'bread-like crag', C. *carn bara*.

Carn Bean (SW 3833): 'little tor', C. *carn byan*. [**Carn Byan**]. Evidence from 1852 suggests that the hill's original name was *Carn Yorgh* (see **Carnyorth**).

Carn Boel (SW 3423): 'axe-shaped crag', C. *carn bol.*

Carn Creagle (SW 3528): 'spider-crab's/cricket's crag', C. *carn crygell.*

Carn Du (SW 4523): 'black/dark crag', C. *carn du.*

Carn Eanes (SW 3833): *Carn-inis* 1584, 'isolated/remote tor', C. *carn enys.* Also called *Carnmele* 1578, *Carn Michael* 1699, 'Michael's tor', C. *carn Myhal.*

Carnelloe (SW 4438): 'little crags', C. *carnellow.*

Carnequidden (SW 4635): *Kernekwyn* 1367, 'white/fair corner', C. *kernyk wyn* (LC *widn*).

Carn Euny (SW 4028): 'St Euny's tor', C. *carn Ewny.*

Carn Galva (SW 4335): 'lookout tor', C. *carn golva.*

Carn Gloose (SW 3531): *Careg Glouse* 1584, 'grey rock', C. *carrek los.*

Carn Greeb (SW 3424): 'crest crag', C. *carn cryb.*

Carn Guthensbras (SW 3762): *Guthen Brose* 1751, 'great tidal ledge', C. *cudhen bras.*

Carnhell Green (SW 6137): *Carnhel* 1302, 'hall tor/cairn', C. *carn hel,* with late addition of E. 'green'.

Carn Kenidjack (SW 3832): *Carn-usack* 1584, *Carnijack* 1700, 'hooting tor', C. *carn ujek,* with additional 'carn' added C18. Early forms show that this does not share the same derivation with the hamlet of **Kenidjack**.

Carn Leskys (SW 3530): 'burnt crag', C. *carn leskys.*

Carn Naun Point (SW 4741): *Carnmen Point* 1839, 'stone crag', C. *carn men,* + addition of E. 'point'. Earlier *Pensowssen* 1580, 'Saxon's headland', C. *pen Sawsen.*

Carn Scathe (SW 3721): 'boat crag', C. *carn scath.*

Carnsew (SW 5537): *Carndu* 1298, 'black/dark crag', C. *carn du.*

Carn Towan (SW 3626): 'crag by sand-dunes', C. *carn tewyn.*

Carn Veslan (SW 4237): 'mussel crag', C. *carn mesclen.*

Carnyorth (SW 3733): 'roebuck's tor', C. *carn yorgh.*

Carrick Gladden (SW 5338): 'rock on a bank/edge', C. *carrek glan* (LC *gladn*).

Carracks, The (SW 4640): C. *carrek,* 'rock', with E. plural. The Little Carracks were *Carrack an Heythen* c1920, 'the birds' rock', C. *carrek an edhyn.*

Castallack (SW 4525): *Castelak* 1284, 'fortified', C. *castelak.*

Castle-an-Dinas (SW 4835): 'castle at the hill-fort', C. *castel an dynas.*

Castle Horneck (SW 4530): *Castelhornek* 1335, 'iron-like castle', C. *castel hornek,* perhaps originally applying to the nearby hill fort of **Lesingey Round**.

Castle Kayle (SW 5835): *Cayl Castelle* 1538, 'castle of concealment/shelter', C. *castel kel.* Earlier, *Castel Treclysten* 1478, 'castel at Treglisson', C. *castel Treglysten.*

Catchall (SW 4227): C19 E. from former public house on a road junction that 'caught all' who passed by. Formerly Lower **Hendra**.

Cathebedron (SW 6236): *Caderbaderen* 1286, 'chair for the backside', C. *cadar bedren.*

Ceres Rock (SW 5741): 'angry one', C. *serrys.*

Chair Ladder (SW 3621): *Tutton Harry an Lader* c1680, 'stool of Harry the Thief', from folk tale of Harry the Hermit; later *Chair Ladder*, 'thief's chair', C. *chayr lader.*

Chapel Carn Brea (SW 3828): *Chapell of Carnbre* c1670, *Chapel Carn Brey* 1700, 'chapel at the hill cairn', C. *chapel carn bre.*

Chapel Jane (SW 4338): *Chapel Innyall* 1580, 'chapel at **Gurnard's Head**', C. *chapel Ynyal*; later *Chapel Jane* c1730, 'cold/bleak chapel', C. *chapel yeyn/jeyn.*

Chenhalls (SW 5535): *Chynals* 1453, 'house at the cliff/slope', C. *chy'n als.*

Chiverton (SW 5429): *Chiwarton* 1311, 'house on pastureland', C. *chy war ton.*

Chun (SW 4034): *Cheiwone* 1283, 'downland house', C. *chy wun.*

Chun Castle (SW 4034): *Castel Choon* c1740, 'castle at **Chun**', C. *castel Chywun.*

Chyandour (SW 4731): 'house at the stream', C. *chy an dowr.*

Chyangweal (SW 5238): 'house at the open field', C. *chy an gwel.*

Chyenhal (SW 4527): 'house at the marsh', C. *chy an hal.*

Chykembro (SW 4437): 'Welshman's house', C. *chy Kembro.*

Chynoweth (SW 5531): 'new house'. C. *chy noweth.*

Chypons (SW 4936): 'bridge house', C. *chy pons.*

Chypraze (SW 3935): 'meadow house', C. *chy pras.*

Chysauster (SW 4734): *Chisalvestre* 1313, 'Sylvester's house', C. *chy Salvester.*

Chytodden (SW 4938): *Chyenton* 1320, 'house at the pastureland', C. *chy an ton* (LC *todn*).

Chyvellan (SW 5232): 'mill house', C. *chy velyn.*

Chywoone (SW 4527): 'downland house', C. *chy wun.*

St Clement's Isle (SW 4726): after St Clement, patron of fishermen, but *Carn Lodgia* C19, 'crag with plants', C. *carn losow* (this name now transferred to a minor rock at the S. end of the island.

Clodgy Point (SW 5041): *Cloygva* 1580, 'place of a lazar-house', C. *clojy-va.*

Cockwells (SW 5234): C17 E., from Cockwell family.

Coldharbour (SW 4937): E. 'cold harbour (i.e. wayside shelter)'.

Colenso (SW 5630): *Kelensou* 1334, 'dark hollies', C. *kelyn dhu.*

Collurian (SW 5234): prob. Gk. *kolorion*, 'eye-salve', from reputed qualities of healing well.

Connerton (SW 5939): river name *Connar*, 'fury' (see **Red River**), with addition of OE *tun*, 'farm, settlement'.

Connor Downs (SW 5939): *Conerton Down* 1580, E. 'hill at **Connerton**'.

Copperhouse (SW 5638): *Copper House* c1810, E. 'copper house' from former foundry and smelting house.

Coswinsawsin (SW 6238): 'Saxon's fair-wood', C. *cos-wyn Sawsen.*

Cowloe (SW 3426): *Cowlo Flatt* 1702, 'curdling', C. *cowla*, from the foam around the reef.

Crankan (SW 4631): *Trevrankan* 1327, 'freemen's farm', C. *tre vrankyon.*

Crankan (SW 4633): *Caranken* 1346, 'fort of misery', C. *ker/cayr anken.*

Crean (SW 3924): *Kacregan* 1238, 'hedge by a small barrow/tumulus', C. *ke crugyn*.

Cribba Head (SW 4022): 'crests, reefs', C. *crybow*, with addition of E. 'head(land)'.

Cripples Ease (SW 5036): E. 'cripple's ease', an ironic name for a location at the top of a long, tortuous hill.

Crowlas (SW 5133): *Croures* 1327, 'ford with stepping stones', C. *crew-res*.

Crows-an-Wra (SW 3927): 'the hag's cross', C. *crows an wragh*.

Cudden Point (SW 5427): *Cudan* 1580, 'tresses, lock of hair', C. *cudyn*, presumably from the headland's distinctive shape.

Derval (SW 4130): *Deverell* 1323, 'watery', C. *devrel*.

Deveral (SW 5939): 'watery', C. *devrel*.

Dorminack (SW 4423): 'stony ground', C. *dor meynek*.

Dowran (SW 3830): 'watering place', C. *dowr-an*.

Drannack (SW 5936): *Dreynek* 1284, 'thorny', C. *dreynek*.

Drewollas (SW 6135): *Trewollas* 1655, 'lower farm', C. *tre woles*.

Drift (SW 4328), properly Lower Drift, *Drefbyghan* 1262, 'little Drift', C. *an dref vyan*. Drift is C. *an dref*, 'the farm'. Higher Drift, *Drefmur* 1327, 'the great farm', C. *an dref vuer*, lies close by.

Dry Carn (SW 4032): *Tricarn* c1300, 'three cairns', C. *try carn*, from destroyed archaeological sites. Normally, this should have spirantised to *try harn* but five historic forms fail to show this.

Ebal Rocks (SW 4338): *An Eball* 1580, 'the colt', C. *an ebol*.

Embla (SW 4837): *Emle* 1301, 1342, river name **Amal**, C. *amal*, 'edge, boundary, slope' (see **Amalebra, Amalveor, Amalwhidden** and **Red River**).

Ennestreven (SW 4130): 'isolated spot with houses', C. *enys treven*.

Ennis (SW 4428): 'isolated, remote', C. *enys*.

Ennys (SW 5532): 'isolated, remote', C. *enys*.

Enys, The (SW 3735): *Enys* 1839, 'island', C. *enys*.

Enys Dodnan (SW 3424): *Enys Tone* 1580, 'turf island', C. *enys don* (LC *dodn*).

St Erth (SW 5535):, after the male saint Erch. The churchtown was also *Lanuthinoc* 1200, 'Guethenoc's church enclosure', C. *lan Wedhenek*, later shortened to *Lanuthno*.

St Erth Praze (SW 5735): *Praze* c1870, 'meadow', C. *pras*.

Escalls (SW 3626): *Eskeles* 1281, 'place of thistles', C. *askall-ys*.

Faugan (SW 4528): *Fawgan* 1689,'white/fair beeches', C. *faw gan*.

Foage (SW 4637): *Bos* 1315, 'dwelling', C. *bos*.

Four Parishes Stone (SW 4235): now E. 'stone where four parishes meet' but *Meane Crouse* 1613, 'cross stone', C.*men crows*.

Frythens (SW 5433): *Breghtyn* 1306, 'dappled rounded hill', C. *bregh-tyn*.

Gala Rocks (SW 4529): *Carlow Rocks* c1813–1870, 'rayfish', C. *carlyth*, with common dropping of final *–th*.

Gamper (SW 3425): 'meeting of currents', C. *kemper*.

Gazell (SW 4423): 'the inlet', C. *an gasal* (literally 'armpit'). The Ordnance Survey has transposed this cove name with that of an adjacent reef, Le Scathe, *Lech Skath* 1778, 'boat ledge', C. *legh scath.*

Gazick (SW 3529): now given to a cove but originally a rock name, 'the mare', C. *an gasek.*

Gear (SW 4437): *Kaer* 1327, 'fort, enclosed farm', C. *ker/cayr.*

Gear (SW 4633): *Caer* 1323, 'fort, enclosed farm', C. *ker/cayr.*

Gear (SW 5734): *Kaer* 1384, 'fort, enclosed farm', C. *ker/cayr.*

Geevor Mine (SW 3734): *Wheal an Giver* 1716, 'the goats' mine workings', C. *whel an gever.*

Georgia (SW 4836): *The Gorga Croft* c1696, 'rough pasture enclosed by a low/ruinous hedge', C. *croft gor-ge.*

Godrevy (SW 5842): 'homesteads', C. *godrevy.*

Goldsithney (SW 5430): *Golsithny* 1409, 'St Sythni's feast', C. *gol Sydhny* (traditional feast transferred from Sithney to here in C13).

Gribba Point (SW 3530): 'the reefs', C. *an grybow*, with addition of E. 'point'.

Grumbla (SW 4029): *Gromlogh* 1498, 'the dolmen', C. *an gromlegh* (the dolmen remains stand at SW 405295).

Gulval (SW 4831): *S. Welvela* 1301–1440, from female saint Guolvel. The church site and manor were *Lanystly* 1365, 'Istli's church enclosure', C. *lan Ystly.*

Gurland (SW 3648): *Gorlan* 1284, 'the sheepfold', C. *an gorlan.*

Gurlyn (SW 5632): *Gorlyn* 1284, 'high pool', C. *gor-lyn.*

Gurnard's Head (SW 4328): now E. 'gurnard's head' after the likeness of its profile to that of a red gurnard. Its C. name was *Innyall* 1580, 'desolate one', C. *ynyal.*

Gwallon (SW 5231): *Wallen* 1338, 'little wall', C. *gwalyn.*

Gwavas (SW 4628): 'winter dwelling', C. *gwavos.*

Gwavas Lake (SW 4728): *Dour Gwavas* c1680, 'Gwavas water', C. *dowr Gwavos.*

Gwennap Head (SW 3621): a baffling name, perhaps that of a local family, replacing the name **Tol Pedn Penwith** from 1888.

Gwenver (SW 3627): 'white sea', C. *gwyn-vor.*

Gwinear (SW 5937): *Gwynyar* 1580, after St Guinier.

Gwithian (SW 5841): *Gothyan* 1535, after St Guidian.

Hailglower (SW 3832): *Halagalower* 1841, 'willow garden', C. *helyg-lowarth.*

Halamanning (SW 5630): *Penhalamanyn* 1651, 'good pasture at Penhale', C. *Penhal amanyn. Penhal* is 'end of a marsh', C. *pen-hal*, while *amanyn* literally means 'butter'.

Halsetown (SW 5038): C19 E. 'settlement founded by James Halse'.

Hannibal's Carn (SW 4336), 'Hannibal's tor', C. *carn Honybal*, possibly after Hannibal Thomas of Bosporthennis C18 and now in E. word order.

Hayle (SW 5637): *Heyl* 1265, 'inlet/estuary with tidal flats', C. *heyl.*

Hayle River: *Heyl* 1265, 'estuary with tidal flats', C. *heyl*. The eastern branch of the two-pronged estuary, now called Copperhouse Pool, was *Est Lo* 1762, 'eastern inlet', C. *yst-logh*.

Heamoor (SW 4631): *Enhee* 1560, 'the enclosure/holding', C. *an hay* (borrowed from OE *(ge)haeg*), with later addition of E. 'moor', i.e. 'marsh'.

Hellangove (SW 4834): 'the smith's hall', C. *hel an gof*.

Hellesvean (SW 5040): 'little Henlys', C. *Henlys vyan*. *Henlys* is 'old court/ruin', C. *hen-lys*.

Hellesveor (SW 5040): 'great Henlys' (see Hellesvean), C. *Henlys vuer*.

Hendra (SW 4227): 'home farm', C. *hen-dre*.

Hendra (SW 5138): 'home farm', C. *hen-dre*.

St Hilary (SW 5531): *S. Elarius* 1229, *Seynt Eler* c1680, after the C4 bishop Hilarius of Poitiers.

Hor Point (SW 4941): 'ram's headland', C. *hordh* + E. 'point'.

Horrace (SW 3921): 'rams', C. *hordhas*.

St Ives (SW 5140): *Porthia* 1272–1695, 'St Ia's landing place', C. *porth Ya*.

St Ives Head (SW 5140): *Dynas Ia* 1513, 'St Ia's fort', C. *dynas Ya*. Also called *Pendinas* 1539, 'fort head(land)', C. *pen dynas*; and *Enys* 1583, 'island', C. *enys*.

Joppa (SW 3829): perhaps C19 (Methodist) Biblical name, or 'workshop', C. *shoppa*.

St Just (SW 3731): *Lanuste* 1396, 'St Just's church enclosure', C. *lan Ust*.

Keigwin (SW 3934): *Kegwyn* 1302–1539, 'white/fair hedge', C. *ke gwyn*. The local pronunciation is 'gwidn' (LC *gwidn*, 'white, fair').

Kelynack (SW 3729): 'holly grove', C. *kelynak*.

Kemyel (SW 4524-4624): a name that had defied all attempts to translate it satisfactorily, C. *ke* 'hedge' + uncertain word or name: *Myhal*, 'Michael' and *mel* 'honey' have been suggested.

Kenegie (SW 4832): 'reed-beds', C. *kenegy*.

Kenidjack (SW 3632): *Kynygiek* 1326, 'fuel-rich ground', C. *cunyjak*.

Kerris (SW 4427): 'fort-place', C. *ker-ys/cayr-ys*.

Kerrow (SW 3827): 'forts, enclosed farms', C. *kerrow/cayrow*.

Kerrow (SW 4134): 'forts, enclosed farms', C. *kerrow/cayrow*.

Kerrow (SW 5734): 'forts, enclosed farms', C. *kerrow/cayrow*.

Kerrowe (SW 4537): *Nancarrow* 1738, 'stag's valley', C. *nans carow*.

Lamorna (SW 4424): *Nansmorno* 1302, 'valley of the stream called Morno' (see **Lamorna Stream**).

Lamorna Cove (SW 4523): *Port of Nansmorno* 1302, 'cove/landing place at Lamorna', C. *porth Nansmorno*.

Lamorna Stream: *Morno* 1302, *Mornou* 1319, meaning unknown unless the form *Morana* 1387 can be accepted. This suggests 'berry-place', C. *moren-a*.

Land's End (SW 3425): E. 'end of the land', the C. equivalent also being recorded as *Pen an ulays* 1504, 'end of the land', C. *pen an wlas*.

Lanyon (SW 4234): *Lynyeyn* 1326, 'cold pool', C. *lyn yeyn*.

Leah/Leha (SW 4027): *Legha* 1318–1504, 'place of stone slabs', C. *legh-a*.

Lelant (SW 5437): *Lananta* c1150–1511, *Erony Lanante* 1522, 'St Anta's church enclosure', C. *lan Anta*, with addition of the Celtic saint's name *Erony*, to whom the church was dedicated.

Lescudjack (SW 4731): *Lanscoisek* 1302, 'wooded valley', C. *nans cosek*.

Lesingey (SW 4530): *Lyssungy* 1326, 'Iunci's court/ruin', C. *lys Ungy*.

Leswidden (SW 3930): *Leswen* 1302, 'white/fair court or ruin', C. *lys wyn* (LC *widn*), or 'white mud', C. *lys wyn* (LC *widn*). Both would fit the site: a now destroyed earthwork stood nearby and china clay was quarried here.

St Levan (SW 3822): *Selevan* 1523, 'St Selevan' (the C. form of Solomon).

Logan Rock (SW 3921): *The Logan Stone* 1754, 'rocking stone', dialect *logging*. The C. name is *Men Amber* 1870, 'balance stone', C. *men omborth*.

Long Rock (SW 4931): E. 'long rock', after an offshore reef.

Longships (SW 3225): E. 'long ships'. Individual rocks of the reef are: Cein, 'back', C. *keyn*; Farkell Carn, 'forked crag',C. *carn forhel*; Tal-y-maen, 'brow of the stones', C. *tal an meyn*; Carn Bras, 'great crag', C. *carn bras* (on which the lighthouse stands); Herly, 'long ledge', C. *hyr-legh*; Plassek, 'foul one', C. *plosek* and Meinek, 'stony', C. *meynek*

Ludgvan (SW 5033): *Ludewan Eglos* 1289, *Lusewan* 1454, 'church at a place of cinders', C. *eglos lusow-an* (corrected from E. word order).

Ludgvan Leaze (SW 5132): 'manor-court of Ludgvan', C. *lys Lusowan*.

Madron (SW 4531): *Eglosmadern* 1394, 'St Madern's church', C. *eglos Madern*. Also called *Landythy* 1616, C. *lan* 'early church enclosure' + uncertain personal name, possibly *(St) Tetha*.

Maen Dower (SW 3529): 'water stone', C. *men dowr*.

Marazion (SW 5130): formerly the site of two markets: *Marghasyou* 1331, 'Thursday market', C. *marhas Yow*; and *Marghasbian* 1359, 'little market', C. *marhas vyan*.

Mayon (SW 3523): *Mayn* 1284, 'stone', C. *men* (after the celebrated stone called Table Men).

Men-an-Tol (SW 4235): *Meane an toll* 1613, 'stone of the hole', C. *men an toll*.

Mennor (SW 5236): *Meneth* 1625, 'hillside', C. *menedh*.

Men Scryfa (SW 4235): *Mean Scriffez* c1670, *Men Skrepha* 1700, variously 'stone of writing', C. *men screfa*; and 'written stone', C. *men screfys*.

Merry Maidens (SW 4324): E. 'merry maidens' from C18 Methodist tale. Formerly *Daunce Mine* c1680, *Dons Mine* 1862, 'dance of stones', C. *dons meyn*.

Merthen Point (SW 4122): *Merthen* 1732, 'sea-fort', C. *merdhyn*.

St Michael's Mount (SW 5130): E. 'mount of St Michael', but *Carrack Looes en Coos* c1680, 'grey rock in the wood', C. *carrek los y'n cos* (the Mount stood in an extensive forest inundated by the sea c2500BC).

Minack Theatre (SW 3821): E. 'theatre at Minack Point', named after a rock called The Minack, 'stony one', C.*meynek*.

Morvah (SW 4035): *Morveth* 1327–1584, 'sea-grave', C. *mor vedh* (the existence of a supposed St Morwetha is in considerable doubt).

Mousehole (SW 4626): *Musehole* 1284, 'mouse's hole', OE *mus hol*, (after a nearby sea cave or the small size of the original harbour) or possibly 'gull's hollow', OE *maewes holh*. The C. name was *Porthenys* 1310, 'landing place by an island', C. *porth enys*.

Mulfra (SW 4534), 'bare-hill'(after the hill above the farm), C. *mol-vre*.

Nancherrow (SW 3731), *Nansserou* 1400, apparently 'valley with an acre (of cultivated land)', C. *nans erow*. A Cornish acre was considerably larger than an E. one.

Nancledra (SW 4936): *Nanscludri* 1302, 'Clodri's valley', C. *nans Clodry*.

Nanjizal Bay (SW 3523): E. 'valley at Nanjizal'. Nanjizal, *Nansusal* 1302, appears to be 'windpipe valley', C. *nans usel*. 'Low valley', C. *nans ysel* would make little sense.

Nanjulian (SW 3529): *Nanselin* 1301, 'elbow-shaped valley' or 'valley of the stream called Elyn ('elbow-shaped')', C. *nans elyn*.

Nanquidno (SW 3628): *Nansgwynyou* 1327, 'Gwinyou's valley', C. *nans Gwynyow*.

Nanseglos (SW 4431): 'church valley', C. *nans eglos*.

Nathaga Rocks (SW 5943): *Lethegga* 1848, 'milky ones', C. *lethegow*.

Navax Point/Knavocks, The (SW 5943): 'autumn farm', C. *kynyavos*.

Newbridge (SW 4231): E. 'new bridge' since 1841; formerly *Hallentacken*, *Hallantegan* C19, 'marsh on the stream called Tegen ('pretty one')', C. *hal an Tegen*.

Newlyn (SW 4628): *Lulyn* 1290–1368, 'fleet pool', C. *lu-lyn*.

Newlyn River: now E. 'river of Newlyn' but the former name of **Newbridge** seems to preserve an older name *Tegen*, 'pretty one', C. *tegen*.

Newmill (SW 4534): *Mulfra Newe Mill* 1621, E. 'new mill at Mulfra'. The C. name was *Choynoy* 1668, 'Noy's house', C. *chy Noy*.

Ninnes (SW 4434): *Enes* 1327, 'isolated, remote', C.*enys*, from old detached portion of Madron parish.

Ninnes (SW 5135): *Enes* 1311, 'isolated, remote', C. *enys*.

Noon Billas (SW 4836): 'the downs where naked oats grow', C. *an wun bylas*. 'Pillas' (*Avena Nuda*) was once widely grown for fodder, but is now almost extinct.

Noongallas (SW 4633): *Goongallish* 1687, 'hard/difficult downs', C. *gun gales*.

Numphra (SW 3829): *Nomfra* 1589, 'the hill downs', C. *an wun-vre*.

Parc-an-Growes (SW 4430), 'field of the cross', C. *park an grows*.

Paul (SW 4627): named after St Paul Aurelian. The churchtown was *Breweny* 1284–1480, C. *bre*, 'hill' or C. *brew*, 'fragment of land' + unknown word or name, although C. *en-y*, 'ash-trees stream' is possible.

Pednavounder (SW 3922): 'end of the lane', C. *pen* (LC *pedn*) *an vownder*.

Pedn Kei (SW 4338): 'dog's head', C. *pen* (LC *pedn*) *ky*.

Pedn-men-du (SW 3426): 'black-stone headland', C. *pen* (LC *pedn*) *men-du*.

Pedn Olva (SW 5240): 'lookout headland', C. *pen* (LC *pedn*) *golva*.

Penbeagle (SW 5139): *Penbegel* 1257, 'top of a hillock', C. *pen begel*.

Penberth Cove (SW 4122): *Porth Penbyrthe* 1580, 'cove/landing place at Penberth', C. *porth Benbreyth*. **Penberth**, *Benberd* 932, *Penbreth* 1461, is 'foot of the river called Breyth ('dappled one')', C. *ben Breyth*.

Penberthy (SW 5533): *Penbyrghi* 1309, 'head of the stream called Bryghy ('speckled one')', C. *pen Brygh-y*.

Pendeen (SW 3834): the village has only been so named since the mid C19: properly, it is *Higher Boscaswell* c1800 (see **Boscaswell**). Pendeen itself is the C17 house at SW 3835 and is itself named after the headland of **Pendeen Watch**.

Pendeen Watch (SW 3736): *Pendyn* 1284, 'fort head(land)', C. *pen dyn*.

Pendour Cove (SW 4438): 'foot of a stream', C. *ben dowr* + E. 'cove'.

Pendower Cove (SW 3622): *Porpendore* 1700, 'stream's foot cove', C. *porth ben-dowr*.

Pendrea (SW 4025): 'principal farm', C. *pen-dre*.

Pen Enys Point (SW 4941): 'isolated/remote headland', C. *pen enys* (there is no appreciable island, also *enys*, here).

Penhale (SW 4232): 'top of a marsh', C. *pen-hal*.

Penlee Point (SW 4726): *Penlegh* 1359, 'slab/ledge head(land)', C. *pen legh*.

Pennance (SW 4437): 'end of a valley', C. *pen-nans*.

Pennance (SW 5940): 'head of a valley', C. *pen-nans*.

Penolva (SW 4627): *Penwolva* 1352, 'lookout head(land)', C. *pen golva*.

Penrose (SW 3725): 'end of a hillspur', C. *pen-ros*.

Penzance (SW 4730): 'holy/sacred head(land)', C. *pen sans*.

Penzer Point (SW 4624): 'steep head(land)', C. *pen serth*.

Perran Sands (SW 5429): *Porth Perane* 1580, 'St Peran's cove/landing place', C. *porth Peran* (see **Perranuthnoe**).

Perranuthnoe (SW 5329): 'St Peran in the manor of Uthno'. The manor name *Odenal* 1086, *Hutheno* 1235, is of unknown meaning but may contain C. *hueth*, 'happy, pleasant'.

Phillack (SW 5638), after the church saint Felec. An alternative C. name, still current in C19, was *Egglosheil* c1170, 'church on the Hayle estuary', C. *eglos Heyl* (see **Hayle**).

Plain-an-Gwarry (SW 5331): 'arena, amphitheatre', C. *plen an gwary*.

Pleming (SW 4931): *Plemmen* 1386, 'plum tree', C. *plumen*.

Polgigga (SW 3723): *Pensiger* 1327, 'head of a stream called Syger ('lazy one')', C. *pen Syger*.

Polhigey (SW 4835): 'ducks' pool', C. *pol heyjy*.

Polkinghorne (SW 4732): 'Cynhoern's pool', C. *pol Kynhorn*.

Polkinghorne (SW 5937): 'Cynhoern's pool', *pol Kynhorn*.

Polmanter (SW 5038): *Porthmanter* 1298, C. *porth*, 'gate' + lost place name *Mentyr*, "stone-land', C.*men-tyr*.

Polpeor (SW 5136): 'clean pool', C. *pol pur.*

Polpry Cove (SW 3530): 'clay/earth pit', C. *pol pry.*

Poniou (SW 4438): 'bridges', C. *ponjow.*

Ponsandane (SW 4731): 'Endean's bridge', C. *pons,* 'bridge' + C. surname *Endean* from C. *an den,* 'the man'.

Pontshallow (SW 4333): 'marshes bridge', C. *pons hallow.*

Pordenack Point (SW 3424): *Poynt Pendenack* 1580, 'fortified head(land)', C. *pen dynek* + addition of E. 'point'.

Porn Boe (SW 4624): 'the buck's cove', C. *porth an bogh.*

Porth Chapel (SW 3821): now 'chapel cove', C. *porth chapel* but formerly *Porth Sellevan* 1580, 'St Selevan's cove', C. *porth Selevan.*

Porthcollum (SW 5533): *Polkellom* 1317, 'shelterless pool', C. *pol kel-lom.*

Porthcurno (SW 3822): *Porth Cornow* 1580, 'cove of horns/pinnacles', C. *porth cornow,* from surrounding rock formations. The name *Kernow,* 'Cornwall' is not involved in this name.

Portheras Cove (SW 3835): *Portheres* 1317, 'ploughland cove', C. *porth erys.*

Porthguarnon (SW 4123): 'alder-tree cove', C. *porth gwernen.*

Porthgwarra (SW 3731): *Porthgorwithou* 1302, 'cove by wooded slopes', C. *porth gorwedhow.* The present form, resembling C. *porth gwartha,* 'higher cove', is merely a corruption of the original.

Porthgwidden (SW 5241): 'white/fair cove', C. *porth gwyn* (LC *gwidn*).

Porth Kidney (SW 5438): *Polkemyas* 1580, *Porthkidny* 1725, 'cove of leave-taking', C. *porth cumyas* (LC *kibmias*).

Porthledden (SW 3532): 'wide cove', C. *porth ledan.* It was also called *Porth Caniack* 1699, 'cove/landing place at Kenidjack', C. *porth Cunyjak.*

Porth Loe (SW 3621): 'cove in a deep inlet', C. *porth logh.*

Porthmeor (SW 42/4337): 'great cove/landing place', C. *porth muer.*

Porthmeor Beach (SW 5140): *Porthmeer* 1826, 'great cove/landing place', C. *porth muer.*

Porthminster (SW 5240): 'cove of an endowed church', C. *porth mynster.*

Porth Nanven (SW 3530): *Porthangwin* 1396, 'Angwin's cove', C. *porth,* 'cove, landing place' + C. surname *Angwin* ('fair-haired man').

Porthzennor Cove (SW 4539): 'cove/landing place at Zennor', C. *porth Senar* + unnecessary addition of E. 'cove'.

Pridden (SW 4126): *Penryn* 1363, 'hillspur', C. *pen-ryn* (LC *pen-ridn*).

Priest's Cove (SW 3531): Anglicised form of *Porthuste* 1396, 'cove/landing place at St Just', C. *porth Ust.*

Progo (SW 3530): 'cove with a cave', C. *porth ogo.* Sadly, the natural arch that accounted for this name collapsed in 1998.

Prussia Cove (SW 5528): E., after the C18 arch-smuggler John Carter, nicknamed 'the King of Prussia'. Its true name was *Portlegh* 1345, 'slab/ledge cove', C. *porth legh.*

Pulsack (SW 5839): *Polsulsek* 1334, 'Sulleisoc's pool', C. *pol Sulsek.*

Raftra (SW 3723): *Raghtre* 1302, 'facing a farm', C. *rag-tre*.
Raginnis (SW 4625): *Ragenys* 1340, 'facing an island', C. *rag-enys*.
Reawla (SW 6036): *Reaulu* 1455, 'royal place', MF. *reial leu*.
Receven (SW 4132): *Resseuen* 1481, 'yew ford', C. *res ewen*.
Red River (Towednack to Mount's Bay): now E. 'red river' but stated to have been the *Lid* 1580 by an external writer. This would be OE *hlyde*, 'torrent' but Dr Borlase c1750 was adamant that this name was not known locally. The C. name is preserved by the collection of place names on its upper course with a prefix in *Amal-*, 'edge, boundary, slope', C. *amal* (compare the river **Amble**, North Cornwall).
Red River (Redruth to Gwithian): now E. 'red river' which, like its namesake above, derives from former discoloration due to intensive tin mining on its upper course. Its C. name was *Dour Conor* c1540, 'fury water', C. *dowr connar*.
Rejarne (SW 5235): *Rosenhoern* 1317, C. *rosyn*, 'little hillspur' + C. *horn*, iron' or Celtic personal name *Hoern*.
Relistian (SW 6036): *Rysclystyn* 1342, C. *res*, 'ford' + unknown word or name.
Relubbus (SW 5631): *Reslehoubes* c1250, 'Lehoubed's ford', C. *res Lehoubes*.
Retallack (SW 5631): *Restalek* 1311, 'Taloc's ford' or 'roach ford', C. *res talek*.
Rissick (SW 3936): *Resegh* 1312, 'dry ford', C. *res segh*.
Roseangrouse (SW 5335): *Reysangrous* 1520, 'watercourse at the cross', C. *reys an grows*.
Rosecadghill (SW 4630): *Roscaswal* 1316, 'Cadwal's roughland', C. *ros Caswal*.
Rosemergy (SW 4136): 'roughland with stables', C. *ros merghjy*.
Rosemodress (SW 4423): 'Modret's roughland', C. *ros Modres*.
Rosemorran (SW 4732): *Rosmoren* 1227, C. *ros*, 'hillspur' + either *moren*, 'berry' or Celtic personal name *Moren*.
Rosevidney (SW 5334): *Rosevynny* 1306, 'roughland with moorgrass', C. *ros fynny* (LC *fydny*).
Rosewall (SW 4939): *Ryswal* 1327, 'ford by a wall', C. *res wal*.
Rosewarne (SW 6136): 'roughland with alder trees', C. *ros (g)wern*.
Roseworthy (SW 6139): *Reswori* 1289, 'Gorhi's ford', C. *res Wory*.
Roskennals (SW 4230): *Resconwals* 1372, 'Cynval's ford', C. *res Kenwal*.
Roskestal (SW 3722): 'castle roughland', C. *ros castel*.
Roskilly (SW 4727): 'coastal slope with a grove', C. *ros kelly*.
Rospannel (SW 3926): 'roughland with broom plants', C. *ros panadhel* (frequently shortened to *panal*).
Rospeath (SW 5232): *Rospygh* 1391, 'little hillspur', C. *ros pygh*.
Rospletha (SW 3822): *Rosplethe* 1278, 'wolf's roughland', C. *ros pleydh*.
Rosudgeon (SW 5631): 'ox's roughland', C. *ros ojyon*.
Sancreed (SW 4229): *Eglus-sans* 1289, 'holy church' or 'Sant's church', C. *eglos sans*; later *Egglossan(c)res* 1443, 'St Sancret's church', C. *eglos Sancres*. The church saint is Sancret and not, as some would have it, Credan.

Sellan (SW 4230): *Seghlan* 1361, apparently 'dry enclosure', C. *segh-lan*.

Sennen (SW 3525): *Senan* 1480, after St Senan, arguably a female saint.

Sennen Cove (SW 3526): *Porth Gone Hollye*, *Gonhellye under Meen* (Mayon) 1580, 'cove/landing place serving **Ganilly** (Isles of Scilly)', C. *porth Gunhyly*.

Sheffield (SW 4526): *Sheffield Terrace* 1841, C19 E. after a group of Yorkshire quarrymen.

Silena (SW 4023): *Sulghene* 1291, *Sulghenegh* 1321, a name that has so far eluded all attempts to translate it.

Skewjack (SW 3624): *Skewyek* 1329, 'place of elder trees', C. *skewyek*.

Sparnon (SW 3924): 'thorn bush', C. *spernen*.

Sperris Croft (SW 4738): *Croft Speris* 1838, 'ghost's enclosed rough pasture', C. *croft sperys*.

Splattenridden (SW 5336): 'the bracken plot', C. *splat an reden*.

Stennack (SW 5140): 'tin-streaming works', C. *stenak*.

Street-an-Nowan (SW 4628): 'street of the river', C. *stret an awan*.

Taskus (SW 5835): *Talscus* 1317, 'hillbrow providing shade', C. *tal scues*.

Tater Du (SW 4423): *Tortell Dewe* 1580, 'black loaf', C. *torthel du*.

Tolcarne (SW 4629): *Talcarn* 1316, 'brow tor', C. *tal-carn*.

Tol Pedn Penwith (SW 3621): 'Penwith's hole-headland' (referring to the great funnel hole in the cliff), C. *toll-pen* (LC *toll-pedn*) *Penwyth*.

Tol Plous (SW 3622): 'filthy hole', C. *toll plos*.

Tolver (SW 4932): *Talvargh* 1284, 'horse's (or Meirch's) hillbrow', C. *tal vargh*.

Towednack (SW 4838): *Tewynnoc* 1335, 'thy St Winnoc', C. *te Wynnek* (LC *Wednak*), a pet form of the saint's name *Winwalo* (see **Landewednack**, Kerrier).

Trannack (SW 4130): *Trevranek* 1302, 'Branoc's farm', C. *tre Vranek*.

Trannack (SW 4731): *Trewethenec* 1342, 'Guethenoc's farm', C.*tre Wedhenek*.

Trannack (SW 5633): *Trevranek* 1325, 'Branoc's farm', C. *tre Vranek*.

Treassowe (SW 4933): *Trevrasowe* 1422, 'Brasou's farm', C. *tre Vrasow*.

Treave (SW 3827): *Treyuff* 1302, 'Yuf's farm', C. *tre Yuf*.

Trebehor (SW 3724): *Trebuer* 1284, 'cow-yard farm', C. *tre buorth* (with common dropping of final *–th*).

Tredavoe (SW 4538): *Treworthavo* 1328, 'Gorthafo's farm', C. *tre Worthavo*.

Tredinneck (SW 4434): *Tredenek* 1457, 'fern-brake farm', C. *tre redenek*.

Treen (SW 3923): *Trethyn* 1284, 'farm by a fort', C. *tre dhyn*.

Treen (SW 4337): *Trethyn* 1314, 'farm by a fort', C. *tre dhyn* (both this and **Treen** above lie close to famous Iron Age cliff castles).

Treeve (SW 3525): *Treyuf* 1334, 'Yuf's farm', C. *tre Yuf*.

Tregadgwith (SW 4225): 'farm by a thicket', C. *tre gajwydh*.

Tregaminion (SW 4035): *Tregemynyon* 1327, 'commoners' farm', C. *tre gemynyon*.

Treganhoe (SW 4229): *Tregenhogh* 1504, 'Cynhoch's farm', C. *tre Genhogh*.

Tregarthen (SW 4932): *Tregeuvran* 1262, 'Gafran's farm', C. *tre Gavran*.

Tregavarah (SW 4429): *Tregouvoro* 1316, *Govarrowe* 1628, 'farm by streams', C. *tre goverow*.

Tregembo (SW 5731): *Trethygember* 1321, 'farm by a double confluence', C. *tre dhy-gemper*.

Tregender (SW 5134): *Tregeneder* 1284, 'Cynheder's farm', C. *tre Geneder*.

Tregenhorne (SW 5634): 'Cynhoern's farm', C. *tre Gynhorn*.

Tregenna (SW 5139): 'Ceneu's farm', C. *tre Genow*.

Tregerest (SW 4032): 'Cerest's farm', C. *tre Gerest*.

Tregerthen (SW 4639): *Tregyrthyn* 1519, 'rowan-trees farm', C. *tre gerdhyn*.

Tregeseal (SW 3731): *Tregathihael* 1284, 'Catihael's farm', C. *tre Gathyel*.

Tregiffian (SW 3627): *Tregivyen* 1327, 'tree-stumps farm', C. *tre gyfyon*.

Tregiffian (SW 4323): *Tregguhion* 1331, 'wasp-infested farm', C. *tre guhyen*.

Tregilliowe (SW 5332): 'groves farm', C. *tre gellyow*.

Treglisson (SW 5836): *Treglistyn* 1326, C. *tre*, 'farm, settlement' + unknown word or name.

Tregonebris (SW 4128): *Tregenhebris* 1342, 'Conhibrit's farm', C. *tre Genebrys*.

Tregurtha (SW 5331): *Tregurthan* 1358, 'rowan-trees farm', C. *tre gerdhyn*.

Trelew (SW 4227): *Treliw* 1291, C. *tre*, 'farm, settlement' + apparently C. *lyw*, 'colour', rather than personal name *Leu*.

Trelissick (SW 5436): *Treweleseкwarheil* 1356, 'Trelissick on the Hayle river', C. *Trewolesyk war'n Heyl*. Trelissick is 'Woledic's farm', C. *tre Wolesyk*.

Trembath (SW 4429): *Trenbagh* 1327, 'farm in a corner' (it lies in the sharp bend of a valley), C. *tre'n bagh*.

Trembethow (SW 5035): 'farm at the graves', C. *tre'n bedhow*.

Tremeader/Tremedda (SW 4638): *Trevemeder* 1269, 'Emeder's farm', C. *tref Emeder*.

Tremelling (SW 5534): *Tremelyn* 1327, 'mill farm', C. *tre melyn*.

Tremenheere (SW 4833): 'standing stone farm', C. *tre menhyr*.

Tremethick (SW 4430): 'physician's farm', C. *tre medhek*.

Trencrom (SW 5136): *Trencrom* 1333, *Trecrobum* 1696, 'farm at the curve/hunch (of a hill)', C. *tre'n crom* (LC *crobm*).

Trencrom Hill (SW 5136): *Torcrobm* 1758, 'hunched bulge (*tor* is literally 'belly')', C. *tor crom* (LC *crobm*).

Trendrennen (SW 3823): 'farm at the thorn bush', C. *tre'n dreynen*.

Trendrine (SW 4739): *Trendreyn* 1302, 'farm at the thorns', C. *tre'n dreyn*.

Trendrine Hill (SW 4738): *Carnminnis* 1700, 'little tor', C. *carn munys*.

Treneere (SW 4631): *Trenyer* 1280, 'the hens' farm', C. *tre'n yer*.

Trengothal (SW 3724): 'farm at the thicket', C. *tre'n godhel*.

Trengwainton (SW 4431): *Trethigwaynton* 1309, C. *tre*, 'farm, settlement' + *dhy* (an intensive prefix) + *gwaynten* 'springtime', perhaps 'farm of everlasting spring'.

Trenhayle (SW 5635): *Trewarneil* 1302, 'farm on the Hayle river', C. *tre war'n Heyl*.

Trenowin (SW 4835): *Treneuwyn* 1300, 'trough farm', C. *tre newyn*.

Trenuggo (SW 4227): *Trewarnogou* 1336, 'farm on the cave', C. *tre war'n ogo*. The cave, now buried, was used as a dairy store as late as C19.

Trereife (SW 4529): *Treruf* 1226, 'king's farm', C. *tre ruyf* (although *ruyf* may also be a personal name).

Trerice (SW 4229): *Treres* 1359, 'farm at a ford', C. *tre res*.

Treryn Dinas (SW 3922): *Castle of Trethyn* 1478, 'castle at Treen', C. *castel Tredhyn* (see **Treen**). The name now contains C. *dynas*, 'fort'.

Tresvennack (SW 4428): *Tressevenek* 1302, 'Sefinoc's farm', C. *tre Sevenek*.

Trethewey (SW 3823): 'Dewi's farm', C. *tre Dhewy*.

Trethingey (SW 5736): *Trethinegy* 1259, 'farm by fortified places', C. *tre dhynegy*.

Trevail/Treveal (SW 4740): 'Mael's farm', C. *tre Vayl*.

Trevalgan (SW 4940): 'Maelgon's farm', C. *tre Valgon*.

Trevarnon (SW 5940): *Treveranon* 1370, 'Meranon's farm', C. *tre Veranon*.

Trevarrack (SW 5137): *Trevorek* 1284, 'Moroc's farm', C. *tre Vorek*.

Trevaylor (SW 4632): *Treveller* 1245, 'Melor's farm', C. *tre Velor*.

Trevean (SW 4228): 'little farm', C. *tre vyan*.

Trevean (SW 4332): 'little farm', C. *tre vyan*.

Trevear (SW 3726): 'great farm', C. *tre vuer*.

Trevedra (SW 3627): *Treverdreth, Trewardraght* 1668, 'farm on a beach', C. *tre war dreth*.

Trevedran (SW 4123): *Trewydren* 1284, 'Guitren's farm', C. *tre Wydren*.

Trevega/Trevessa (SW 4839): *Trevysa* 1507, 'lowest farm', C. *tref ysa*.

Treveneague (SW 5432): *Trevanahek* 1356, 'monastic farm', C. *tre vanahek*. The farm was once owned by the priory of St Michael's Mount.

Treverven (SW 4123): *Treverwyn* 1380, 'Berwyn's farm', C. *tre Verwyn*.

Trevescan (SW 3524): *Trefescan* 1302, 'sedge farm', C. *tref hesken*.

Trevethoe (SW 5336): 'farm by graves', C. *tre vedhow*.

Trevider (SW 4326): *Trevehether* 1500, 'Gorheder's farm', C. *tre Worhedher*.

Trevilley (SW 3524): Beli's farm', C. *tre Vely*.

Trevithal (SW 4626): *Trevethegal* 1315, 'farm with a surgery', C. *tre vedhegel*.

Trevorgans (SW 4025): *Treworgans* 1356, 'Uuorcant's farm', C. *tre Worgans*.

Trevorian (SW 3726): *Treveryan* 1296, 'Beriana's farm', C. *tre Veryan*.

Trevorian (SW 4228): *Treverthion* 1384, 'Meirchyon's farm', C. *tre Verghyon*.

Trevorrian (SW 4226): *Treworyan* 1323, 'Uuorien's farm', C. *tre Woryan*.

Trevorrow (SW 5233): *Treworveu* 1299, 'Gorfeu's farm', C. *tre Worvow*.

Trevowhan (SW 4035): *Treveuan* 1283, 'Euan's farm', C. *tref Ewan*.

Trewarveneth (SW 4627): 'farm on a hillside', C. *tre war venedh*.

Trewellard (SW 3733): *Trewylard* 1327, 'Guilart's farm', C. *tre Wylard*.

Trewern (SW 4232): *Treyouran* 1302, 'Youran's farm', C. *tre Youran*.

Trewey (SW 4538): *Trethewy* 1314, 'Dewi's farm', C. *tre Dhewy*.

Trewhella (SW 5532): *Trewhyla* 1357, 'beetle-infested farm', C. *tre whyl-a*.

Trewidden (SW 4429): 'white/fair farm', C. *tre wyn* (LC *widn*).

Trewinnard (SW 5434): *Trewynard* 1319, 'Guinart's farm', C. *tre Wynard*.

Trewoofe (SW 4325): *Trewoyf* 1302, 'winter farm', OC *tre woyf*. A rare survival of Old Cornish so far west.

Trezelah (SW 4733): 'farm in a waterless place (i.e remote from the nearest water supply)', C. *tre segh-la*.

Trink (SW 5137): *Trefrynk* 1333, 'Frenchman's/freeman's farm', C. *tre frynk*.

Trowan (SW 4940): *Trevowan* 1327, 'oxen farm', C. *tref ohen*.

Trungle (SW 4627): *Trevonglet* 1283, 'farm by an open-cast mine', C. *tre vongledh*.

Truthwall (SW 3632): *Trewothwall* 1495, 'Gudual's farm', C. *tre Wodhwal*.

Truthwall (SW 5232): *Treuthal* 1086, 'Iudhael's farm', C. *tre Yudhal*.

Trye (SW 4535): *Trevry* 1325, C. *tre*, 'farm, settlement' + either Celtic personal name *Fri*, or C. *fry*, 'nose, hillspur'.

Trythall (SW 4433): *Trewreythel* 1289, 'farm where root-crops grow', C. *tre (g)wreydh-yel*.

Varfell (SW 5032): *Varwell* 1568, after the C16 Varwell family.

Vellandreath (SW 3626): 'beach mill', C. *melyn dreth*.

Vellandruchia (SW 4226): *Mellintrucke* 1652, 'tucking/fulling mill', C.*melyn drokkya*.

Vellanoweth (SW 5033): *Melynnoweth* 1520, 'new mill', C. *melyn noweth*.

Vellansagia (SW 4225): *Melyn Saya* 1590, 'sifting mill', C. *melyn saya*.

Ventonleague (SW 5738): 'slab well/spring', C. *fenten legh*.

Venton Vision (SW 5040): 'acorn well/spring', C. *fenten vesen*.

Venwyn (SW 5137): *Menven* 1327, *Venwin* 1659, apparently 'white stone', C. *men wyn*.

Vorvas/Worvas (SW 5138): *Gorvos* 1258, 'high dwelling', C. *gor-vos*.

Watch Croft (SW 4235): now E. 'watch' + C. *croft* 'enclosed rough grazing', from the hill's use as a Napoleonic Wars lookout. Formerly *Carnonbigh* 1584, *Carn an Vyth* 1752, 'little cairn', C. *carnen bygh*.

Westway (SW 5137), *Westva* 1659, 'lodging house', C. *gwestva*.

Wheal Bal (SW 3533): *Whele an Bal* 1780, 'mine workings at the diggings', C. *whel an bal*.

Wheal Buller (SW 4031): C. *whel*, 'mine workings' + family name, from a short-lived C19 mining venture. Formerly *Goonevas* 1841, 'shieling downs', C. *gun havos*.

Wheal Owles (SW 3632): 'cliff mine', C. *whel als*.

Wheal Reeth (SW 5036): 'red mine', C. *whel rudh*.

Wherry Town (SW 4629), E. 'wherry town', after a type of small working boat.

Whitesand Bay (SW 3527): E, 'white-sand bay' since C16 (*Whitsande Bay* 1582); formerly *Porthsenan* 1370, 'cove/landing place at Sennen', C. *porth Senan* (also see **Sennen Cove**).

Wicca (SW 4739) *Wicke* 1545, named after the de Wyket (1327)/de Wykke (1420) family whose name derives from an OE place name *wic*, 'farmstead, dairy farm', possibly **Week St Mary**, North Cornwall.

Wolf Rock (SW 2611): *The gulfe* 1588, possibly 'the beak', C.*an gelf*, otherwise E. 'gulf'.

Woon Gumpus (SW 3833): *Nun Compez* 1782, 'the level downs', C. *an wun gompes.*

Wra, The/Three Stone Oar (SW 3836): *Guyahore* (for *Enys Hore*) 1580, 'ram island', C. *enys hordh.*

Zawn a Bal (SW 3633): 'cliff-chasm at the mine', C. *sawan an bal.*

Zawn Brinny (SW 3634): 'crows' cliff-chasm', C. *sawan bryny.*

Zawn Bros (SW 4740): 'great cliff-chasm', C. *sawan bras.*

Zawn Gamper (SW 4323): 'cliff-chasm where currents meet', C. *sawan gemper.*

Zawn Kellys (SW 3522): 'hidden cliff-chasm', C. *sawan kelys.*

Zawn Organ (SW 4624): 'pennyroyal cliff-chasm', C. *sawan orgel.*

Zawn Peggy (SW 3523): 'cliff-chasm by pointed rocks', C. *sawan pygow.*

Zawn Pyg (SW 3523): 'point(ed) cliff-chasm', C. *sawan pyg.*

Zawn Reeth (SW 3523): now 'red cliff-chasm', C. *sawan rudh*; formerly *Savan Marake* 1580, 'horseman's cliff-chasm', C. *sawan marhak* (a pinnacle within the zawn is still called 'Diamond Horse')

Zawn Wells (SW 3424): 'cliff-chasm with grass', C. *sawan (g)wels.*

Zennor (SW 4538): *Senar* c1509, *Eglos Senor* 1869, 'St Senara's church', C. *eglos Senar.* St Senara might have been Azenor of Brittany, mother of St Budoc.

Zennor Hill (SW 4638): now E. 'hill at Zennor'; formerly *Carne Marrack* 1822, 'horseman's tor', C. *carn marhak.*

Penwith: Signpost at Drift

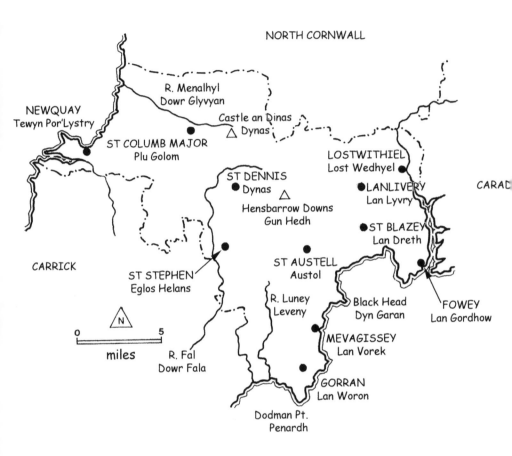

NORTH CORNWALL

R. Menalhyl
Dowr Glyvyan

NEWQUAY
Tewyn Por'Lystry

Castle an Dinas
△ Dynas

ST COLUMB MAJOR
Plu Golom

LOSTWITHIEL
Lost Wedhyel

ST DENNIS
Dynas
△

●LANLIVERY
Lan Lyvry

CARAD

Hensbarrow Downs
Gun Hedh

●ST BLAZEY
Lan Dreth

CARRICK

ST STEPHEN
Eglos Helans

ST AUSTELL
Austol

R. Luney
Leveny

Black Head
Dyn Garan

FOWEY
Lan Gordhow

N

0   5

MEVAGISSEY
Lan Vorek

miles   R. Fal
Dowr Fala

GORRAN
Lan Woron

Dodman Pt.
Penardh

Borough of RESTORMEL
Burjestra ROSTORMOL

Place Names of the Borough of RESTORMEL

Henwyn Plasow an Burjestra
Rostormel

Arrallas (SW 8853): *Arganlis* 1086, 'silver court', OC. *arhant-lys*.

St Austell (SX 0152): *Austol* c1150, after St Austol.

St Austell River: in addition to the present name, E. 'river at St Austell', this has no less than three alternative names: Clissey, 'sticky, clinging', C. *clyjy*; Winnick, 'the little white one', C. *an wynnyk*; and Gover, 'stream', C. *gover*.

Bargoes (SX 0361): *Crukbargos* 1424, 'buzzard's barrow/tumulus', C. *crug bargos*.

Belowda (SW 9661): *Boloude* c1240, *Bolowsa* 1503, 'Louda's dwelling', C. *bos Lowsa*.

Benallack (SW 9249): *Benathelek* 1244, 'broom-brake', C. *banadhlek*.

Benhurden (SW 9942): *Benhordon* 1329, apparently 'foot of a ram-fort', C. *ben hor'dhyn*.

Berryl's Point (SW 8467): E. 'Burrell's head(land)' after a local family.

Bethel (SX 0353): C18/19 Biblical name from a Methodist chapel.

Bilberry (SX 0160): *Billebery* c1280, 'Billa's barrow/tumulus', OE *Billa beorg*.

Biscovey (SX 0553): *Bosconevey* 1201, 'Cunefei's dwelling', C. *bos Conevey*.

Biscovillack (SW 9954): *Boscovelec* 1306, 'Cofelec's dwelling', C. *bos Covelek*.

Black Head (SX 0447): *Blak-hed* c1540, E. 'black head(land)'. Place name evidence indicates that the Iron Age cliff castle here was **Dyngaran*, 'crane's/heron's fort', C. *dyn garan* (see **Trenarren**).

St Blazey (SX 0654): after St Blaise. The C. name was *Landrethe* 1369, 'church enclosure at a beach/ferry', C. *lan dreth*.

Bodardle (SX 0960): *Bodardel* 1284, 'high-stream dwelling', OC *bod ard-el*.

Bodelva (SX 0554): *Bodelwyth* 1327, 'dwelling by elm trees', OC *bod elwedh* (with common dropping of final *–th, -dh*).

Bodinnick (SW 9552): *Bodythenec* 1281, 'furzy dwelling', OC *bod eythynek*.

Bodrugan (SX 0143): *Bodrygan* 1329, 'Rigan's dwelling', OC *bod Rygan* (the OC form *bod*, later *bos*, is usually retained before an initial R, even into West Cornwall – see **Bodrifty**, Penwith).

Bodwen (SX 0660): *Boswyn* 1296, 'white/fair dwelling', or 'Gwyn's dwelling', C. *bos wyn*.

Bogee (SW 9069): *Bosyuf* 1340, 'Yuf's dwelling', C. *bos Yuf*.

Bojea (SX 0154): *Bosyuf* 1340, 'Yuf's dwelling', C. *bos Yuf*.

Bolingey (SW 8866): *Melyndy* 1216, 'mill house', C. *melynjy*.

Borlase (SW 9566): *Borlas* 1290, 'green hummock', C. *bor las*.

Borlasevath (SW 9466): *Borlas Margh* 1335, 'Meirch's (or 'horse's') **Borlase**', C. *Borlas vargh*.

Boscoppa (SW 0453): *Boscoppe* 1284, 'Coppe's dwelling', C. *bos Coppa*.

Boscundle (SX 0453): *Botconwall* 1201, 'Cynval's dwelling', C. *bos Kenwal*.

Bosinver (SW 9951): *Bosgenver* 1327, 'Cynvor's dwelling', C. *bos Genvor*.

Bosithow (SW 9952): *Bosithiow* 1523, 'dwelling of ivy plants', C. *bos ydhyow*.

Bosoughan (SW 8760): *Boshoghan* 1311, 'piglet's dwelling', C. *bos hoghen*.

Bospolvans (SW 9063): *Bospalven* 1371, 'dwelling at a pillar-stone', C. *bos puel-ven*.

Bosue (SW 9847): *Boshu* 1290, *Boshugh* 1319, 'Huw's dwelling', C. *bos Huw*.

Boswinger (SW 9941): *Boswengar* 1301, 'Uuencar's dwelling', C. *bos Wengar*.

Bosworgey (SW 9063): *Bosworgy* 1327, 'Wurci's dwelling', C. *bos Worgy*.

Brannel (SW 9551): *Bernel* 1086, *Branel* 1201, 'place of hills', C. *bron-el*.

Breney (SX 0660): *Brenou* 1327, 'hills', C. *bronow, brenow*.

Brownqueen (SX 1062): *Brounkun* 1334, 'dogs' hill', C. *bron cuen*.

Brynn (SX 9862): *Bren* 1244, 'hill', C. *bren*.

Bugle (SX 0158): C19 E. 'bugle' from the name of an inn built c1840.

Burgotha (SW 9255): *Bargoythou* 1327, 'top of streams', C. *bar godhow*.

Burngullow (SW 9852): *Brongolou* 1296, *Bronwolou* 1311, 'hill of light', C. *bron wolow*.

Cadythew Rock (SX 0140): *Carn-due* 1584, *Carrack Due* 1699, originally 'black/dark crag', C. *carn du*; then 'black/dark rock, C. *carrek du*.

Caerhayes (SW 9741): *Karihaes* 1259, *Carihays* 1379, seemingly C. *ker/cayr*, 'fort, enclosed farm' + unknown name or word. This name appears to be parallel to Carhaix, Brittany, which also currently defies translation.

Cannis Rocks (SX 1049): *Canis* 1699, 'white place', C. *can-ys*.

Carbean (SX 0056): *Carnbyan* 1356, 'little tor', C. *carn byan*.

Carbis (SW 9959): *Carbons* 1303, 'paved road, causeway', C. *car-bons* (literally 'cart-bridge').

Carclaze (SX 0254): *Cruklas* c1500, 'green barrow/tumulus', C. *crug las*.

Carhurles (SX 1054): C. *ker/cayr*, 'fort, enclosed farm' + unknown word or name.

Carloggas (SW 8765): *Cruclogas* 1284, 'barrow/tumulus of mice', C. *crug logos*.

Carloggas (SW 9063): *Kaerlogoos* c1320, 'fort of mice', C. *ker/cayr logos*.

Carloggas (SW 9554): *Cruglogos* 1282, 'barrow/tumulus of mice', C. *crug logos*.

Carluddon (SX 0255): *Crucledan* 1364, 'wide barrow/tumulus', C. *crug ledan*.

Carnanton (SW 8764): *Carnetone* 1086, C. *carn*, 'tor' + addition of OE *tun*, 'farm, settlement'.

Carne (SW 9558): 'tor', C. *carn*.

Carnsmerry (SX 0158): *Carne Rosemerry* 1660, 'tor at **Rosevear**', C. *carn Rosvuer*.

Carpalla (SW 9654): *Carnpalla* 1336, C. *carn*, 'tor' + unknown word or name.

Carrancarrow (SW 9955): *Nanskerou* 1366, perhaps 'stag's valley', C. *nans carow*, this name being preceded by *Caven-* (meaning unknown) in 1522.

Carrickowel Point (SX 0350): *Carrick Owl Rock* c1810, 'weather rock', C. *carrek awel.*

Carruggatt (SX 0857): *Carhulgat* c1170, 'high-wood fort', OC *ker/cayr uhel-guyt.*

Carthew (SX 0055): *Cartheu* 1201, 'black/dark fort', C. *ker/cayr dhu.*

Carvinick (SX 0041): *Carveynek* 1333, 'stony fort', C. *ker/cayr veynek.*

Castilly (SX 0362): 'castles', C. *castylly.*

Castle-an-Dinas (SW 9462): *Dynas* 1345, *Castle of Dynas* 1478, 'fort', C. *dynas*, with later additions: E. 'castle of', then C. *castel an*, 'castel of/at the' forming a somewhat tautologous name.

Castle Dore (SX 1054): *Castledour* 1540, 'earthen castle', C. *castel dor.*

Castle Gotha (SX 0249): *Castelgothou* 1338, the site suggests 'castle of geese', rather than 'castle of streams', both C. *castel godhow.*

Chapel Point (SX 0243): E. 'chapel point (headland)' since at least C16 but an undated C. name *Goelhofna* may be a corrupt form of C. *golowva*, 'beacon'.

Charlestown (SX 0351): now E. 'Charles's town', after Charles Rashleigh (C18); formerly *Portmoer* 1354, *Polmere* 1584, 'great cove/landing place', C. *porth muer.*

Cheesewarne (SX 0045): *Chisorne* 1588, 'house at a nook', C. *chy sorn.*

Chegwins (SW 9654): 'wind(y) house', C. *chy gwyns.*

Chytane (SW 9155): *Tywarton* 1296, *Chyton* 1543, 'house on pastureland', C. *chy war ton.*

Cleers (SW 9758): *Clehar* 1518, possibly C. *clegar*, 'crag'.

Colan (SW 8661): after St Colan. The C. name was *Plewe-Golen* 1501, 'St Colan's parish', C. *plu Golan.*

Coldvreath (SW 9858): *Kellyvregh* 1281, 'dappled grove', C. *kelly vregh.*

Colona Beach (SX 0243): E. 'beach at Colona'. Colona, *Caerlaenou* 1329, is 'fort at strip fields', C. *ker/cayr leynow.*

St Columb Major (SW 9163): *S. Columba majore* 1339, Lat. 'greater St Columb'. The C. name was *Plewgolom* 1543, 'parish of St Columb', C. *plu Golom.* St Columb(a) was perceived to be a female saint.

St Columb Minor (SW 8362): *S. Columbe minor* 1284, Lat. 'lesser St Columb'. *Colom* 1742, represents the C. form of the name.

St Columb Porth (SW 8362): now 'St Columb's cove/landing place' (with C. *porth*) in E. word order. The C. name was *Porbyhan* 1284, 'little cove/landing place', C. *porth byan.* A further name was *Por Pennalls* 1699, 'cove at Penalls ('end of a cliff ', C. *pen als*).

St Columb Road (SW 8159): C19 E. 'road to St Columb', given after construction of railway station.

Colvithick (SX 1253): *Colvethicke* 1613, 'place of hazel trees', C. *collwedhek.*

Conce (SX 0362): *Cawnce* 1613, 'paved road, causeway', C. *cauns.*

Coombe (SW 9551): 'valley', OE *cumb* (borrowed from C. *com*/W. *cwm*).

Corgee (SX 0460): *Corngae* 1279, 'corner of a hedge', C. *corn ge.*

Cornakee (SX 0559): 'crane's stream', OE *cornuc ea.*

Coswarth (SW 8659): *Gudiford* 1086, *Cudyford* 1340, *Coswarthe* 1561, the present name is a Cornucised form of the original which seems to be 'Coda's ford', OE *coda ford*.

Cotna (SX 0042): *Cruckonnar* 1289, 'Conor's barrow/tumulus', C. *crug Conor*.

Crantock (SW 7960): *Seyntkarantoc* 1373, after St Carantoc. The C. name of the churchtown was *Langorroc* 1086, 'St Correc's church enclosure', C. *lan Gorrek*, Correc being a pet form of Carantoc.

Creak-a-Vose (SW 9353): *Crucgkeyrvos* 1346, 'barrow/tumulus at a fort rampart', C. *crug ker-fos/cayr-fos*.

Creed (SW 9347): after St Crida.

Crift (SX 0659): *Croft* 1609, 'enclosed rough grazing', C. *croft*.

Criggan (SX 0160): *Crugan* 1533, 'little barrow/tumulus', C. *crugyn*.

Crinnis (SX 0552): *Caryones* 1477, uncertain derivation, perhaps C. *ker/cayr*, 'fort, enclosed farm' + an archaic plural of C. *on*, 'lamb'.

Cuddra (SX 0452): *Crukdur* 1299, 'earthen barrow/tumulus', C. *crug dor*.

Currian Vale (SW 9656): now E. 'vale at Currian' but *Venton Currian* 1695, perhaps 'traders' well/spring', C. *fenten wycoryan*.

Demelza (SW 9763): *Dynmaelda* 1309, 'Maelda's fort', C. *dyn Malsa*.

St Dennis (SW 9557): not named after St Dionysius or St Denis, but C. *dynas*, 'fort', the churchyard preserving the shape of an Iron Age fort (the name of which might have been **Din Milioc* – see **Domellick**).

Denzell (SW 8866): *Dynesel* C12, 'little fort', C. *dynasel*.

Dodman, The (SX 0039): *Dudman Point* 1562, E. 'Dudman's point (headland)', after a C15 family.

Domellick (SW 9455): *Dynmyliek* 1284, 'Milioc's fort', C. *dyn Mylyek*.

Drinnick (SW 9655): *Dreynek* 1370, 'thorny', C. *dreynek*.

Duporth (SX 0351): *Deuborth* 1338, 'two coves/landing places', C. *dew-borth*.

Enniscaven (SW 9659): *Enescauen* 1357, 'isolated place with an elder tree', C. *enys scawen*.

Ennisworgey (SW 9361): *Enisworgy* 1332, 'Wurci's isolated spot', C. *enys Worgy*.

St Enoder (SW 8957): *Eglos Enoder* 1416, 'St Enoder's church', C. *eglos Enoder*.

St Ewe (SW 9746): *Lanewa* 1302, 'St Ewa's church enclosure', C. *lan Ewa*.

Fal (river): an ancient name that was *Faele* 969, *Fala* 977–c1540. This is an early Celtic name, the meaning of which has become lost. Its source, now **Pentevale**, was *Penfenten fala* 1320, 'spring-head of the Fal', C. *penfenten Fala*. The Fal might have been the *Cenionis fluvii* of Ptolemy C2 AD, placed by him in the approximate position of the Fal.

Fire Beacon Point (SX 1092): *Fire Beacon* 1795, C18 E, 'fire beacon', with addition of E. 'point (headland)'.

Fistral Bay (SW 7961): *Fistal Bay* 1813, E. 'fish-tail bay', from shape of bay and flanking headlands.

Fowey (SX 1251): *Fawi* c1200, 'beech-trees river', C. *faw-y*. An alternative name was *Langorthowe* 1378, 'church enclosure of the clans/war-hosts', C. *lan gordhow*.

Fowey (river): *Fawe* c1210–1306, *Fawi* 1241, *Fawy* 1241–1339, 'beech-trees river', C. *faw-y*. Some modern sources give **Fawydh* but this is not borne out by historical references except the late *Foath* c1600, c1680. A late name for the estuary, *Uzell* c1680, may be an LC or dialect word meaning 'windpipe'.

Foxhole (SW 9654): E. 'fox-hole', after a C17 tinwork.

Fraddon (SW 9158): *Frodan* 1321, 'stream-place', OC *frod-an*.

Galowras (SW 9944): *Golowres* 1428, 'light/clear-ford', C. *golow-res*.

Gamas Point (SX 0247): C. *camas*, 'bay' + E. 'point (headland)'.

Gannel (river): *Ganal Creek* 1748, 'the channel', C. *an ganel*. A possible early name is suggested by the place name **Gwills** (*Willit* 1258) at SW 8259, and the river Guelit where St Carantoc (**Crantock**) is said to have landed on his arrival from Wales. The name appears to be 'among open fields', C. *gwelys*.

Gargus (SX 9446): *Cargus* 1334, 'fort at a wood', C. *ker/cayr gos*.

Garker (SX 0454): *Karker* 1354, 'pillory', C. *carhar*.

Garlenick (SW 9450): *Corlennek* 1334, 'hedge by a strip-field system', C. *cor leynek*.

Gaverigan (SW 9359): *Govergwyn* 1302, 'white/fair stream', C. *gover gwyn*.

Gazzle (SW 8062): 'indented cove', C. *an gasal* (literally, 'the armpit').

Gluvian (SW 8666): *Gliwian* 1325 *Glyvion* C12/13, this and Gluvian (SW 9164) are at either end of the river now called **Menalhyl**, and appear to take an early river name perhaps containing C. *glew*, 'clear, bright'.

Goenrounsan (SW 8855): 'ass's/nag's downs', C. *gun rounsyn*.

Golant (SX 1254): *Golenance* 1457, 'feast/festival valley', C. *gol-nans*.

Goonabarn (SW 8954): apparently C. *gun an*, 'downs of the' + E. 'barn'.

Goonamarris (SW 9555): *Guenenmarges* 1290, 'downs of the horses', C. *gun an marghes*.

Goonamarth (SW 9954): *Goenenmargh* 1345, 'downs of the horse', C. *gun an margh*.

Goonhoskyn (SW 8757): 'sedge downs', C. *gun heskyn*.

Gorran/Goran Churchtown (SW 9942): *S. Goran* 1306, after St Goron (Guron). The C. name was *Langoron* 1373, *Laworran* 1717, 'St Goron's church enclosure', C. *lan Woron*.

Gorran Haven (SX 0141): E. 'haven at **Gorran**'. The C. name was *Porthjust* 1374, *Porteuste* 1576, *Portheast* 1587, 'St Just's cove/landing place', C. *porth Ust*.

Goss Moor (centred at SW 9360): *Gosmour* 1502, perhaps 'goose marsh', OE *gos mor*, although the nearby farm of Tregoss (*Tregors* 1210, 'fen farm', C. *tre gors*) suggests that 'Goss' may be an Anglicisation of C. *cors*, 'fen'.

Gothers (SW 9658): *Gothfos* 1334, probably 'stream by a wall/bank', C. *godh fos*.

Goverseth (SW 9654): 'dry stream', C. *gover segh*.

Grampound (SW 9348): *Grandpont* 1401, 'great bridge', F. *grand pont*. The C. equivalent was found from 1296–1308 as *Ponsmur*, 'great bridge', C. *pons muer*.

Gready (SX 0658): *Gredyou* 1400, 'stock sheds', OC *gredyow*.

Greensplat (SW 9955): C18 E. 'green' + dialect *splat* 'plot of land'.

Gribbin Head (SX 0049): *Grebin* 1699, 'little crest/reef', C. *crybyn*. This name properly belongs to the point now called Little Gribbin (SX 0850) which was *Gribbin* 1794. The main headland was *Pennarthe* 1525, 'prominent headland', C. *penardh*.

Griglands (SX 0162): 'clump of heather', C. *gruglon*.

Gunheath (SW 9956): *Goenheth* 1310, 'red deer's downs', C. *gun hedh* (see **Hensbarrow Downs**).

Gunwen (SX 0560): *Goynwen* 1483, 'white/fair downs', C. *gun wen* (fem. form of *(g)wyn*, 'white/fair').

Gwindra (SW 9552): probably 'white/fair land', C. *gwyn-dyr*.

Gwineas/Gwinges (SX 0342): 'windswept', C. *gwynsys/gwynjys*.

Hallaze (SX 0256): *Halelase* 1503, 'green marsh', C. *hal las*.

Hallew (SW 9556): 'marshes', C. *hallow*.

Heligan (SW 9946): *Helygan* 1330, 'willow tree', C. *helygen*. Properly pron. 'h'lig'en', with stress on middle syllable.

Helman Tor (SX 0661): *Helman* 1541, *Helman Tor* 1696, E. 'crag belonging to the Helman family'.

Hendra (SW 9557): 'home farm', C. *hen-dre*.

Henmoor (SW 9957): *Hyndemor* 1261, 'hind's moor', OE *hinde mor*.

Hensbarrow (SW 9957): *Hyndesbergh* 1284, 'hind's barrow/tumulus', OE *hindes beorg*.

Hensbarrow Downs (SW 9957): *Goenheyth* 1660, 'red deer's downs', C. *gun hedh* (also see **Gunheath**).

Hewas Water (SW 9649): E. 'stream at Hewas'. Hewas (*Hayves* 1370) is 'shieling, summer grazing', C. *havos*.

Holmbush (SW 0352): E. 'holly bush', OE *holegn bysce*.

Indian Queens (SW 9158): *Indian Queen* c1870, named after a former post-house and public house called *The Queen's Head* 1780, *The Indian Queens* 1802.

Innis (SX 0262): *Enys* 1554, 'isolated/remote place', C. *enys*.

Innisvath (SX 0261): 'horses' isolated place', C. *enys vergh*.

Karslake (SW 9856): 'cress stream', OE *caerse lacu*.

Kernick (SX 0559): *Kernyk* 1279, 'little corner', C. *kernyk*.

Kestle (SW 8559): *Castel* 1194, 'castle', C. *castel*.

Kestle (SW 9945): *Kestel* 1327, 'castle', C. *castel*.

Kilgogue (SX 0934): *Kelligog* 1235, 'cuckoo's grove', C. *kelly gog*.

Kilhallon (SX 0754): *Kellyhon* c1180, probably 'grove of ash trees', C. *kelly on*.

Killaganogue (SW 9465): *Killignowek* 1388, 'nut-producing grove', C. *kelly gnowek*.

Killaworgey (SW 9060): *Kylworge* c1320, 'Wurci's ridge', C. *kyl Worgy*.

Kilmarth (SX 0952): *Kylmergh* 1329, 'horses' ridge', C. *kyl mergh*.

Lamellyn (SX 0652): *Nansmelyn* 1296, 'mill valley', C. *nans melyn*.

Lamledra (SX 0140): *Lamleder* 1617, 'leap-cliff', C. *lam-leder*.

Lanescot (SX 0755): *Lysnestoch* 1086, 'Nestoc's court', C. *lys Nestek*.

Lanhadron (SW 9947): *Nansladron* 1302, 'thieves' valley', C. *nans ladron*.

Lanhainsworth (SW 9264): *Lanhensuth* 1278, 'kinsmen's church enclosure', C. *lan henseth*.

Lanherne (SW 8765): *Lanherno* 1257, 'Herno's church enclosure', C. *lan Herno*.

Lanjeth (SW 9752): *Nanshirgh* 1332, *Nansyrgh* 1356, 'valley of roe deer', C. *nans yergh*.

Lankelly (SX 1151): *Lengelly* 1308, 'pool by a grove', C. *lyn kelly*.

Lanlivery (SX 0859): *Lanlyvri* c1170, 'Lifri's church enclosure', C. *lan Lyvry*.

Lantyan (SX 1057): *Lantien* 1086, 'cold valley', OC *nant yeyn*.

Lanvean (SW 8766): *Lanvyghan* 1302, 'small church enclosure', C. *lan vyan*.

Lanwithan (SX 1059): *Lankewythan* 1355, 'Cywoethgen's church enclosure', C. *lan Kewothgen*.

Lawhibbet (SX 1055): *Languebat* 1305, 'valley of gnats', OC *nant gwybed*.

Lawhyre (SX 1151): *Lanwoer* 1303, 'sister's church enclosure', C. *lan whor*.

Legonna (SW 8359): *Lyngone* 1330, 'downland pool', C. *lyn gun*.

Levalsa (SW 9948): *Avalde* 1086, *Avalsa* 1302, 'apple store', C. *aval-jy*.

Little Hell (SX 0852): E. 'little' + C. *heyl*, 'inlet with tidal flats' (this was a former estuary that extended as far inland as **Ponts Mill** (SX 0756).

Lockengate (SX 0361): C18 E. 'locking gate', referring to a former toll gate.

London Apprentice (SX 0049): C19 E. from a former inn called 'The London Apprentice', itself named after a folk song.

Lostwithiel (SX 1039): *Lostuuidiel* c1194, 'tail-end of a place of trees', C. *lost wedhyel*.

Luney (river):*Lyfni* 1293, *Lyveny* 1318, 'smooth river', C. *leven-y*.

Lusty Glaze (SW 8262):, perhaps 'little green tail of land', C. *lostyn glas*.

Luxulyan (SX 0558): *Lauxsilyen* 1330, *Lansulyen* 1335, originally 'Sulgen's chapel/cell', C. *lok Sulyen*; then 'Sulgen's church enclosure', C. *lan Sulyen*. The name is pronounced 'luk-zil'yen'.

Luxulyan River: in addition to the present name, E. 'river at Luxulyan', two others are recorded: *Wermen* c1200 and *Pellin* 1748. The meanings of both are uncertain although Wermen might contain C. *gwer*, 'green' or be a corruption of C. *gwernen*, 'alder marsh'. Pellin could be 'little hill', C. *pelyn*.

Maenease Point (SX 0141): seemingly 'corn stone', C. *men ys* + E. 'point (headland)'. Also called Pen-a-maen , *Penarmene* 1699, 'head(land) facing a stone', C. *pen ar men*.

Maen-lay Rock (SW 9939): 'slab/ledge stone', C. *men legh* + addition of E. 'rock'.

Manheirs (SW 9347): *Menhir* 1327, 'standing stone', C. *menhyr*.

St Mawgan-in-Pydar (SW 8765): *S. Mauganus* 1260, after St Maugan and including the old Hundred name **Pydar** (see **The Cornish Hundreds**). The C. name of the churchtown was *Lanherno* 1257, 'Herno's church enclosure', C. *lan Herno* (see **Lanherne**).

Mawgan Porth (SW 8467): *Porthmawgan* 1755, 'cove/landing place at St Mawgan', C. *porth Maugan*, rendered into E. word order c1830. An earlier name was *Porthglyvyan* 1334, 'cove of the stream called Glyvyan', C. *porth Glyvyan* (see **Gluvian** and **Menalhyl**).

Melancoose (SW 8662): *Melyncoys* 1334, *Mellangoose* 1655, 'mill at a wood', C. *melyn gos*.

Meledor/Melbur (SW 9254): *Meinleder* 1201, 'slope stones', C. *meyn leder*.

Mellanvrane (SW 8160): *Melyn Bran* 1343, 'crow's mill' or 'Bran's mill', C. *melyn vran*.

Menabilly (SX 1051): *Mynnybelly* 1573, 'colts' stone', C. *men ebylly*.

Menacuddle (SX 0153): *Menequidel* 1250, *Menedcudel* 1284, 'hillside with a small wood', OC *mened cuydel*.

Menadue (SX 0359): *Menethdu* 1279, 'black/dark hillside', C. *menedh du*.

Menagwyns (SX 0150): 'wind(y) hillside', C. *menedh gwyns*.

Menalhyl (river): a misspelling of *Mellynheyl* C19, 'mill on tidal flats', C. *melyn heyl*, probably a settlement name rather than a river name. The likely name for the river is indicated by two settlements called **Gluvian** at either end of its course. Both were *Glyvion* in C12/13, the meaning of which is not known unless it contains C. *glew*, 'clear, bright'.

Menear (SX 0354): *Menhyre* 1525, 'standing stone', C. *menhyr*.

Methrose (SX 0556): *Methros* 1277, 'middle hillspur', C. *medh-ros*.

Mevagissey (SX 0144): *SS Meva & Ide* 1420, 'Saints Meva and Idi', C. *Meva hag Ysy*. The churchtown was also *Lannvorech* 1230, 'Moroc's church enclosure', C. *lan Vorek*.

Mevagissey Bay (SX 0244): *Porthiley* 1694, 'salt-water cove/landing place', C. *porth hyly*.

St Mewan (SW 9951): *S. Mewen* 1380, after St Mewen.

St Michael Caerhayes (SW 9642): *S. Michael of Karihaes* 1259, after St Michael + place name **Caerhayes**. The C. name was *Lanvyhaill* 1473, 'St Michael's church enclosure', C. *lan Vyhal*.

Molingey (SX 0050): *Melyngy* 1302, 'mill-house', C. *melynjy*.

Molinnis (SX 0159): *Molenys* 1502, 'bare isolated/remote place', C. *mol-enys*.

Mountjoy (SW 8760): *Meyndy* 1284, 'house of stones', C. *meynjy*.

Mulvra (SX 0050): *Molvre* 1370, 'bare hill', C. *mol-vre*.

Nankelly (SW 9061): *Nanskelly* 1330, 'grove valley', C. *nans kelly*.

Nankervis (SW 9053): *Nanskerwes* 1284, *Nanscervys* 1564, 'stags' valley', C. *nans kervys*.

Nanpean (SW 9656): *Nanspyan* 1380, 'little valley', C. *nans pyan* (the *–s* of *nans* hardening the *b–* of *byan*, 'small, little').

Nanphysick (SW 9851): *Nansfusik* 1359, 'happy/fortunate valley', C. *nans fusyk*.

Nanscawen (SX 0555): 'elder tree valley', C. *nans scawen*.

Nansladron (SX 0048): 'thieves' valley', C. *nans ladron*.

Nanswhyden (SW 8762): *Nanswethan* 1428, 'tree valley', C. *nans wedhen*.
Newquay (SW 8061): E. 'new quay' since at least 1602 (although the quay was built in 1440). The original settlement here was *Tewyn* 1289, 'sand dunes', C. *tewyn*, to which was added in C14 C. *por(th) lystry*, 'cove/landing place for ships', seen as *Towenplystre* 1530. A rock named Listrey, 'ships', C. *lystry*, is still marked just north of the harbour. (NB. O.J.Padel has doubts that the final word is C. *lystry*, but he may, in this case, be applying linguistic rules too rigidly within a field where those rules tend to be historically relaxed).
Newton (SX 0155): *Neweton* 1296, 'new farm/settlement', OE *niwe tun*.
Ninnes (SW 9750): *Enys* 1305, 'isolated/remote place', C. *enys*.
Par (SX 0753): *Porth* 1327, 'cove/landing place', C. *porth*.
Paramoor (SW 9749): *Pale Moore* 1659, E. 'marsh where poles/pales are cut'.
Pelyn (SX 0958): *Penlyn* 1296, 'head of a pool', C. *pen lyn*.
Penare Point (SX 0245): *Pennare* 1866, 'prominent headland', C. *penardh*.
Pencoose (SW 9646): 'end/top of a wood', C. *pen-cos*.
Pendine (SW 9560): *Pendyn* 1303, 'head fort', C. *pen dyn*.
Pengelly (SW 9649): 'top/end of a grove', C. *pen gelly*.
Pengrugla (SW 9947): *Pengregell* 1608, 'hilltop with a small barrow', C. *pen grugel*.
Penhale (SX 1052): 'top of a marsh', C. *pen-hal*.
Penhaver Point (SX 0142): 'head(land) at summer fallow land', C. *pen havar*. An alternative name (for Great Penhaver Point) was *Carlescas Point* 1866, perhaps 'burnt crag', C. *carn leskys*.
Penhellick (SW 9464): *Penhelek* 1327, 'top of willow trees', C. *pen helyk*.
Penknight (SW 1059): *Penknegh* 1284, 'top of a hillock', C. *pen knegh*.
Pennant (SX 0759): *Pennant* 1549, 'head of a valley', OC *pen-nant*.
Pennare (SW 9940): *Penarth* 1306, 'prominent headland', C. *penardh*. This was certainly the original name of The **Dodman**.
Pennatillie (SW 9166): *Penansdelyowe* 1618, 'head of the valley called Nansdelyow', C. *pen Nansdelyow*, the valley name being 'valley of leaves', C. *nans delyow*.
Penpillick (SX 0856): *Penpelic* 1302, 'top of a small hill', C. *pen pellyk*.
Penpoll (SW 7960): *Penpol* 1216, 'head of a creek', C. *pen-pol*.
Penquite (SX 1155): *Penquid* 1327, 'top of a wood', OC *pen-cuyt*.
Penrice (SX 0249): *Penres* 1262, 'end of a ford', C. *pen res*.
Penrose (SW 8462): *Penros* 1327, 'top of a hillspur', C. *pen-ros*.
Penrose (SX 0457): *Penros* c1200, 'top of a hillspur', C. *pen-ros*.
Pensagillas (SW 9746): *Pensugelis* 1525, 'end of rye-growing land', C. *pen sugal-ys*.
Penscawn (SW 8755): *Penscawen* 1306, 'hilltop with an elder tree', C. *pen scawen*.
Penstrassoe (SW 9849): 'head of flat-bottomed valleys', C. *pen strassow*.
Penstraze (SW 9961): *Penstras* 1340, 'head of a flat-bottomed valley', C. *pen stras*.
Pentevale (SW 9958): *Penfenton fala* 1320, 'spring-head (source) of the river Fal', C. *pen-fenten Fala*.

Pentewan (SX 0147): *Bentewyn* 1297, 'foot of the stream called Tewyn', C. *ben Tewyn*. The stream in question is that flowing into Pentewan from the north, a farm near its source being **Towan**. This is likely to be the river name **Tewyn* (analogous to W. *tywyn* 'radiance'), rather than C. *tewyn*, 'sand dunes'.

Pentire, East (SW 7861): *Pentirbighan* c1270 'little Pentire', C. *Pentyr byan*, this being a headland name with *pentyr* translating as 'promontory'.

Pentire West (SW 7761): *Pentir* c1270, promontory', C. *pentyr*.

Penventinue (SX 1153): *Penfentenyou* 1284, 'spring-heads', C. *pen-fentynyow*.

Penwarne (SX 0144): *Penwern* 1327, 'end/top of alder trees', C. *pen wern*.

Penwithick (SX 0256): *Penwythek* c1550, 'end/top of a place of trees', C. *pen wedhek*.

Peruppa (SX 0046): *Beaurepeir* 1313, 'fair retreat', F. *beau repair*.

Pill (SX 1058): 'creek', C. *pyll* (borrowed from OE *pyll*).

Pits Mingle (SW 9860): 'quarry pits', C. *pyttys mengledh*.

Place House (SX 1251): 'mansion', C. *plas*.

Poldew (SX 0960): *Poldu* 1446, 'black/dark pool', C. *pol du*.

Polgassick (SX 0859): *Polgasick* 1841, 'mare's pool', C. *pol gasek*.

Polglaze (SX 1052): *Polglas* 1386, 'blue/green pool', C. *pol glas*.

Polglaze (SX 0248): *Polglas* 1296, 'blue/green pool', C. *pol glas*.

Polgooth (SW 9950): *Polgoyth* 1500, 'goose pool', C. *pol godh*, originally the name of a tin-work.

Polkerris (SX 0952): *Polkerys* 1585, apparently 'fortified pool/cove', C. *pol kerys*. As no historic form has yet been found to predate the Tudor period, it may be that the name derives from a planned (but never built) Tudor fortification.

Pollawyn (SW 8860): *Penhalwyn* 1302, 'end/top of a white marsh', C. *pen hal-wyn*.

Polmassick (SW 9745): *Ponsmadek* 1301, 'Madoc's bridge', C. *pons Masek*.

Polmear (SX 0853): *Porthmuer* 1403, 'great cove/landing place', C. *porth muer*.

Polridmouth (SX 1050): *Porthredeman* 1443, 'stone-ford cove', OC *porth red-men*.

Polrudden (SX 0247): *Polreden* 1321, 'bracken pool', C. *pol reden*.

Polscoe (SX 1152): *Polkoth* 1314, 'old pool', C. *pol coth*.

Polstreath (SX 0145): 'pool/cove with a stream', C. *pol streth*.

Poltarrow (SW 9951): *Poltarou* 1327, 'bull's pool', C. *pol tarow*.

Pont's Mill (SX 0756): *Pontes Mulle* 1366, probably OC *pont*, 'bridge' + E. 'mill'.

Porcupine (SX 0755): C19 E. named after the Porcupine Inn, built on the site of the Tywardreath Sessions.

Portgiskey (SX 0146): *Portkiskey* 1760, C. *porth*, 'cove/landing place' + unknown word or name.

Porthluney (SW 9740): 'cove/landing place at the river **Luney**', C. *porth Leveny*.

Portholland (SW 9541): *Portalan* 1288, probably C. *porth*, 'cove/landing place' + Celtic river name *Alan*.

Porthpean (SX 0350): *Porthbyhan* 1297, 'little cove', C. *porth byan*.

Portmellon (SX 0143): *Porthmelyn* 1539, 'mill cove', C. *porth melyn*.

Prideaux (SX 0556): *Prydias* 1249, uncertain derivation, perhaps 'copses', OC *prydyes*.

Quintrell Downs (SW 8460): E. 'Cointerell's/Coyntrel's downs' from family recorded from C12.

Quoit (SW 9261): *Coyt* 1450, 'dolmen', C. *coyt*.

Readymoney Cove (SX 1151): *Mundy* 1811, 'mineral-house ford', OC *ret mondy*.

Redmoor (SX 0860): *Redemor* 1301, 'reed marsh', OE *hreod mor*.

Rescassa (SW 9842): *Roscada* 1269, *Roscasa* 1390, 'Cada's hillspur', C. *ros Casa*.

Rescorla (SW 9848): *Roscorlan* 1370, 'hillspur with a sheep-fold', C. *ros corlan*.

Rescorla (SX 0257): *Roscorle* 1360, probably 'hedge-place hillspur', C. *ros cor-la*.

Resparva (SW 8854): *Rosperveth* 1341, 'middle hillspur', C. *ros perveth*.

Restormel (SX 1061): *Rostormel* 1175, 'hillspur at a bare eminence', C. *ros tor-mol*.

Restowrack (SW 9457): *Rosdowrack* 1357, 'watery roughland', C. *ros dowrak*.

Resugga (SW 9452): *Rosogou* 1304, 'hillspur with a cave', C. *ros ogo*.

Resugga (SX 0356): *Rosogou* 1317, 'hillspur with a cave', C. *ros ogo*.

Resurrance (SW 8854): *Resgerens* 1321, 'Gerent's ford', C. *res Gerens*.

Retallack (SW 9365): *Reshelec* C13, 'ford by willow trees', C. *res helyk*.

Retallick (SW 9759): *Retelek* 1304, *Restelek* 1370, 'ford by willow trees', C. *res helyk*.

Retew (SW 9257): *Retteu* 1320, probably 'black/dark ford', OC *ret du*.

Retyn (SW 8858): *Restyn* 1334, 'ford by a rounded hill', C. *res tyn*.

Rialton (SW 8462): *Ryalton* 1283, C. *ryal*, 'royal, regal' + addition of OE *tun*, 'farm, settlement'.

Roche (SW 9860): *Rupe* 1201, *La Roche* 1201, 'the rock', Lat. *rupes*, F. *la roche*.

Rosedinnick (SW 9165): *Rosidenoch*, 'furzy hillspur', C. *ros eythynek*.

Rosemelling (SX 0457): *Rosemelyn* 1296, 'roughland at a mill', C. *ros melyn*.

Rosemellyn (SX 0059): *Resmelin* 1233, 'ford by a mill', C. *res melyn*.

Rosenannon (SW 9566): *Rosnonnen* 1326, 'hillspur of the ash tree', C. *ros an onnen*.

Rosevallen (SW 9454): *Rosavallen* c1350, 'apple-tree hillspur', C. *ros avallen*.

Rosevath (SX 0261): 'horses' roughland', C. *ros vergh* (see **Savath**).

Rosevean (SX 0258): *Rosvyan* 1327, 'little Ros', C. *Ros vyan* (*ros* here means 'hillspur').

Rosevear (SX 0258): *Rosveour* 1523, 'great Ros', *Ros Vuer* (see **Rosevean**).

Rosewin (SW 8954): *Reswyn* 1450, 'white/fair ford', C. *res wyn*.

Ruddlemoor (SX 0055): *Rydel* 1296, name of uncertain meaning, perhaps E. 'rye dale' + OE *mor*, 'marsh'.

Ruthern (river): *Roythan* 1296, *Ruthen* 1412, *Rothyn* 1494, perhaps 'little red one', C. *rudhyn*.

Ruthvoes (SW 9260): *Ruthfos* 1296, 'red wall/bank', C. *rudh-fos*.

Ruzza (SX 0760): *Rosou* 1696, 'hillspurs', C. *rosow*.

St Sampson (SX 1255): *S. Sampson* 1255, after St Sampson of Dol.

Savath (SX 0261): *Enysvergh* 1423, 'isolated place with horses', C. *enys vergh*.

Sconhoe (SX 0146): *Heskennou* 1302, 'sedges', C. *heskennow*.

Skewes (SW 9665): *Skewys* 1408, 'place of elder trees', C. *skewys*.

Stenalees (SX 0157): *Stenaglease* 1621, 'tin-stream at a ruin', C. *stenak lys*.

Stepaside (SW 9454): E. name for a narrow thoroughfare.

St Stephen-in-Brannel (SW 9453): after St Stephen and including the manorial name **Brannel**. The C. name was *Eglosselans* 1297, *Egloshellans* 1379, 'Helant's church', C. *eglos Helans*.

Sticker (SW 9580): *Stekyer* 1319, 'tree-stumps', C. *stekyer*.

Strickstenton (SX 0857): *Tregestentyn* 1387, 'Constantine's farm', C. *tre Gostentyn*.

Summercourt (SW 8856): C18 E. 'summer courtyard'. An earlier name was *Longaferia* 1227, E. 'long fair', OE *langan feire*, slightly altered in 1351 to *Langchepyng*, E. 'long market', OE *lang cieping*.

Sweetshouse (SX 0861): E. 'Swete's house' after John Swete, recorded in 1302.

Talskiddy (SW 9165): *Talskedy* 1300, apparently 'hill-brow of shadows', OC *tal scuedy*.

Terras (SW 9353): *Terres* 1306, 'three fords', C. *teyr-res*.

Tolcarne (SW 8161): *Talcarn* 1309, 'brow-crag', C. *tal-carn*.

Tolgarrick (SW 9352): *Talgarrek* 1327, 'brow-rock', C. *tal garrek*.

Torfrey (SX 1154): *Torfre* 1284, 'bulge/hump hill', C. *tor-vre*.

Towan (SX 0149): *Tewyn* 1331, from the name of the stream running from here to **Pentewan**. This is likely to be a cognate of W. *tywyn*, 'radiance', rather than C. *tewyn*, 'sand dunes'.

Trebilcock (SW 9960): *Trebilcok* 1380, C. *tre*, 'farm, settlement' + unknown word or name, possibly C. *pyl-caugh*, 'dung-heap'.

Trebudannon (SW 8961): *Trepydannen* 1395, 'Pidannen's farm', C. *tre Pydannen*.

Treesmill (SX 0855): an Anglicised form of *Melyntrait* 1150, 'beach mill', C. *melyn dreth*.

Tregamere (SW 9264): *Tregamur* 1422, 'great dwelling', C. *tregva muer*.

Tregaminion (SX 0952): *Trekeminyon* 1284, 'commoners' farm', C. *tre gemynyon*.

Tregargus (SW 9453): *Tregargos* 1433, perhaps C. *tre* 'farm, settlement' + place name *Gargus*, 'fort at a wood', C. *ker/cayr gos*.

Tregarrick (SW 9960): 'farm at a rock', C. *tre garrek*. The rock in question is Roche Rock.

Tregaswith (SW 8962): *Tregaswyth* 1302, 'farm at a thicket', C. *tre gaswyth*.

Tregatillian (SW 9263): *Trengentulyon* 1327, 'farm of the assemblies', C. *tre'n guntellyon*.

Tregerrick (SW 9943): *Tregeryek* 1305, 'Cerioc's farm', C. *tre Geryek*.

Tregidgeo (SW 9647): *Tregrisyow* 1338, 'farm of folds/wrinkles (in the landscape)', C. *tre grysyow/gryjyow*.

Tregiskey (SX 0146): *Tregesky* 1284, C. *tre*, 'farm, settlement' + unknown word or name (see **Portgiskey**).

Tregonetha (SW 9563): *Tregenhetha* 1341, 'Cynhedda's farm', C. *tre Genhedha*.

Tregongeeves (SW 9951): *Tregenseves* 1409, 'Cyndefyd's farm', C. *tre Genseves.*
Tregonissey (SX 0253): *Tregenedwith* 1224, 'Cyneduit's farm', C. *tre Geneswyth.*
Tregoose (SW 8861): *Tregoys* 1397, 'farm at a wood', C. *tre gos.*
Tregorrick (SX 0151): *Tregorrec* 1258, 'Correc's farm', C. *tre Gorrek.*
Tregoss (SW 9660): *Tregors* 1210, 'fen farm', C. *tre gors.*
Tregrehan (SX 0553): *Tregrechyon* 1304, 'farm of folds/wrinkles (in the landscape)', C. *tre gryghyon.*
Tregurrian (SW 8565): *Tregurien* 1232, 'Coryen's farm', C. *tre Goryen.*
Trekenning (SW 9062): *Trehepkenyn* 1294, apparently 'farm without wild garlic', C. *tre heb-kenyn*, although a personal name may be involved (the surname Tripconey originates from this place name).
Trelavour (SW 9557): *Trelowargh* 1331, 'farm with a garden', C. *tre lowargh.*
Trelion (SW 9352): *Trefleghion* 1334, *Trelyghon* 1483): 'farm by slabs of stone', C. *tre(f) leghyon.*
Trelowth (SW 9850): *Trelewyth* 1306, 'Leuit's farm', C. *tre Lewyth.*
Tremodrett (SX 0061): *Tremodret* 1086: 'Modret's farm', OC. *tre Modret.*
Trenance (SW 8161): *Trenans* 1327, 'valley farm', C. *tre nans.*
Trenance (SW 8568): *Trenans* 1277, 'valley farm', C. *tre nans.*
Trenance (SW 9864): *Trenans* 1356, 'valley farm', C. *tre nans.*
Trenance (SX 0053): *Trenans* 1380, 'valley farm', C. *tre nans.*
Trenant (SX 1052): *Trenant* 1305, *Trenans* 1334, 'valley farm', C. *tre nans* (OC *nant*)
Trenarren (SX 0348): *Tyngaran* 1304, 'crane's/heron's fort', C. *dyn garan*, after the Iron Age fort on **Black Head**.
Trencreek (SW 8260): *Trencruc* 1216, 'farm at the barrow/tumulus', C. *tre'n crug.*
Treneague (SW 9353): *Trevanek* 1379, *Treneneyke* 1381, *Trenanek* 1380, C. *tre*, 'farm, settlement' + unknown word(s) or name.
Trenithan (SW 8955): *Treneythin* 1259, 'farm at the furze', C. *tre'n eythyn.*
Trenoon (SW 8664): *Trenoen* 1426, 'farm at the downs', C. *tre'n wun.*
Trenovissick (SX 0653): *Trenevesek* 1428, 'farm in a place of sacred groves', C. *tre nevesek.*
Trenowth (SX 0458): *Trenewyth* 1327, 'new farm', C. *tre noweth.*
Trenowth (SW 8964): *Trenewyth* 1428, 'new farm', C. *tre noweth.*
Trenython (SX 0154): *Treneithen* 1201, 'farm at the furze', C. *tre'n eythyn.*
Treringey (SW 8060): *Trevrengy* 1404, 'Brenci's farm', C. *tre Vrengy.*
Tretherras (SW 8261): *Tretheyris* 1284, *Tretheyres* 1312, 'farm at three fords', C. *tre dheyr-res.*
Trethew (SX 0758): 'dark farm', C. *tre dhu.*
Trethosa (SW 9454): *Trewythoda* 1327, C. *tre*, 'farm, settlement' + unknown word or name.
Trethowell (SX 0158): *Treworthual* 1302, 'very quiet farm', C. *tre wor-thawel.*

Trethurgy (SX 0355): *Tretheverki* c1230, 'Dofergi's farm', C. *tre Dhevergy* (C. personal name meaning 'otter').

Trevarren (SW 9160): *Treveren* 1244, 'Meren's farm', C. *tre Veren.*

Trevarrian (SW 8566): *Treveryan* 1345, 'Merien's farm', C. *tre Veryen.*

Trevarrick (SW 9843): *Trevarthek* 1332, 'Arthoc's farm', C. *tref Arthek.*

Trevelgue (SW 8363): *Trevelgy* 1284, 'Maelgi's farm', C. *tre Velgy.*

Trevemper (SW 8159): *Trevymper* 1360, C. *tre,* 'farm, settlement' + unknown word or name.

Treverbyn (SX 0157): *Treverbin* 1086, 'Erbin's farm', C. *tref Erbyn.*

Treviscoe (SW 9456): *tref otcere* 1049, *Trevyscar* 1327, 'Otcer's farm', C. *tref Osker.*

Trevithick (SW 8662): *Treweythek* 1392, 'farm at a place of trees', C. *tre wedhek.*

Trevithick (SW 9645): *Trevethik* 1303, 'Budoc's farm', C. *tre Vudhek.*

Trevornick (SW 9265): *Trefornek* c1350, 'farm with a bakehouse', C. *tre fornek.*

Trewan (SW 9164): *Treiowan* 1327, 'Ieuan's farm', C. *tre Yowan.*

Trewhiddle (SX 0151): *Trewydel* 1262, 'Guidel's farm', C. *tre Wydel.*

Trewince (SW 8563): *Trewynt* 1284, 'wind(y) farm', C. *tre wyns.*

Trewollack (SX 0042): *Trewolak* 1426, perhaps 'farm with a view', C. *tre wolok.*

Trewoon (SW 9952): *Trewoen* 1284, 'downland farm', C. *tre wun.*

Trezare (SX 1153): *Reswor* 1302, perhaps 'sister's ford', C. *res whor.*

Trezaise (SW 9959): *Treseys* 1303, 'Saxon's farm', C. *tre Seys.*

Troan (SW 8957): *Treiowan* 1327, 'Ieuan's farm', C. *tre Yowan.*

Tucoyse (SW 9645): *Tucoys* 1428, 'side wood', C. *tu-cos.*

Tywardreath (SX 0854): *Tywardraeth* c1200, 'manorial centre on a beach', C. *ty war dreth.*

Ventonwyn (SW 9646): *Fentenwyn* 1370, 'white/fair spring', C. *fenten wyn.*

Ventonwyn (SW 9550): *Fentenwyn* 1442, 'white/fair spring', C. *fenten wyn.*

Victoria (SW 9861): C19 E. 'Victoria', from public house named after Queen Victoria.

Vose (SW 9546): *la Vos* 1301, *Voos* 1409, 'the wall/bank', C. *fos.*

Vounder (SX 0454): *Vounder* 1743, 'the lane', C. *an vownder.*

Watergate Bay (SW 8364): C19 E. 'bay at Watergate (i.e. 'sluice gate')', replacing *Tregorrian Cove* 1699, 'cove at Tregurrian'.

St Wenn (SW 9664), after St Wenna.

Winnard's Perch (SW 9266): E. 'redwing's perch', *winnard* being the local dialect term for a redwing.

Winnick (SW 0146): 'the little white one' (a stream name), C. *gwynyk.*

Restormel: guide stone marked FOY (for Fowey)

INDEX OF
CORNISH PLACE NAME ELEMENTS
Rol a'n Elvennow Henwyn Plasow Kernuak

a, prep	at, of	bahow, pl.	nooks, corners
-a, desc. suff.	place of	bagyl, f.	crook, crozier
ajy, f.	gap	bal, m.	mine workings
-ak, adj. suff.		ban, f. (LC badn)	a height
alow, m.pl.	water lilies	bannek, adj.	prominent
als, f. (OC alt)	cliff, shore, slope	banadhel, f. coll.	broom plants
alsyow, pl.	cliffs, slopes	banadhlek, adj.	broom-brake
alter, f.	altar	banadhlen, sg.	broom plant
amal, m.	edge, boundary,	bar, m.	summit, top
	slope	bar-drogh, comp.	broken-summit
amanyn, m.	butter, lush pasture	bara, m.	bread
an, def. art.	the, of the, at the	bargos, m.	buzzard
-an, adj. suff.	place of	bas, adj.	shallow
ancar, m.	hermit	bedh, m.	grave, tomb
anet, f.	guillemot	bedhow, pl.	graves, tombs
anken, m.	grief	begel, m.	mound, hillock
anneth, f.	dwelling	beler, f. coll.	water cress
anter, f.	retreat	beleryon, f.	cress-bed
ar, prep.	facing	belerak, adj. n.	cress-bed
ardar, m.	plough	ben, m.	foot (of)
ereder, pl.	ploughs	benegys, adj.	blessed
ardh, m (OC ard)	a height	ber, adj.	short
ardhow, pl.	heights	ber-res, comp.	short-ford
ardhek, adj.	elevated	bery, f.	kite
ardhyn, dim.	little height	besek, adj.	finger-like
argel, f.	retreat	besowen, f.	
arhans, adj.	silver	(OC bedowen)	birch tree
argantel (OC)	silver stream	besow	
arluth, m.	lord	(OC bedow)	birches
askall, f. coll.	thistles	bleydh, m.	wolf
atal, m. coll.	mine waste	bleydhek, adj.n.	wolf territory
aval, m.	apple	blogh, adj.	bare, bald
avallen, f.	apple tree	blou, adj.	blue
avon, awan, f.	river	blyn, m.	point, tip
awel, f.	breeze, weather	bodhowr, m.	foul water, polluted
aweth, f.	watercourse,		water
	stream	bogh, m.	buck, he-goat
bagh, m.	hook, nook,	bolgh, m.	gap, pass
	corner	bolghen, dim.	little gap

bor, f.	swelling, hump	calgh, m.	lime
bos, m. (OC **bod**)	dwelling	cam, adj. (OC cabm)	bent, crooked
bodyn, dim.	little dwelling	camas, f.	bend, bay
bosow, pl.	dwellings	can, adj.	white
both, f.	hump, boss	canel, f.	channel, gutter
bothek, adj.	humped	cant, m. (OC)	border, host
bowjy, m.	cow-shed	capa, m.	cape, headland
bowlan, f.	cattle-pen	carbons, m.	paved road
bownder, f.	lane	carjy, m.	cart-shed
bran, f.	crow	carn, m.	crag, tor, cairn
bryny, pl.	crows	carnek, adj.	craggy
bras, adj.	large, great	carnel, carnen,	
bre, f.	hill	dim.	little crag, cairn
bregh, f.	arm	carneth, adj.	craggy
bregh, adj.	speckled, dappled	carow, m.	stag
bren, f.	hill	kervys, pl.	stags
brenyow, pl.	hills	carrek, f.	rock
brew, f.	fragment of land	carregy, pl.	rocks
breyn, adj.	foul, polluted	casek, f.	mare
bro, f.	land, region	casal, f.	armpit, indented
brogh, m.	badger		cove
bron, m.	hill	castel, m.	castle
bronek, adj.	hilly	castelak, adj.	castled
bronnow,		castelyk, dim.	little castle
bronyon, pls.	hills	castylly, pl.	castles
bronnen, f.	a rush	caswydh, m.	
bron, coll.	rushes	(LC cajwydh)	thicket
bronek. adj. n.	rush-bed	cath, f.	cat
bryally, f. coll.	primroses	caugh, m.	dung
brygh, adj.	speckled, dappled	cauns, m.	paved way,
bryth, adj.	speckled, dappled		causeway
bugel, m.	shepherd		
bugeles, f.	shepherdess	cayr (see **ker**)	
bugh, f.	cow	chapel, m.	chapel
bukka, m.	goblin, scarecrow	chayr, m.	chair
buorth, f.	cow-yard	choca, choha, m.	jackdaw, chough
buorthow, pl.	cow-yards	chy, m. (OC ty)	house
buthyn, f.	meadow	cledh, m.	ditch
buthynyow, pl.	meadows	clegar, m.	cliff, precipice
byan, adj.	small, little	cleys, f.	ditch
bygh, adj.	small, little	clog, m	crag
cadar, f.	chair, seat	clogh, m.	bell
cad-lys, m. (OC		cloghprenyer, m.	gallows, gibbet
comp.)	courtyard	clojy, m.	lazar-house,
cagel, m.	dung, manure		hospital
cal, m.	penis (pointed	clun, f.	meadow
	feature)	clunyek, adj. n.	meadow-place
cales, adj.	hard, difficult	clyjy, m.	marshy place
		cog, f.	cuckoo

cog, adj.	blind, empty	crows, f.	a cross
coger, adj.	winding	cruen, m.	artificial pool,
coll, f. coll.	hazel trees		reservoir
collen, sg.	hazel tree	crug, m.	mound, barrow
colles, f.	hazel grove	crugel, dim.	liitle mound
collwedh, f. coll.	hazel trees	crugow, pl.	mounds
com, m.	small valley	crugyn, dim.	little mound
commow, pl.	small valleys	cryb, f.	crest, reef
compes, adj.	level, flat	cryben, f.	little crest, reef
conna, m. (LC codna)	neck	crybow, pl.	crests, reefs
connar, f.	rage, fury	crygh, m.	fold, wrinkle
cor, cordh, m.	clan, tribe, army	crygh-ton, m.	wrinkled pasture
cordhow, pl.	clans, tribes, armies	crys, m.	fold, wrinkle
cor, m.	hedge, boundary	cul, adj.	narrow
cores, f.	weir, dam	culyek, m.	cockerel
corlan, f.	sheep-fold	cumyas, m. (LC	
corn, m.	horn, corner	kibmias)	leave-taking
cornel, dim.	little horn/corner	cuntell, m.	gathering, assembly
cornow, pl.	horns, corners	cuntellyon, pl.	gatherings,
cors, f. coll.	reeds		assemblies
corsek,		cunys, f. coll. (LC	
kersek, adjs.	reedy, reed-bed	kidnis)	fuel
kersys, f.	place of reeds	cunyjak, adj.	fuel-ground
cos, m. (OC cuyt)	a wood	dar, m. coll.	oak trees
coth, adj.	old	derow, pl.	oak trees
cough, adj.	scarlet, blood-red	derowen, sg.	oak tree
coyt, f.	dolmen	derves, m.	oak wood
crak, m.	crag	davas, f.	sheep
craken, dim.	little crag	del, m. coll.	leaves
cran, f.	bracken, scrub	delyow, pl.	leaves
crannow, pl.	bracken-brakes	den, m.	man
cren, f. coll.	aspen trees	dever, m.	water, river
crenwedh, f. pl.	aspen trees	deverys, adj.	well-watered
cres, adj.	middle, centre	devrel, adj.	watery
crew, f.	weir, stepping	devrak, adj.	watery
	stones	devryon, pl.	waters, rivers
croft, m.	enclosed rough	dew, m.	god
	grazing	dewyow, pl.	gods
croftow, pl.	rough grazing	dew, card. no.	two
	enclosures	dons, m.	dance
crogen, f.	skull, shell	dor, m.	ground, earth
crom, adj. (LC		dorn, m.	hand, fist
crobm)	curved, crooked	down, adj.	deep
cromlegh, f.	dolmen	down-nans, m.	deep valley
cronak, m.	toad	dowr, m.	water, river
cronogow, pl.	toads	dowrak, adj.	watery
crow, m.	hut, sty, shed	dowran, m.	watering place
crowjy, m.	hut, hovel	dowrow, pl.	waters, rivers

dres, prep.	across, beyond, over	**evor**, m.	cow-parsley, yew
dreyn, m. coll.	thorns	**ewen**, f.	yew tree
dreynak, adj.	thorny	**ew**, f. coll.	yew-trees
dreynen, sg.	thorn tree	**ewnter**, m.	uncle
dreynys, m.	thorn-brake	**ewyk**, f.	hind, doe
dreys, f. coll.	brambles	**ewegy**, pl.	hinds, does
dreysak, adj.	brambly	**eythyn**, f. coll.	furze
dreysen, sg.	bramble bush	**eythynek**, adj.	furzy
du, adj.	dark, black	**eythynen**, sg.	furze bush
dy-, int. pref		**faw**, f. coll.	beech trees
dyjy, m.	cottage	**fawen**, sg.	beech tree
dy-les, adj.	profitless, worthless	**fawedh**, pl.	beech trees
		fe, m.	feudal estate
dyn, m.	fort	**fenten**, f.	spring, well
dynan, dim.	little fort	**fentynyow**, pl.	springs, wells
dynas, m.	fort	**fog**, f.	forge, furnace
dynek, adj.	fortified	**fogo**, f.	cave
dy-serth, adj.		**fold**, m.	fold, pen
(OC **dy-sert**)	very steep	**fordh**, f.	road, way
dywys, adj.	burnt	**fos**, f.	wall, dyke, bank
ebol, m.	colt, foal	**fosyn**, dim.	little wall/bank
ebylly, pl.	colts, foals	**fow**, f.	cave
ebry, adj.	lower	**fros**, m. (OC **frod**)	stream, current
edhel, f. coll.	poplars, aspens	**frosow**, pl.	streams, currents
edhlen, sg.	poplar, aspen	**fry**, m.	nose, hillspur
edhen, f.	bird	**frynk**, m.	freeman, French-man
edhyn, pl.	birds		
eglos, f.	church	**fusyk**, adj.	happy, pleasant
egorow, m. pl.	openings	**fyn**, f.	end, boundary
-ek, adj. suff.		**fynweth**, f.	end, limit
-el, dim. suff.		**gahen**, f.	henbane
elergh, m. pl.	swans	**ganow**, m.	mouth
elester, f. coll.	flag irises	**garan**, f.	crane, heron
elestrek, adj.n.	flag marsh	**garow**, adj.	rough
elestren, sg.	flag iris	**garth**, m.	yard, enclosure
elow, f. coll.	elm trees	**garth**, f.	ridge, promontory
elowen, sg.	elm tree	**gavar**, f.	goat
elwedh, pl.	elm trees	**gever**, pl.	goats
elyn, m.	elbow, bend	**gawl**, f.	fork
-en, fem. sg.	plant-name suffix	**gel**, f.	leech
enys, f.	island, isolated spot	**geler**, f.	coffin
epscop, m.	bishop	**gen**, m.	wedge, chisel
er, m.	eagle	**genow**, pl.	wedges, chisels
er, adj.	fresh, green	**gesys**, adj. (LC **gejys**)	left behind/dry
erow, f.	acre	**glan**, f. (LC **gladn**)	bank, waterside
erys, f.	ploughland	**glas**, adj.	blue, green, grey
-esyk, adj. suff.		**glasen**, f.	greensward
		glasnedh, m.	verdure

glastan, f. coll. — holm oaks
glastanen, sg. — holm oak
glegh, m. — moisture
glow, m. — charcoal
glow-wedh, f.pl. — charcoal wood
glyn, m. — deep valley
glynen, dim. — small deep valley
glyn-wedh, f. — valley wood
go-, dim. pref — slight, sub-
gobans m. — litle hollow, dell
godh, f. — goose
godhow, pl. — geese
godh, f. — stream
godhek, adj. — stream abundant
godhel, f. — watery ground
godhow, pl. — streams
godref, f. — homestead
godrevy, pl. — homesteads
gof, m. — smith
gol, m. — feast, festival
goles, adj. — lower
golow, m., adj. — light, bright
golva, f. — watchplace
golvan, m. — sparrow
golytha, m. — cataract
gor-, int. pref — over-, very-, high-
gor-dre, f. — principal farm
gor-ge, f. — low/broken hedge
gorhel, m. — ship, vessel
gorm, adj. — brown, dark
gortharap, adj. — very pleasant
gortos, v.n — waiting
gorwedh, f. — wooded slope
gorwedhow, pl. — wooded slopes
gosa, v.n. — bleeding, bloody
gover, m. — stream, brook
goverow, pl. — streams, brooks
gras, m. — grace, virtue
gre, f. — flock, herd
gre-dy, m. — cattle-shed
gre-lyn f. — stock pond
gwreyth, f. — roots, root crops
gronen, f. — grain
grow, m. coll. — gravel
growyn, m. — granite
grug, m. coll. — heather
gruglan, m. — heather bush
gun, f. — downland, open

moorland
gonyow, pl. — downs, moors
gwaf, m. (OC goyf) — winter
gwavos, m. — winter dwelling
gwag, adj. — empty, weak
gwal, m. — wall
gwallek, adj. — walled
gwallen, dim. — little wall
gwallow, pl. — walls
gwan, adj. — weak, poor
gwaneth, f. coll. — wheat
gwarth, m. — top
gwartha, adj. — upper, higher
gwas, m. — fellow, servant
gwaynten, m. — springtime
gwedh, f. coll. — trees
gwedhek, adj. — tree-grown
gwedhel, dim. — sapling
gwedhen, sg. — tree
gwedh-yel, f. — place of trees
gwel, m. — open field
gwella, adj. — best
gwels, f. coll. — grass
gwelsek, adj.
(LC gweljak) — grassy
gwen, f. adj. (LC
gwedn) — white, fair
gwennol, f. — swallow
gwennyly, pl. — swallows
gweres, m. — slope
gwer, gwerth, adj. — green
gwern, f. coll. — alder trees
gwernak, adj.n. — alder grove/marsh
gwernen, sg. — alder tree
gwestva, f. — lodging house
gwlas, f. — land, country
gwragh, f. — hag, crone, witch,
wrasse, (LC giant)
gwya, v.n. — weaving
gwybes, f. coll.
(OC gwybed) — gnats
gwybesek, adj. — gnat-infested
gwybesen, sg. — gnat
gwycor, m. — trader, merchant
gwycoryon, pl. — traders, merchants
gwyk, f. — forest settlement
gwykel, dim. — small forest
settlement

gwylgy, f.	ocean	hordh, m.	ram
gwyn, m. adj. (LC		hordhas, pl.	rams
gwidn)	white, fair, holy	hor-dhyn, comp.	ram-fort
gwynyon, pl. adj.	white, fair, holy	hordh-lys, comp.	ram-court
gwynek, adj.	whitish	horn, m.	iron
gwyns, m.(OC gwynt)	wind	hornek, adj.	iron-like
gwynsek, adj.		hos, m.	duck
(LC gwynjak)	windy	heyjy, pl.	ducks
gwys, f.	a sow	heyjygow, pl.	ducklings
ha, hag, cons.	and	hot, m.	hat
haf, m.	summer	howl, m.	sun
havar, f.	fallow land	howlak,	
havos, m.	summer grazing,	howlyak, adjs.	sunny
(OC hafod)	shieling	hueth, adj.	peaceful, happy
havrak, f.	fallow land	hueth-nans,	
hagar, adj.	ugly, rough, cruel	comp.	happy valley
hal, f.	marsh, moor	hyly, m.	brine, salt water
hallek, adj.	marshy	hyn, m.	border, boundary
hallow, pl.	marshes, moors	hynsa, m. pl.	fellows, kinsmen
hay, m.	enclosure, holding	hyr, adj.	long, tall
hanter, adj.	half	hyr-drum, comp.	long-ridge
heb, prep.	without, lacking	hyr-ven, comp.	longstone
hedh, m.	stag	hyr-yarth, comp.	long-ridge
hel, m.	hall	ke, f.	hedge
helgh, m.	hunt	keak, adj.	hedged
helghy, v.n.	hunting	keow, pl.	hedges
helygen, f.	willow	keber, f.	timber, beam
helyk, f. coll.	willows	keberek, adj.	timber-strewn
helygy, pl.	willows	kegyn, f.	ridge
hen, adj.	old, ancient	kel, m.	shelter,
hen-dre, f.	old farm, home		concealment
	farm	kelgh, m.	circle
hen-fordh, f.	old road	kellestron, m.	pebble
henjy, m.	old/ruined house	kellester, coll.	pebbles
hen-lan, f.	disused church	kelly, f.	grove, copse
	enclosure	kelly-wedh, f.	grove of trees
hen-lys, f.	ancient court, ruin	kelly-wyk, f.	forest grove
hens, m.	way	kellyen, dim.	little grove
henscath, f.	slipway	kellyow, pl.	groves
henkyn, m.	iron peg	kelyn, f.	holly
hesken, f.	sedge	kelynak, adj. n.	holly grove
heskennow, pl.	sedges	kelynen, sg.	holly tree
heyl, m.	estuary with	kelynnow, pl.	holly trees
	tidal flats	kelys	lost, hidden
hogen, f.	hawthorn berry	Kembro, m.	Welshman
hogen, f.	pastry, pasty	kemper, f.	confluence of
hogh, m.	pig		streams/currents
hoghen, dim.	piglet, porker	kemyn, m.	commoner

kemynyon, pl.	commoners	ladron, pl.	thieves
kendevryon, m.	confluence	ladres, m.	sluice
kendowrow, m.	confluence	lam, m. (LC labm)	leap
kenyn f. coll.	wild garlic	lan, f.	early church
kenynek, adj.n.	where wild garlic		enclosure
	grows	lanergh, m.	clearing
ker, cayr, f.	fort, enclosed	lanerhy, pl.	clearings
	farm	ledan, adj.	wide, broad
kerrow, cayrow,		leder, f.	cliff, steep slope
pls.	forts	lefans, m. (OC lefant)	toad, frog
kerys, adj.	fortified	legh, f.	slab, ledge
kerdhyn, f.	rowan tree	lehen, dim.	little slab, slate
kerdh, coll.	rowan trees	lehow, leghyow,	
kerhyth, f.	heron	leghyon pls.	slabs, ledges
kernyk, m. dim.	little corner	leryon, n. (OC)	floods
kest, f.	pouch, basket	leskys, adj.	burnt, swaled
kevar, m.	joint tillage	losk, adj.	burnt, swaled
keverang, f.	Hundred, cantref	lester, m.	vessel, ship
keverangow, pl.	Hundreds	lestry, lystry, pls.	vessels, ships
kevyl, m.	horse	leth, m.	milk
kew, f.	enclosure, paddock,	lety, m.	dairy
	hollow	leven, adj.	smooth
kewesyk, adj.	hollowed	levryth, m.	sweet milk
kew-nans, m.	enclosed valley	lewyador, m.	pilot, steersman
kew-res, f.	hollow ford	lewyth, m.	pilot, steersman
keybalhens, m.	ferry	leyn, f.	strip-field, stitch
keyn, m.	back, ridge	leynow, pl.	strip-fields
keynek, adj.	ridged	logh, f.	pool, deep water
keynans, m.	ravine		inlet/estuary
knogh, m.	hillock	logosen, f.	mouse
know, f. coll.	nuts, nut-trees	logos, coll.	mice
knowen, sg.	nut, nut-tree	logosek, adj.	mouse-infested
kuen, f. pl.	reeds, rushes	lok, f.	chapel, cell
kenak, f.	reed bed	lom, adj.	bare
kenegy, pl.	reed beds	lon, m.	grove, thicket
ky, m.	dog	lonow, pl.	groves, thickets
cuen, pl.	dogs	lonk, m.	gully, ravine
cuen-jy, m.	kennels	lonken, dim.	gully
kyf, m.	stump	los, adj.	grey
kyl, m.	nook	losow, f.pl. (LC lojow)	plants
kyl, m.	back, ridge	losowek, adj.	plant-rich
kyl-godh, f.	goose-back	losowen, sg.	plant
kyl-margh, f.	horse-back	lost, m.	tail
kylen, f.	creek, inlet	lostek, m.	fox
kynyavos, m.	autumn dwelling	lovan, f.	rope, cord
kyogh, f.	snipe	lowarn, m.	fox
-la, -le, suff.	place	lewern, pl.	foxes
lader, m.	thief	lowarth, m.	garden

lowen, adj.	happy		melyn-jy, m.	mill-house
lu, m.	host, army, fleet		melyn-wyns, f.	windmill
luegh, m.	calf		men, m.	stone
luehy, pl.	calves		mengledh, m.	quarry
luryk, m.	breastplate,		menhyr, m.	standing stone
	rampart		menhyryon, pl.	standing stones
lus, f. coll.	bilberries		menow, pl.	stones
lusek, adj.	bilberry patch		meyn, pl.	stones
lusow, f.pl. (LC lijiow)	ashes, cinders		meyndy, m.	stone house
lyn. m. (LC lidn)	pool, pond		menawes, m.	
lynnek, adj.			(OC menawed)	awl
(LC lidnak)	place of pools		menedh, f. (OC	
lynnow, pl.			mened)	hill, hillside
(LC lidnow)	ponds, pools		menedhek, adj.	hilly
lynas, f. coll.	nettles		menedhyow,pl.	hills
lys, m.	mud		meras, v.n..	watching
lys, f.	court, ruin		merther, m.	place of a saint's
lyw, m.	colour			grave or relics
lywek, adj.	coloured		merdhyn, m.	sea-fort
ma, -va, f.	place		mes, m.	open field/land
magor, f.	ruin		mesak, adj.n.	open place
mam, m.	mother		mesclen, f. coll.	mussels
managh, m.	monk		meskel, sg.	mussel
manahek, adj.n.	monastic land		mogh, m. pl.	pigs
menegh, pl	monks		mol, adj.	bare
menehy, m.	church land		mol-ardh, m.	bare height
manal, f.	sheaf, stack		mol-enys, f.	bare isolation
manalys, adj.	stacked		mol-vre, m.	bare hill
margh, m.	horse		molgh, f.	thrush, blackbird
marhak, m.	horseman, rider		mols, m.	wether sheep
marhes, pl.	horses		mon, adj.	thin, slender
mergh, pl.	horses		mon, m.	ore, mineral
mergh-jy, m.	stables		mon-dy, m.	ore-house
marhas, f.	market		mon-gledh, m.	open-cast mine
medh, adj.	middle		mor, f. coll.	berries, black-
medh-le, m.	middle place			berries
medh-lyn, m.	middle pool		morek, adj.	blackberry patch
medh-ros, m.	middle hillspur		moren, sg.	berry, blackberry
medh-ryn, m.	mid-slope		mor, m.	sea
medhek, m.	doctor		morhogh, m.	dolphin, porpoise
medhegel, m.	surgery		morreb, m.	seaside, shore
mejer, m.(OC meder)	harvester, field		morva, f.	marsh
	mouse		morvyl, m.	whale
mel, m.	honey		mosek, adj.	stinking
melek, adj.	honeyed		muer, adj.	great, large
melen, adj.	yellow		mullyon, f. coll.	clover
melyn, f.	mill		mullyonek, adj.	clover patch
melynder, m.	miller		munys, adj.	small, little

muryon, f. coll.	ants		end, top, principal
muryonek, adj.	ant-infested	pen-ardh, m.	prominent
mylgy, m.	greyhound,		headland
	hunting dog		or hillspur
myn, m.	edge, tip, muzzle	pen-cos, m.	
mynster, m.	endowed church	(OC pen-cuyt)	end/top of a wood
myth, m.	whey	pen-dre, f.	principal farm
nans, m. (OC nant)	valley	pen-fenten, f.	spring-head
nath, m.	hewn stone	pen-gelly, f.	end/top of a grove
naw, card. no.	nine	pen-hal, f.	end/top of a marsh
nessa, adj.	nearest, next	pen-lyn, m.	end of a pool
neth, adj (OC)	?clean	pen-nans, m.	
neves, m. (OC neved)	sacred grove	(OC pen-nant)	end/head of a
newl, m.	mist, fog		valley
newlak, adj.	misty, foggy	pen-pol, m.	head of a creek
newyn, f.	trough	pen-ryn, m.	promontory, hill-
neyth, m.	nest		spur
nor, m.	land, mainland	pen-tyr, m.	promontory
noweth, adj.	new	pennek, m. (LC	
ogas, adj.	near	pednek)	tadpole
ogo, f.	cave	perth, f.	bush, thicket
ojyon, m.	ox	perveth, adj. (OC	
ohen, pl.	oxen	pervet)	middle, inner
olcan, m.	metal, tin	peskys, v.n.	feeding, grazing
omborth, m.	balance	plas, m.	place, mansion
on, en, f. coll.	ash trees	plen, m.	arena
enwedh, pl.	ash trees	plos, adj.	foul, filthy
onnek, adj.	ash grove	plu, f.	parish
onnen, sg.	ash tree	plumen, f.	plum tree
on, m.	lamb	pol, m.	pool, creek, cove,
en, pl.	lambs		pit
orgel, m.	pennyroyal	pol-gruen, m.	gravel pit
orth, prep,	at, by	pol-pry, m.	clay pit
own, m.	fear, dread	pol-ros, m.	wheel pit
ownek, adj.	fearful, dreadful	pol-sten, m.	tin pit
oy, m.	egg	pons, m. (OC pont)	bridge
pajer, m. card. no.	four	ponjow, pl.	bridges
pans, f. (OC pant)	hollow, dingle	porhel, m.	young pig
park, m.	field	porth, m.	cove, landing
peder, f. card. no.	four		place, entrance
pedreda, f. (OC)	four fords	post, m.	post, pillar
pedren, m.	backside	poth, adj.	burnt, scorched
pel, f.	ball, rounded hill	pow, m.	land, country
pellek, adj.	ball-like	pras, m.	meadow
pellen, dim.	little ball/hill	pren, m. (LC predn)	tree, timber
pellow, pl.	balls, rounded hills	pry, m.	clay
pell, adj.	far, distant	prys, prysk, f.	copse, thicket
pen, m.	head, headland,	pryven, m.	worm

pronter, m.	preacher, priest	scath, f.	boat
puelven, m.	pillar	scathow, pl.	boats
pur, adj.	clean, pure	scaw, f. coll.	elder trees
pybel, f.	conduit, pipe	scawen, sg.	elder tree
pyber, m.	piper	skewys, f.	elder grove
pybyth, m.	piper	skewyek, f.	
pyg, m. (OC pyk)	point	(LC skewjak)	elder grove
pygow, pl.	points	scorya, m.	mine waste
pyl, m.	mound, heap	scoul, m.	kite
pyllek, adj.	heaped	scovarn, f.	ear
pylas, m.coll.	naked oats	screfa, v.n.	writing
pyll, m.	creek	screfys, adj.	written
pyn, m. coll. (LC pidn)	pine trees	scubys, adj.	swept
pynnek (LC		scues, m.	shade, shadow
pidnek)	pine grove	scuesek, adj.	
pystyl, m.	waterfall	(LC scujak)	shady
pyt, m.	pit	scuesy, pl.	shadows
pyttys, pl.	pits	segh, adj.	dry
pyth, m.	a dug well	sehen, f.	dry/waterless place
rajel, m.	boulder field	sehor, m.	dryness
rag, prep.	for, before, facing	segh-nans, m.	dry valley
reb, prep.	beside	sehys, adj.	dried
reden, f.coll.	bracken, ferns	serrys, adj.	angry
redenek, adj.	fern-brake	serth, m. (OC sert)	steep slope
res, f. (OC red, ret)	ford	seth, f.	arrow
rew, m.	slope	sethow, pl.	arrows
reys, m.	watercourse	sethyn, dim.	little arrow, dart
ros, f.	wheel	sevy, f. coll.	strawberries
ros, f.	promontory, coastal	sevyek, adj.	strawberry fields
	slope, hillspur,	sevyen, sg.	strawberry
	roughland, uncult-	sewya, v.n.	following
	ivated valley	sewys, m.	stitcher
rosow, pl.		Seys, m.	Saxon, Englishman
rosyn, dim.	little promontory	shoppa, m.	shop, workshop
rounsyn, m.	nag, ass	skyber, f.	barn
rudh, adj.	red	skyberyow, pl.	barns
ruen, m.	seal	slynkya, v.n.	sliding
run, m.	slope, spur	sorn, m.	nook, corner
ruyf, m.	king	sowl, f. coll.	stubble
ryll, m.	cleft	spedhes, f. coll.	briars, brambles
ryn, m. (LC ridn)	slope, spur	spern, f. coll.	thorn trees
sans, adj. (OC sant)	holy	spernek, adj.	thorny
sans, m. (OC sant)	saint, holy man	spernen, sg.	thorn tree
sens, syns, pls.	saints, holy men	spern-gor, f.	thorn hedge
sawan, f.	coastal chasm	sperys, m.	spirit, ghost
Sawsen, m.pl.	Saxons, English-	spyrysyon,	
	men	spyryjyon, pls.	spirits, ghosts
saya, v.n.	sifting	splat, m.	plot of land

stag, m.	mud, tether
stampys, m.pl.	tin-stamping mills
starn, f.	frame
sten, m.	tin
stenak, f.	tin-stream
stok, m.	stump
stekyer, pl.	stumps
stras, m. (OC strad)	flat-bottomed valley
strayl, m.	mat, tapestry
streyth, f.	stream
stret, m.	street
stronk, adj.	dirty, polluted
stum, m.	bend, turn
suent, adj.	level, even
sugal, f. coll.	rye
sugal-dyr, m.	rye-land
syger, adj.	lazy
tagell, f.	noose, choker
tal, m.	brow
tal-carn, m.	brow-tor
talek, adj.	big-browed
tal-van, f.	brow-height
talar, f.	auger, sea-stack
tam, m. (LC tabm)	morsel, crumb
tanow, adj.	thin, narrow
taran, f.	thunder
tardh, m.	burst, explosion
tarow, m.	bull
tarow-vyr, f.	bull-baiting show
tavas, m.	tongue
tawel, adj.	quiet
te, pron.	thy, thou
teg, adj.	beautiful, pretty, fair
tegen, dim.	pretty thing, jewel
tenewan, m.	side
tenow, m.	valley, side-valley
tevy, v.n.	growing, planting, cultivating
tevys, adj.	grown, planted, cultivated
tewel, m.	pipe, conduit
tewl, adj.	dark
tewyn, m.	sand dunes
teyr, f. card. no.	three
toll, m.	tithe/tax boundary
toll, m.	hole

toll-gos, m	hole-wood
tollven, m.	holed stone
tom, adj. (LC tubm)	warm
tomen, f. (LC tubmen)	mound
ton, m. (LC todn)	pastureland, lea-land
tor, f.	belly, eminence
tor-mol f.	bare eminence
torn, m.	turning
torthel, f.	loaf
towargh, f.coll.	peat, turf
tre, tref, f.	farm, settlement
tregva, f.	dwelling
treven, m.pl.	houses
trevow, pl.	farms, settlements
tregh, m.	cut wood
treth, f.	ferry
treth, m.	sand, beach
trethen, m.	sandbar
trogh, adj.	cut, broken
trokkya, v.n.	fulling
tron, m.	nose, promontory
tron-gos, m.	promontory wood
tros, m.	foot
treys, pl.	feet
tru, prep.	beyond, yonder
trum, m.	ridge
try, m. card. no.	three
try, adj. pref.	triple, very
tryg, m.	low water
tu, m.	side
tus, m. pl. (OC tud)	men, people
tuska, adj.	mossy
tutton, m.	seat
ty, m. (OC)	house, manorial centre
tyn, f.	rump, rounded hill
tyny, adj.	rump-like
tyr, m.	land
tyreth, m.	territory
ugh, adj.	high
uh-gos, m.	high-wood
uhel, adj.	high
ujek, adj.	hooting, shrieking
ula, m.	owl
usel, m.	throat, gullet
usyon, m. coll.	chaff

ussa, adj.	topmost, outer-most	**ydh**, f. coll.	ivy
		ydhyow, f. coll.	ivy
usys, adj.	well-used	**yet**, m. (LC **jet**)	gate
uthek, adj.	terrible, awful	**yeyn**, adj. (LC **jeyn**)	cold, bleak
war, prep,	on, upon	**yeyn-jy** (LC	
wast adj.		**jeyn-jy**)	ice-house
west, m & adj.	west	**yfern**, m.	hell
whel, m.	mine workings	**ygolen**, f.	whetstone
whethlow, m. pl.	tales, stories	**yn**, **y'n**, prep,	in, in the
whevrer, adj.	lively	**ynyal**, adj. (LC	
whor, f.	sister	idniall)	desolate, wild
whyl, m. coll.	beetles	**yorgh**, m.	roe deer
whylen sg.	beetle	**yergh**, pl.	roe deer
-y, suff.	place/river name suffix	**yorhel**, dim.	young roe deer
		Yow, m.	Thursday
yar, f.	hen	**ys**, adj.	lower
yer, pl.	hens	**ysa**, adj.	lowest
-yek, suff.	adj. suffix	**ysel**, adj.	low
-yel, suff.	adj. suffix	**ys**, m.	corn
-yer, suff.	pl. suffix	**ysek**, adj.	corn-rich, cornfield
-yk, suff.	dim. suffix	**yslonk**, m.	chasm
-yn, suff	dim. suffix	**yst**, m. & adj.	east
-ys, adj. suff.	place of	**yurl**, m.	earl

Kerrier: signpost near Mawnan

Craig Weatherhill *is an author and historian and presently the Chairman of the Cornish language society* Agan Tavas – Our Language. *His previous books include two standard works on Cornish archaeology:* Belerion *and* Cornovia *and two novels based upon Cornish legends. Now a freelance architectural designer and keen horseman, he has frequently featured in radio and television programmes such as* Westcountry Tales *and* Time Travels.